Dear Rhoda,
my good friend
who I have enjoyed
wonderful outings with!
May your journey of Self Love
be joy filled. All the best!
Cindy

CLEAR CONNECT CREATE

A Powerful Path to Self-Love

CINDY PAINE

WITH MARGARET A. BROWN

BALBOA
PRESS

A DIVISION OF HAY HOUSE

Balboa Press books may be ordered through booksellers or by contacting:

Balboa Press
A Division of Hay House
1663 Liberty Drive
Bloomington, IN 47403
www.balboapress.com
1 (877) 407-4847

Because of the dynamic nature of the Internet, any web addresses or links contained in this book may have changed since publication and may no longer be valid. The views expressed in this work are solely those of the author and do not necessarily reflect the views of the publisher, and the publisher hereby disclaims any responsibility for them.

The author of this book does not dispense medical advice or prescribe the use of any technique as a form of treatment for physical, emotional, or medical problems without the advice of a physician, either directly or indirectly. The intent of the author is only to offer information of a general nature to help you in your quest for emotional and spiritual well-being. In the event you use any of the information in this book for yourself, which is your constitutional right, the author and the publisher assume no responsibility for your actions.

Any people depicted in stock imagery provided by Thinkstock are models, and such images are being used for illustrative purposes only.
Certain stock imagery © Thinkstock.

Printed in the United States of America.

ISBN: 978-1-4525-8824-7 (sc)
ISBN: 978-1-4525-8826-1 (hc)
ISBN: 978-1-4525-8825-4 (e)

Library of Congress Control Number: 2013923375

Balboa Press rev. date: 5/7/2014

ACKNOWLEDGEMENT

by Cindy Paine

first want to thank Divine Consciousness, my whole team of guides, and their never ending nudges for me to complete this book and get this message out there. In reviewing the book, Margaret and I laughed at times, saying "Where did this come from? I don't remember saying that!" I know that God and my Team had such a big hand in it!

I want to thank all of my teachers who have guided me along my spiritual path. You have inspired me and awakened within me my own knowing. My work and this book are the culmination of those teachings. I want to thank my friends and family members who encouraged me along the way asking me, "when is that book going to be done?" Specifically, I want to acknowledge three people close to me who have been an integral part of my life journey and supported me in my own personal growth from which this book was conceived: Susan Henkels, Gail London, and my niece Liza Stewart. June Rouse, an editor, a beautiful spirit who passed away during the beginning of this process was the first to make me believe in this book and its possibility. I know she is proud of my accomplishment. America Martinez has held a never-ending vision that I was going to do this book and many more to come. She continued to remind me that this is my destiny. Thanks to Jane Perini for your fabulous cover and mid-wifing; Balboa Press for being so easy to work with; and Deb Pinsoff for your edits and enthusiasm.

And then of course there is Margaret. Margaret Brown took this book from my spoken word to the written word. This book would not have happened without our collaboration. She stepped in about 8 years ago and has been a constant support on an almost daily basis to take my words and transcribe them into the language of this book. She organized, detailed, and grounded it with her eight planets in Virgo; not my forte. Our two sides of the brain allowed this book to be birthed.

To you, my dear Readers, I am so happy that you have decided to take the Self-Love journey. My labor of love can now be a part of your path to discover your own beauty and power. I feel that it is your birthright to discover who you really are. The path that I have found to awaken this truth is Self-Love. You will be guided step-by-step to release anything in the way of your full knowing of your divinity. Congratulations on taking the first step!

FOREWORD

by Co-Author, Margaret Brown

I f you are like me, Reader, you are thinking, "Great, another book about manifestation – let me just skip to the back to the Create section and see what the magic incantation is to get what I want!" What Cindy and I propose here is that getting all you desire is not necessarily what you do-do-do, but *who you are*. As one of my favorite teachers, Iyanla Vanzant says, "You've got to do your work!" This is a difficult proposition in an instant gratification society. Need to lose weight - take a pill! Want to buy something but do not have the money - put it on a credit card! Don't feel like cooking - drive-thru!

Self-Love is the process of really getting in touch with who you are. Creating a deep relationship with Self involves taking the time to work the clearing and connecting sections to prepare the way so your innermost desires *can* come forth. One stop on the path leads to the next, the final homecoming is You!

This powerful path is a process to move you from *pain* to *gain*. If you find value in your Self, if you are excited by the prospect of self-illumination and being supported by the abundant Universe, if you are open to the possibility of miracles of transformation, then the path is laid out before you! Welcome to that journey and Bon Voyage!

NOTE TO READER:

You will notice throughout this book that we have taken the liberty of capitalizing a few words not normally capitalized. For instance, Self is capitalized throughout because the self we are referring to herein encompasses the God, Universal, life-force energy. That delineation of the "little self" vs. the "the bigger Self' deserves special handling. We have also capitalized Spirit as writers would capitalize God. Spirit, that energy of everything that is everywhere present, is used universally throughout as describing the active aspect of God. And lastly, because this book is about Self-Love we felt the action of recognizing, acknowledging and loving yourself is the most important work one can do. By embracing the action of Self-Love you also embrace your highest Self, the essence of who you truly are.

To love oneself is the beginning of a life-long romance.
~ OSCAR WILDE

I don't like myself, I'm crazy about myself.
~ MAE WEST

"You, yourself, as much as anybody in the entire universe, deserve your love and affection."
~ BUDDHA

Contents

CONNECT

CREATE

Preface

t is my belief that from the so-called advancements in our society we have become disconnected - disconnected from ourselves, and from a higher power (Universe, Source, God, whatever you want to call it). A mere few hundred years ago, for example, the Native Americans and indigenous tribes everywhere were very connected to Mother Earth; living off the land, simply, taking only what they needed, honoring the spirit of the food, the animals and the earth. Take a look at the world now. We walk down the street talking on our cell phones, or not even talking, texting one another, spending hours sitting in front of a computer. We are absorbed in technology, taking us further and further away from nature, Spirit, and our Self, and our love of Self. In the original design, man and woman were created to have and maintain a connection with Spirit. Because of all the distractions and noise in our technological world, we are separated from the Divine, from our Selves. We have lost touch with that which grounds us, leading to disillusionment, aberrant behavior, and addiction. This disconnection can cause the individual to derail, to "fall off the path," to become depressed and stagnant, broken, and in pain. It has been my experience that regardless of a person's spiritual life, there has been an underlying cause for that disconnection, and that is a *resistance to Self-Love*. This book is a journey back. When we strip away technology, we embark on a journey to re-connect with that original design. When we stop, slow down, and listen to our thoughts, and the mind chatter running in our minds, we begin the process of re-connecting with our Self and Spirit, recreating the initial intention of being One on this planet. When that happens, it is transformational! When you are "hooked up" with Spirit, you operate from your authentic Self, you come from a place of trust and empowerment, you have a deeper relationship with yourself and create healthy relationships, work that you love, a healthy body, abundance, joy and peace. I am not advocating completely "unplugging" from technology, but by embarking on this journey of Self-Love you can reconnect with your Self, Earth, and Spirit.

> *Love of Self creates love for everything else and*
> *brings us closer to the sacred oneness.*
> *~Coyote Thunder*

Introduction

My First Retreat

This body of work originated many years ago with my first retreat to myself. I call it my first retreat because over the years and as a result of this experience I created hundreds of retreats to help others get in touch with their Highest Self and begin the journey of Self-Love. I was in my late twenties, and I had just broken up with a man who had been in and out of my life for the previous six years. It was around the Christmas holidays and friends were asking me to parties and I was down for the count, completely unable to be with people. I was depressed, I hit my rock bottom. I retreated to my own personal cave and surrendered. It wasn't just the relationship with the boyfriend that ended, I was questioning everything... what was my purpose in life, what is my contribution, why wasn't I happy? I began having realizations about my life. I did not have an addictive personality, but that does not mean that I did not find other ways to abuse myself: I was constantly talking negatively to myself; I made poor decisions about food and exercise; I was not clear about a career; I was making bad money decisions. I had just had this breakup, but in general my relationships were a mess, problems with my parents, friends, and siblings. This can only be classified as the proverbial "dark night of the soul." It was a time to be with myself and it lasted for months. My time was spent alone, walking, journaling, praying, meditating and reading. One book suggested an exercise for mirror work. I was in so much despair, I would have tried anything at this point. The process is to look at one's self, your eyes only, and notice your thoughts. Eventually I started talking to myself in the mirror daily... looking into my eyes and having a conversation with myself. I was beginning to be conscious of seeing something more in my eyes... some energy, some light, something.

I liked it. I did it more.

An awareness came to me that God, this energy, life force, or whatever you want to call it, is all around us, therefore it must live within us ... within our own being and in our own hearts. Your body, my body - this body - houses the Divine. I am the sacred vessel! How incredible! It became this funny thing to me ... I remember I started laughing in the mirror and thinking, "Since I was born I have been spending all this time chasing these men, searching for the perfect career, striving for money, beauty, acceptance..." Standing there, in front of the mirror, I knew the cosmic joke. How funny that I have *not* nurtured this being, my body, myself, this sacred temple that houses God. The most divine and sacred thing I could have done was to be loving and nurturing to myself, and put myself first. If God is within me, I am the vessel that holds the Divine. What could be more sacred than caring for that vessel?

In the following months I continued the walking, writing, and mirror work. I noticed I was being more loving and nurturing with myself. I began to feel that I *deserved* to be loving to myself. I felt stronger! Out of this, I can create a powerful relationship with myself and with Spirit. I can take that out to all my relationships. I can transform what is broken in my life. I wanted to shout it from the roof tops! "This is the key, people! Self-Love is the key!"

Do you want to meet the love of your life? Look in the mirror. ~Byron Katie

So that is what I did, and now 30 years later, hundreds of clients later, here is the book that describes the process from beginning to end.

The Journey Back to Self

Do you value yourself enough to take this journey? *That*, is the question.

We are born pure, a slate for our parents, our peers, our whole environment to write on. Some of us make it to adulthood without many issues, our proverbial "baggage." Most people, however, carry a caravan of issues by the time they reach puberty. Our wounds begin at a very early age, when we begin to experience trauma, loss, or fear. We shove our wounds down deep, so deep no one will see how much pain we are in. We develop unhealthy coping mechanisms, such as overworking; abusing alcohol or drugs; developing eating disorders or dependence on unhealthy relationships. We are expected to go through life broken, in pain, to keep working, producing, giving, until there is nothing left. No dreams, no self-respect, no integrity, no true authentic self, no me! The coping mechanism or choices we made that got us where we are now worked for awhile. Those choices are no longer working and now the cost of remaining in pain is greater than the fear of diving in, and freeing ourselves. Are you ready to put yourself first, to put your dreams first? To stand up and say, "I am not willing to continue along this path that I am on for one moment longer!" This is true self-responsibility. However we got here, whatever part we each, individually played, the choices we made (or refused to make) got us to the here and now. And now is when we will begin to make the changes that support ourselves to transform our life and become the Divine Self – the person we desire to be.

> *Only by seeing how in the past we have allowed problems to control us, and forgiving ourselves, can we really change and be free to go forward in life feeling more powerful, able to create the success and happiness we want.*

I will ask you in this book to become your own therapist. You are the sole authority on you. All the answers are already within you and you know how to navigate this path. You are the 'Psyche Detective' - examining your thoughts, your belief systems, looking at your life with fresh eyes and with an intention to discover what is working and what is not. The human psyche has been compared to an onion. You have to peel layer upon layer to get to the heart, to get to your true essence. This book will be your powerful path to return to Self. I will take you through many writing, meditation, and self-examination exercises to identify your issues, to "look in the baggage." Through my own personal stories and my teachings, I hope you will be able to see yourself and know you are not alone. You will get the most out of this book if you stop, and actually do the exercises and/or visualizations when prompted. Each of the writing exercises is notated with a ✎; each meditation is notated with an ☙; and each interactive exercise has a ➷.

There are three stops on our journey back to Self. *Clearing* is the first and most important step. This work will help complete the past and release the blocks of emotion that are limiting your life experience. We will be letting go of the thoughts and patterns that no longer serve. You will forgive yourself for the choices that have derailed you, and clear what is in the way of manifesting the life you love.

Connecting is our second stop on the path. By doing this clearing, by wiping the slate clean, by forgiving and acknowledging yourself, you can connect to a higher power and/or to your true authentic self. I will teach you how to ground yourself, to have compassion for your journey, and unite with your Spirit. By following the Connecting exercises we will experience what it feels like to be anchored to our Divine Self. This internal connection empowers us to move forward and make the changes necessary to progress to the next step.

Creating is our third and final stop on the path. After Clearing and Connecting we are now experiencing ourselves as the Divine Co-Creator of our lives. Knowing that you deserve all that you desire, you can begin to envision the life you were destined to live, before you detoured off the path. In this section's chapters I will share the manifesting tools to help you design and build your new life.

I have worked with hundreds of clients, and it always comes back to these three steps, *Clear – Connect – Create*, as the formula for transformation, change, and flow. There have been countless books written about "creating the life you want," there have been even more written about connecting with God. There have not been many books written about Self-Love. Self-Love is the key people… the missing piece and the path to transformation!

This path back to your Self has many a winding road and each of those roads have avenues of support, techniques, meditations, and actions you can take through the workbook and through my website www.cindypaine.com

to *Clear, Connect and Create*. This path may be difficult and even treacherous for some, and a remembrance for others. Even the most diligent students of this workbook will not clear everything. I have been working with these steps for the better portion of my life and issues still show up. There is no time table, there is no right way to work through the exercises. This, like Self-Love itself, is an organic journey of transformation. A year from now there may be a trigger by something that you believed had been cleared, brought out, lifted into the light, and released. You might say to yourself, "Self, I thought we had dealt with that already." But then it is time to bring out your workbook and peel back another layer of the onion.

This is the knowledge I have gathered over the course of my lifetime and is the basis of this work. In my spiritual journey I have studied with great teachers and masters for their knowledge, wisdom and contribution to consciousness on this planet. For example, even though I am Jewish, I have experienced teachings of Jesus who I consider a great teacher of Self-Love. I have studied the Kabbalah, Peruvian Shamanism, Guided Visualization, Meditation, EST Training, Landmark Education, the teachings of Prem Rwat, and more. My path has been an eclectic mix of all that I have been drawn to on my journey which has culminated in my work and this book.

All roads do lead to the One, but everyone's path is personal. Each individual has his/her own experience and beliefs when it comes to religion and spirituality. Religion is an organized system of beliefs or rituals centered on a supernatural being, as opposed to Spirituality which is similar but non-organized. If we remove the "supernatural" aspect, they are both the pursuit of Spirit, the quest of the soul. Where I use the word God, if you are uncomfortable with that word, substitute the word that works for you, such as Source, Universe, Love, whatever. I use words like God, Divine, Force, Spirit, Universe. For many, even the word "God" holds a charge. It is not my desire to impose or even suggest my own beliefs.

Where appropriate, I have quoted to prove a point, or when my paraphrase could not do the concept justice. The workbook style is designed to be your personal facilitator through this journey back to Self, to the Divine, and as co-creator in your life. Through these techniques, my students have come to feel a power and energy, reconnected with Source ... that Power ... that Spirit that enables people to transform their lives. Many have come to know and to love their true Self, a spiritual being having a physical experience. To love the Self that houses the sacred, the Divine... *that* is worth doing and from that love comes a sacred Oneness. As Coyote Thunder says, as each person transforms one's life, there is a divine rippling effect on all others and the planet.

CHAPTER 1

What Is Self-Love?

What do you think of when you think of Self-Love? Some people might say, Self-Love is taking time for a hot cup of tea, a bubble bath, or a great vacation. It is more than these ideas. Self-Love is a feeling, a consciousness, a practice, an adventure, a discovery, a sacred journey. It is the most important path you can take during your lifetime. It is an organic experience ever-changing; receding, and expanding. Here are examples of what I believe Self-Love is.

Self-Love is Your Relationship with your Self and Spirit:

- Caring for yourself and your body
- Putting yourself and your relationship with God first
- Making healthy choices
- Making conscious choices about how you "hold" your past, how you respond to the present, and how you create your future.

Self-Love is Your Relationship with Others:

- Being in integrity with your beliefs, speech, and the way you walk in the world
- Surrounding yourself with caring loving people
- Being kind to others and expecting the same in return
- Having boundaries and not allowing others (or yourself) to step over them

Self-Love is Expressed through Your Career and Finances:
* Doing what you have a passion for
* Getting paid what you are worth
* Honoring your truth and giving it a voice
* Feeling deserving of success

Self-Love is Allowing and Creating the Time to Step on this Path:
* Working on yourself
* Uncovering your authentic Self (and knowing who that is)
* Getting to the core of your patterns, blocks, and perceived limitations
* Tackling your core beliefs about yourself
* Nurturing your divinity
* Listening to your intuition, the language of your heart
* Coming from a place of strength (and knowing what that means)
* Forgiving yourself for your failures, illness, and for limiting your choices

Self-Love is Change:
* Identifying what you really want
* Creating a life with no regrets
* Having the courage to make choices and take action about all of the above

Self-Love is saying no (loving yourself enough to say no to another).
Self-Love is saying YES!

> *I do believe that the single most important thing I could ever, ever share with you regarding maximizing the health, harmony, and happiness in your life, not to mention expediting the manifestation of your heart's fondest desires, can be summed up in just two words: Love yourself. ~ Mike Dooley, TUT - The Universe*

> **What is Self-Love to you?**
>
> **What are your fears, beliefs, and negative thoughts around the concept of Self-Love? Write about it in a journal.**

From Selfish to Sacred

The notion of Self-Love is not selfish. I have to say that first because numerous people I talk to and work with immediately tell me that they were told growing up that working on their self is indulgent, egotistical, and narcissistic. There are even best-selling religious books about finding your purpose in life which dissuades the reader from doing any work on themselves calling it self-centered and selfish.

Love others as well as you love yourself. – Jesus, Mark 12:31

Most people will focus on the first part of Jesus' command, *love others,* without regard for the second part, *love yourself.* I find it difficult to believe that this master teacher wanted us to pay attention to only one half of his greatest commandment. If loving yourself was not part of the equation, his command would have just stated, "love others." Loving yourself and loving others is a reciprocal relationship. Loving yourself is equally as important and necessary. You cannot have one without the other. It is impossible to love others, if you do not love yourself first.

Women in our society, especially, are taught to care for and focus on everybody else and not think about themselves. In general, men do not take the time to look at themselves; they make work and productivity their priorities. Our Society, as well, with its constant barrage of technical distractions, does not naturally lead inward to self reflection and Self-Love.

Loving yourself, working on yourself, clearing your issues is the most unselfish, sacred thing we can do in a lifetime. It will allow you the freedom to create a life with no regrets. It is imperative that we shift from believing that our personal work is selfish to knowing our personal work is sacred.

The Sacred Journey

 Take a moment of reflection and imagine this:
What if you looked at your life as a journey, a quest for love, joy and peace? What if every person you met on this journey was a piece of the grand design, the puzzle that is your life? Each of them held a clue to solving the mystery of your experience.
What if everything that happened to you, the good and the bad, was part of that journey? The bad things happen so you can uncover for yourself the strength you possess. It also shows you who in your life you can count on and trust for support. The good things happen so you can feel the heights of joy, love, and laughter. Everything, absolutely everything, happens for a reason. It is your job on this journey to fit all the pieces together and understand for yourself WHY, and to give meaning to the journey. Your job is not to understand why other people do what they do, even if they do it to you. Your job is to not even take it personally, but to forgive, and discover what it means, to you. This is the journey of Self-Love. This is your quest for love, joy, and peace. This is the sacred journey.

Why is the Path to Self-Love Important?

So much of our lives are spent in the past. People stew and brew over past events and hurts. Wounds from childhood and adolescence continue to impact the decisions we make today. These early wounds limit us. They limit our ability to move forward, to take risks, to create the life we know, deep down, we deserve. And these are just the wounds that we know about! There are a whole slew of wounds operating in our subconscious that we are not even aware of, yet. There is hope. There is nothing wrong with you.

Everybody experiences wounding at times. We are able to move past our wounds and create a meaningful, authentic life that you enjoy. Within the covers of this book we will be developing new skills to get over and heal the wounded parts of ourselves. Only then can you find the joy that life has to offer. By taking the Self-Love path, you heal and clear the past and you are operating more fully in the present! You can experience what is happening NOW!

When we have cleared the blockages – the wounds, the past, the hurts - we are stronger, more connected with Self and a higher power, or that part of our self that is Spirit. We were designed to be connected to our God-Self. You will have greater creativity and ability to express yourself. You will be in the flow of Spirit. You will be resonating at a higher vibration. You will more easily manifest that which you desire. You will be closer to the original Divine Design that is You! When you love yourself, you are a much better mate, parent, friend, employee, and citizen. You become a greater role model for those around you (especially children). You are filled up; you have more to give. The more you love yourself, the more capacity you have to love others. You have something to give. You have more capacity for joy. You are more alive. You have more appreciation for your life, nature and the life around you.

Self-Love enhances our ability to appreciate what we have and have gratitude for it. Gratitude and Self-Love raise our vibration and this new vibration/energy expands without effort. Because your vibration is higher, lighter, more positive, people want to be around you. Your capacity to receive increases. Your ability to magnetize things, people, and situations to yourself is improved. Therefore, your ability to manifest and create is enhanced. Life becomes easier, less of a struggle. By taking the Self–Love journey, we bring harmony and balance to our lives by being whole, healthy, and nurturing to ourselves and others.

It's not your job to like me - it's mine. ~ Byron Katie

Expressing Self-Love

There are four major areas of your life that we will be focusing on throughout this book: relationships; career and finance; health and well-being; and spirituality. While reading these statements, think about what they mean to you and notice how you feel as you read each one. Self-Love may look like this:

Expressing Self-Love in Relationships:
* Release relationships that no longer serve you, are unhealthy or toxic
* Respect yourself enough to create strong boundaries
* Surround yourself with loving relationships
* Be yourself

Expressing Self-Love in the Area of Career and Finances:
* Receive a fair wage for your efforts
* Manifest your dream job
* Be in integrity with your finances
* Eliminate your credit card debt
* Have an emergency fund

Expressing Self-Love in the Area of Health (Physical, Emotional and Mental) and Well-Being:
* Make healthy food choices and exercising regularly
* Meditate
* Schedule a physical (mammogram, dental appointment, etc.) every two years
* Avoid dependence on addictive substances

Expressing Self-Love in Spirituality:
* Make time and space for nurturing your Spirit
* Attend workshops in the area of spiritual growth
* Feel connected to your Self
* Feel connected to a higher power
* Take time for inspiration, prayer, nature, ritual or meditation

If you were triggered or uncomfortable with any of the statements above, this would be a good place to begin. For example, when you read, Self-Love means making healthy food choices and exercising regularly, and you know that you do not do that for yourself, did you feel uncomfortable? This discomfort might stem from the knowledge that you are not living up to your own expectations. Or, this might be an area where you have some baggage, or as I will call it often throughout this book, you have a "charge" on this topic. For instance, this might be a charged area for you because you are overweight and have been overweight your whole life. Maybe you had experiences of being made fun of as a child, or maybe, your mother was critical about your weight when you were a child. You may have felt unattractive and unloved. So, the idea of loving your body, for example, triggered a response from you. My perspective on identifying and acknowledging this discomfort is "Congratulations!" If you feel uncomfortable, this is a pivotal point where you can say, "Hot Button!" There is a connection between what is happening in the present (unhealthy food choices) and memories of the past." My current charges are connected to my past. This is an area that I may need to look at closer and do some work around.

◆ **Write about anything that "triggered" you from the Expressing Self-Love list. We will go into more depth later, but here, just notice your feelings or any resistance you might have, and write about them.**

I have coined the term "Psyche Detective." I am asking you to become your own Psyche Detective while on this path. The psyche is defined as "the mind functioning as the center of thought, feeling, and behavior." You will investigate the "crimes" perpetrated against you in your past that have in some way colored your thoughts, feelings, and behaviors. Like a detective investigates crimes and uncovers evidence, you will be a detective for your psyche. In the example above related to health, you might describe frustration, sadness, and shame. When working with my clients, I listen and examine the feelings described, and then I ask questions: "What was your parent's relationship to food? What was it like around the dinner table? What are your earliest memories about your body?" And like a detective, I begin to try to make the connections between the current discomfort and the past event. I explore and dig deeper to discover the originating cause, the place where the original decisions, thoughts and feelings about your health were made.

There's always an underlying cause, it came from somewhere.

Somewhere in the past, there was an original wound, experience, or trauma around the body image. You will be uncovering the evidence of why you feel, think, and behave in certain ways. Once you acknowledge these wounds, you can heal and change them. You can create new thoughts, feelings, and behaviors that support the person you want to become. This journey supports you to be the Psyche Detective for yourself!

- **Describe your thoughts and feelings around an area of your life that you currently feel discontent or discomfort.**

Because I have taken this journey myself and worked with a multitude of people with these techniques, I know this works! At the start of this journey, there may be a part of you that does not even believe it is possible for you to transform your life. I will hold the sacred space for each and every one of you to move through what you need to move through in order to heal and fulfill your purpose. Know in your heart there is someone who believes in you, who is committed to your healing, and holds your hand *etherically* throughout this journey.

CHAPTER 2

Stepping on the Path

ur destination is Self-Love and the transformation of our lives. Before we set out on our path, we must prepare. What are we to take with us on our Self-Love journey, and what should we do in preparation?

Journal

There have already been a few writing exercises, and you will find many more. You will want to keep your own journal so that you can review your thoughts and feelings, impressions, and dreams that you have along the way. Purchase a journal that pleases you. Choose one that makes you feel good. Your journal will be one of the most important tools in working through the exercises in this book. You will be chronicling your thoughts and feelings, unedited. Unedited means you will be writing in the stream of consciousness with no attention to grammar or punctuation. Think of journaling as a way to take all the conversations that are continually bouncing around in your head and pour them out from your mind on to the paper. There will be many exercises constructed around journaling your experiences from the past in order to acknowledge what really happened. Often in doing this work, the subconscious gets "activated" in our dreams. Keep your journal by your bed, so you can write about your dreams when they are fresh in your memory. I write in the journal from the front to the back, and chronicle my dreams from the back to the front. The subconscious can show your underlying feelings about a situation through symbols. As a result of this work, you may find your dreams becoming more vivid. Do not limit yourself to just a journal. If an image reoccurs, draw it. If a song will not leave your head, sing it. We all process information differently. One of my clients says she would have never had a conscious thought if she did not have her girlfriend to talk to on the phone... so speak it!

Time

We need to give ourselves some time. Give yourself the permission to make YOU a priority. For this book to be effective you need to be willing to carve out some special *sacred* time to focus on this journey ~ the adventure of you. You do not need to retreat to a cave or withdraw to a mountaintop, but you need to be willing to maybe get up a half hour earlier, or turn off the phone and the television some evenings. It does not matter how fast or slow you work through this book, this work is time released, meaning once you step on the path to healing, it will take as long as it needs to take. This probably is not the type of book you want to read cover to cover, there is a lot in here you will want to savor. Take it slow. When I work with people on these techniques, we have a session each week and then they have a homework assignment to process the depth of their emotions. I tell them to "sit with" a concept for a few days, let it percolate before jumping into an exercise. Give yourself the time to do the work. Give yourself the time to heal.

Intuition

Your intuition is your innate knowing about an event or a person. It is your gut instinct. There are numerous ways to hone and honor your intuition. Do this by giving your intuition credit and validation. Follow your intuition. By following your intuition, you make it stronger. The Psyche Detective is closely linked to your intuition. For instance, throughout the Clearing section, you may be triggered by one of the exercises and not understand why.

There may be an event in your past that your conscious mind has chosen to forget, but that your intuition, your inner knowing, remembers and sends up warning flags. You, your own Psyche Detective, will begin to put together the pieces from where the charge is coming. In the meantime, as you embark on this journey, give yourself the gift of acknowledging when you are triggered by people and experiences. You do not have to know why. Begin by journaling these experiences to clear them out of your head. We will go back to the triggers later with specific exercises to bring them into the light and heal them.

Compassion

Many of you have compassion for your loved ones, but how about compassion for yourself? In order to cultivate the love of Self we will be working on being gentler and more compassionate with you. If this is not the way you currently operate, be open. Compassion is the ability to listen closely to your thoughts and feelings; compassion, then, allows your Self to acknowledge your thoughts and feel what needs to be felt.

It is easier for us to have compassion for the people in our lives, than to have that same compassion for ourselves. When a friend is upset and telling you a problem, you listen deeply, being fully present for them and putting yourself in their shoes. Having compassion for your Self is listening to your needs and feelings, instead of tuning them out, trying to change them, avoid them, drown them in drugs, food, alcohol, shopping, or some other form of distraction.

In this book, when I discuss compassion, it will be the compassion for oneself, allowing the space for yourself to feel whatever you are feeling in the moment. When we acknowledge our feelings, we are present with our feelings as they are. We give our feelings "room to breathe" without getting stuck in them. In our society, there is very little room for people to feel. If you watch a father with his son on a playground, and the little boy falls down and begins to cry, more often than not you will hear, "brush yourself off, boys don't cry, be a man." It is more acceptable for girls to express emotion as children, but any woman in the workplace will tell you that if you want to get ahead, outbursts of any emotion are taboo. We are trained at an early age to not allow room for our feelings. I would like to introduce a core quality of Self-Love: have compassion for *whatever* feelings you are experiencing. If you fully express the emotion, it will complete itself. The following meditation will begin to develop this ability to have compassion for yourself.

Guided Visualization for Compassion

(Reading this meditation slowly into a recording device and playing it back so you can be fully present with yourself while listening is the best way to experience any and all visualizations herein. Reading it and trying to go through it yourself from memory detracts from being able to fully evoke the emotions.) This visualization is about creating a space for your Self without judgment, accepting what is, and lovingly holding yourself in a place of compassion. In this visualization, we will be working with two aspects of your Self; the inner child aspect represents the emotions needing expression and acceptance and the adult aspect represents the nurturing, supportive, compassionate feelings for yourself.

Turn off the phones, get into a comfortable position. Close your eyes and take three slow deep breaths bringing yourself into this moment NOW. Imagine a room, your favorite color on the walls. Imagine soft light streaming in through the windows. In your mind, picture two comfortable chairs facing each other. Imagine yourself as both your adult self and your inner-child self walking hand and hand into the room. You sit down across from each other. You are first going to identify with being the child part which represents the emotions. Think about something from the past or an issue that is currently going on for you that makes you feel sadness, anger, fear, or any other uncomfortable emotion that comes up for you. Think about that experience and allow yourself to really go into the feeling of that emotion that is present for you. Letting it be there. Say anything you need to express about that feeling as the child. When children are angry, they can cry, throw a tantrum, stomp their feet, scream, and throw things. When they are sad, they might crumple up in a ball, cry, or hold their favorite stuffed animal. When they are scared, they may hide, close their eyes, and cover their ears. First identify which emotion is there. Allow the child to act out the emotion that has come up for you. Do not hold back. Visualize the full expression of that emotion. If you are sad, then cry. If you are angry, stomp around. Let your emotions continue to be expressed until you feel complete and return to the chair.

Now focus in as the adult. Remember a time in your life when you were comforted, held by a parent or someone who has loved you unconditionally. Most of us can recall an experience of completely being loved and held, your hair being stroked, the soft soothing words of someone telling you, "it will all be alright." Evoke these feelings for yourself. Really feel the safety, peace, and comfort. Now imagine yourself as that compassionate adult. Visualize yourself leaving the chair and going to comfort the emotional child. You take the child into your arms. Feel free to give your child-self a hug, and imagine that you are holding the child within. You comfort the child and tell her or him that it is o.k. to express their feelings. Let the child know that all of their feelings are good. Comfort the emotional child, the emotional being within yourself, with the nurturing, compassionate, loving energy of acceptance. Continue to express that compassion for your child until you feel complete, and return to your chair. Is there anything more your adult or child would like to say to each other? Let the thoughts, words, or feelings come.

When you are ready, imagine the parent and child getting up and again joining hands. The parent lovingly gazes down at the child and says, "Not to worry, whatever you are feeling is o.k. and I love and accept you." Together they leave the room. Slowly begin to bring your awareness back into your body and open your eyes.

Forgiveness

Forgiveness of others and ourselves is another step on our journey. We will discuss many aspects of forgiveness. First let us briefly discuss a false belief about forgiveness: when I forgive, I condone the bad behavior of another or myself. For example, people do not forgive an abusive father because they think that if they say, "I forgive you," they are saying that it was o.k. what you did to me. This is not true. By forgiving the person that transgressed us, we are not condoning the behavior, the act, the words, or the hurt. The experience happened. By forgiving, we are letting go of the grudge, and some of the feelings that continue to harm us because we are holding on to it. By carrying that story along, we carry that heavy burden of anger, outrage, shame, and any other unresolved feelings into the present. It continues to hold us in the past. By forgiving, we let go of the energy of that experience and find a way to move forward, into the present. The act of forgiveness is truly for the person *doing* the forgiving.

Support

Every person's journey is different. And for some, this work will be difficult. It is very important to have support on this journey. If you have a partner, let them know you are embarking on some interpersonal work, and that you might need some support and/or space. Put together a group of people committed to working through the exercises in the workbook. Let your friends know. Have one person in your life that you absolutely trust and train them in the Re-Creation Process which follows. I learned this process many years ago in a workshop, and have used it regularly with my best friend Susan to clear and complete huge chunks of trauma and emotion from my past. This is not your usual conversation with a friend, there is no typical back and forth banter or advice giving. The Re-Creation Process is a Clearing tool in which we will speak about a situation or experience with an intention to release it, complete it, and leave it behind. If you listen to conversations in the world, there is a lot of "bitching and complaining." The people speaking are not being Re-Created. Complaining feeds the negativity, and keeps you stuck in your story. The Re-Creation Process will bring forth the opposite intention – letting the story go and creating the space to make a new story. Speaking what is going on for you is an integral part of the Clearing process and we will be doing much more of this in the Clearing chapters.

The Re-Creation Process

 Your intention for the Re-Creation Process is to get complete on a situation in your life. It may be a situation that has you stirred up or if your mind is chattering or distracted. Your intention is to clear, release, and get present. It can be used for small, unimportant things that are niggling at you or large issues bothering you. This is a powerful way to keep clear and present in all your relationships. I have trained many couples, for example, to use this exercise to release conversations they are having about the other in their head, and greatly enhance their relationship to be more loving and in the present. You can use this tool with a partner either on the phone or in person. In this communication, the Sender speaks like he/she is taking out the garbage and sending it down a shoot. As the Sender, take your whole story of an experience, wrap it up, and hand it to the Receiver. You will be speaking about what is going on for you, everything you want to say that is rattling around in your mind. You speak about the things you feel you should not say, really getting in touch with your feelings and what is true for you right now in the moment. For example, if you are upset about your boss berating you in front of your co-workers, you would call your friend, and ask if he/she would help you "Re-Create" the experience. You would then tell the whole story that is going on in your head, all the details, the feelings, emotions and thoughts that have you charged or stirred up. You might speak about how you never felt acknowledged by your boss, how you have tried your hardest, how you are a better employee than anyone there. You might speak about how fearful you are that you may be passed over for a promotion, and how this is how you felt when your parents embarrassed you in front of your friends. Keep speaking until you feel complete. By speaking it, something within you has shifted and you no longer have attention on it. This process can complete the experience for you, significantly decreasing the charge or the emotional energy behind the experience. This process lessens the intensity of the feelings and releases them or lightens them to such a degree that they are manageable. This is one of the most powerful processes in the whole book. It can assist you in completing your emotional history, your baggage, and you can transform your relationships and keep them loving. If the Re-Creation process is done well, it can literally make difficult episodes in your life disappear. The Re-Creation process is also a window into your true emotions and allows for great insights.

The role of the Re-Creation Partner is silence. If in person, the Receiver does not touch the Sender or make any facial expressions. The Receiver should receive the communication without judgment. The Receiver is creating a neutral space for the Speaker to communicate into. The Receiver needs to be able to support the Speaker by being silent, not interrupting, not asking questions or adding anything, but only hearing the Speaker's experience. The Receiver is not to give their opinions or advice. When the Speaker stops speaking, the Receiver may ask, "Are you complete?" and then again be silent until the Speaker is silent. The Receiver's job is then done.

First, acknowledge who is the Speaker and who is the Receiver. If you are in each other's presence, sit across from each other. Then you will be doing a closed eye "Be-With" - "breathe with" each other, whether you are on the phone or in person. Close your eyes and take a few deep breaths. Bring yourself into this moment now by noticing your heartbeat, breath, the temperature of the air on your skin. Fully bring yourself into the present moment with an intention for the Speaker to be complete and the Receiver to be fully present and hear the Speaker. Open your eyes and if present with each other, gaze into each other's eyes with the intention to create a safe space. If not together, still hold the intention of a safe container for this work. The acknowledged Speaker will begin sharing until they are complete. Once the Speaker is done, do the "Be-With"- "breathe with" again. Next, the person who was the Speaker is now the Receiver and vice- versa. The new Speaker begins sharing until they have a feeling of being complete. At that point, the Receiver asks, "Is there any more to share?" The Speaker needs to look within to see if they have anything more to say, and if not, both people can now enter into a short Releasing Visualization. Each person should close their eyes, take a deep breath with the intention to release the communication that just took place and allow the energy that was in their head to flow down all the way through their body into the ground.

Sending it deep down into the earth and allow the light from the center of the earth to travel up through the layers of the earth into their feet, legs, trunk of the body, heart, throat, head and out the top of the head and let it go. When ready, each person can open their eyes and acknowledge their partner. The Re-Creation Exercise is now over.

Professional Support

One last word about support, do seek out professional help if you find that you are depressed for a period more than two weeks, if your appetite and sleep are disrupted, or if you have thoughts of harming yourself. Sometimes our burdens are too difficult to deal with on our own. It is Self-Loving to ask for and accept help and support.

Self-Responsibility

I will ask you throughout this book to "own it," to acknowledge and admit to yourself the part you played in any given circumstance. Taking responsibility for yourself, your behaviors, actions, and feelings, removes the word "victim" from your vocabulary. Whether you chose or refused to choose, stuff did not just happen to you. You are where you are as a result of your actions. An act of God can blow down your house, and you may not see your responsibility there. You are responsible for how you respond to that tragedy. The knowledge and growth that occurs in our responses, or our reactions, is what we are here to learn. This level of self-responsibility may be a new concept to some of you. What does it mean to fully take responsibility for yourself?

- You do not blame others for the choices you have made.
- You do not live in the past letting blame, regret, or fear hold you back.
- You choose the direction for your life.
- You are responsible for what you choose to feel and think.

- You teach others how to treat you, and you are responsible for expressing your needs in a relationship.
- You structure your life by managing your time and stress effectively, allowing yourself to rejuvenate and relax when needed.
- You own your own part in the situation. Are you willing to ask yourself, "where am I responsible?" Are you willing to tell others, "I am fully responsible for myself..."

Ready to go! We have our special journal or sketch pad, and we have carved out some sacred time. We acknowledge our feelings in the present moment. We have packed a healthy dose of compassion and forgiveness for ourselves and others. We have alerted our support team or our loved ones that we are embarking on a spiritual path and we are ready to take responsibility and act responsibly on that journey.

Spiritual transformation happens outside of time and space.
You are entering new territory – we will be clearing the past,
connecting in the present, and creating a new future!
Congratulations, and Bon Voyage!

CHAPTER 3

How the Journey Works

We will be taking this journey together. I will be your guide, asking you to notice your thoughts and feelings, urging you to dig deeper in your consciousness for the true source of your behaviors. What is your true purpose?

Our Emotional Body

Science is finally catching up with what Eastern medicine and masters have taught for thousands of years. There is a direct correlation between a person's emotions and the body's physical symptoms that are created if one's feelings are not expressed. I recommend Louise Hay's, *Heal Your Life*, the proverbial "bible" that connects the underlying causal thought patterns to physical symptoms. I propose that our emotions also dictate many of our life experiences as our soul's way of healing events from our past. Our emotions are our bodies' way to guide us and communicate with us. It is our natural energetic response to what we experience. It is our bodies' call to get our attention. When we experience physical pain our brain tells us to move, get out of trouble, and take action. Likewise, when we experience emotional pain, it is our brains' way to wake us up to a stressful relationship, a distressing situation, or an aspect of our life that needs help. Fear, distress, anxiety, worry, and despair are all signposts on the road to health, healing, and balance. It is our soul's way of saying, "It is time to change."

This journey will be taking place on many levels. Physically, I will be guiding you through exercises designed to clear out the blocks, the dense energy that is slowing down your progress towards your goals. Whether that blockage comes from the past, from fear, or from a lack of attention on yourself, we will begin to understand and make different choices. We will also be looking at the way the brain works unconsciously and will retrain the brain's functions to change your behaviors. I will be helping you change your thoughts and attitudes towards your life. The emotions are the conduit through which we will be taking this journey. Spiritually you will be getting in touch with the Divine and experiencing a renewed sense of Self and the sacred in your life.

Energy

This type of metaphysical work is energy-based. We know that the physical universe is made of energy. The constant quality about energy is that it moves. Matter is relatively dense energy. Our thoughts are relatively fine or a light form of energy. Feelings, like thoughts are light or heavy depending on the feeling. Sorrow and fear are heavier, happiness and joy are lighter. All forms of energy are inter-related and can affect one another. Energy is magnetic. *Like energy attracts like energy.* So therefore, if I have a traumatic thought or experience, and I was never encouraged or felt safe to express or cry about that experience, this energy can get stuck. This dense energy of unresolved feelings can become like a *wound* within me or my energy field. If I, consciously or unconsciously, continue those wounded thought patterns, I will *re-create* this experience until it gets healed. Energetically, the energy of the wound sends a signal out and attracts more of the same, setting up life-long wounding patterns that make us feel the same way. We will attract that same or a similar experience that makes us feel the same way until that wound is healed. Clearing, is getting to the root of the original experience. It is a way of actually re-experiencing the experience - expressing, feeling and emoting through a variety of techniques - breaking apart that wound so the signal is neutralized or completed. When you clear that dense energy and you put out a new signal of choosing love, joy, and peace, or anything else your heart desires, then that signal goes out and attracts more of the same and the transformation is complete.

We are all part of one great energy field which is God, He/She, the Universe, the Source, Energy, Creator, Yahweh, Jehovah, Buddha, Spirit... therefore we are a part of God, and God is part of us. That is who we are. We see things as being solid and separate from us through our limited physical senses, when really they are just forms of energy vibrating at different rates of speed, from finer to denser, from lighter to heavier. If that is the truth, and we are made up of that same energy, then we are literally all One. And as you step on this path, *One* will meet you and guide you, regardless of your spiritual upbringing or beliefs.

Intention

Over and over throughout this book you will read...

What you focus on, is what you create.

I will ask you to begin to make choices that are in alignment with your highest purpose and Source's purpose for you. That of course will mean that you have to decide what you want to create. There is a phrase frequently used in Real Estate, the most important thing is, "location, location, location." When I studied shamanism, my teacher explained to us that in this kind of metaphysical work the key phrase is "intention, intention, intention." Your intention includes the commitment you need to focus on your target. Take aim, pull back the bow and then shoot your arrow at the bull's-eye. Creating what you want will require a total commitment of your emotional, mental, spiritual and physical being. A laser-like-focus with a clear and specific goal in alignment with your purpose is the strongest force in the Universe. Miracles happen!

Energy Flow

How do you know if a goal is in alignment with your true heart's desire? We will answer this question in more depth in the Create chapter, but the quick response is to answer the question with another question: Is there flow? Do I feel light or heavy?

To clarify this principle, I will expound on a personal experience of mine from years ago. I had been trying to manifest an events business for a year. I had the contacts and the people, venues, and details in place, and felt this should have been a relatively effortless revenue stream to develop; yet there were obstacles at every turn. We finally had a breakthrough and organized two large weddings. This was going to be our big launch! You can guess what happened. What could go wrong, did go wrong. The energy around this project was heavy and challenging. I got the message that the Universe did not want me to pursue this path. While I was beginning the events business, I began seeing clients privately to do this coaching work. As much as I was "out of the flow" trying to develop this events business (which was definitely not working), I was "in the flow" when I started putting my focus and intention in developing my spiritual coaching business. The energy of being able to assist people in their transformation felt light, joyful, and effortless. Within a week, I had manifested 13 new clients! This showed me that I was on the right path – there was flow!

- Recall an experience when you felt you were definitely NOT in the "flow." When you felt like a person pushing a boulder up a mountain. How did that feel? What was the outcome? Recall an experience when you felt you were in the "flow." How did it feel in comparison? What was the outcome?

Warning: Shift Happens

Once you put forth your intention, the Universe aligns with that intention in order to support you. Be prepared. At this point your thoughts, feelings, and belief systems can get stirred up and things may get worse before they get better. Everything feels exaggerated and everywhere you look, that theme plays out: the music on the radio becomes a soundtrack for your experience; your boss begins to remind you of your father; a single girl longing for relationship sees couples everywhere she looks. When I started to want to do relationship courses, my relationship issues came up, during my abundance courses, money became a big issue. Many would dismiss these events as coincidence. They absolutely are not. Synchronicity is consciousness in action, Spirit guiding us. When you state your intention, you put the spotlight on that area, the laser is on that part of your life, and the Universe brings the awareness to that area for you. Be *aware* of all the little signals the Universe sends you for expansion, healing, and flow. Allow them to comfort you on your journey, and know that your resolve to change has put you in the flow of life-force energy.

The Universe's flow does not always come in positive. For instance, I had a client named Marge who first came to me wanting to work on her finances. Once we began to look at these and some of her other issues, it became apparent to us both that her financial issues were first her mother's issues and many of her beliefs were "inherited." Most people have heard the saying, "what you resist, persists." In her efforts to *not* be like her mother, she was exhibiting many of her mother's destructive behaviors. When she clearly stated her intention to clear up her finances, a firestorm of activity erupted in the financial department: within days she was served a court summons from a debt collector; an old friend whom she owed money and had fallen away, reappeared wanting repayment; and her car broke down and needed several hundred dollars in repair. All of these events forced her to do the hardest thing for her, which was to look at her finances and deal with the reality of them, and to look at herself and what was really going on. As she was going through the experience, though somewhat devastating at the time, she had to knowingly smile to herself because she had, "called it in." All of these events were forcing her to be in integrity with her finances. The Universe was just making sure she was *fully* in integrity, and also fully in the *flow*. Once you state that intention with clarity, watch and see how the Universe responds.

Energy Drains

Commitment and intention to change your life in a new direction is a process of gathering your emotions, mental strength and abilities to focus them towards what you desire to achieve. You can better achieve your goals when you have gathered up your energy. What if you took all the energy that you use for the feelings of worry, regret, and fear that drain you, and gathered up that energy and put it towards your goals? What if you took all the situations, relationships and people in your life that are not sustaining their own energy but pulling energy from you, and used it for your own creation? How much more energy would you have? Scattering our energy keeps us distracted, unclear, and lacking the energy that manifestation requires. Plugging energy drains will require that we become more disciplined in our thoughts, releasing those that you can do nothing about, and allowing other people in your life to take responsibility for themselves.

* **List who or what are the energy drains you can identify in your life. How do they drain you and how does it affect you? How could you use this energy for yourself or for your own goals, dreams, and desires?**

Willingness vs. Will Power

Analyze your perception of change. Everybody prefers to stay in their comfort zone. Most people do not have much flexibility. Change can be uncomfortable, new, and different. We make most of our difficult decisions when we are faced with consequences. The status quo, the ego, our physical senses and old-fashioned instant gratification can override our resolutions for change. Lasting change takes time. In many cases, when one is trying to change a certain aspect of their lives, they tend to rely solely on will power. The word will-power... it is forceful, it is bold, it is conquering... and it does not last. The way we need to approach lasting positive change is not as much through our will as through our *willingness* to change. Will power denotes success or failure, the hand is closed like a fist, forcing change. Willingness is open to experimentation, support, the hand is open to receive, open to advice, and a new way of doing things. Here are a new set of tools to help you make different choices; to help you make lasting change.

Self-discipline

One of the ways to help ourselves begin to change is to strengthen our self-discipline. Self-discipline is like a muscle. If we have given into temptation enough times, that muscle is weak. It is weak from lack of use. You can make that muscle strong by "resistance training." We begin by resisting the desire to do the unnecessary, unimportant, harmful, and useless things in our lives. These too, are energy drains. They can be looked at as that which takes you away from your heart's desire. While you just identified some people or situations that are likely energy drains, now identify the more insidious ways our energy can be drained.

◆   **What experiences or routines do you regularly participate in that are: Unnecessary: Unimportant: Harmful: Useless. Start your resistance training. Write about how can you begin to resist some of these activities in order to make your goals a priority?**

To strengthen self-discipline we must constantly make the choice for our highest good and follow- through with the physical action – the follow through of the action as a result of our intention is the most important part. Start small. Make a small step towards self-discipline to begin building that muscle. For instance, if you drink too much caffeine, go for one day without coffee. Make the choice to not eat after 8pm, and stick to it. This is a conscious, self-loving choice.

Giving Yourself Permission

One of our biggest societal problems is how hard we are on ourselves. We drive ourselves to the point of absolute exhaustion, feeling that we do not deserve to rest and rejuvenate. This is not loving ourselves. Stress is a very real disease and can lead to a multitude of health problems. Just as it is important to begin to exert some self-discipline, it's just as important to give ourselves permission to have fun. Give yourself permission to experience Self-Love. The following is a list of Self-Loving acts. Tab this page to refer back to throughout the reading of this book.

Acts of Self-Love

* If you do not exercise, do 10 sit-ups a day working towards 100
* Get an extra hour of sleep every night for a week
* Say no to an invitation when you really do not feel up to it
* Take the first step, and reach out to a friend you have not spoken to in several months
* Do not say anything negative about yourself to anyone
* Take a real weekend, do not work
* Take a news-fast, no nightly news, internet, or newspapers for a week (start with one night: no media)
* Do not be involved in the gossip at work for a week
* When doing simple tasks, do it mindfully, focusing all your attention on the task at hand (i.e. dishwashing, raking, sweeping, etc.)
* Take three slow focused breaths whenever you have anxiety
* Meditate ten minutes a day and build up
* Take a bath with your favorite scent and candles
* Read a magazine or a light, fluffy novel
* Breathe and meditate
* Play with a child, hold a baby, or look through old photos
* Play your favorite piece of music
* Stretch out in the sun and lay in the grass
* Tend your garden
* Go to a waterfall or fountain and just listen
* Curl up with a blanket and take a nap

- *Buy your favorite flowers*
- *Visit a thrift store, used book store or art supply store*
- *Daydream, look out the window and drink tea*
- *Light candles all over your home*
- *Pull out a coloring book and crayons*
- *Bake a batch of chocolate chip cookies*
- *Spa at home: paint your nails, give yourself a facial, massage your feet*
- *Hang out in a hammock*
- *Eat an ice cream cone*
- *Star gaze*
- *Spend a few minutes in silence, taking some deep breaths*
- *Go to the library and get a great book*
- *Take a walk in your neighborhood, and just listen to the sounds of nature*
- *Watch an old movie*
- *Feel free to make up your own.*

The key here is to do these things guilt-free, knowing you deserve to enjoy yourself and take a break! Notice how you feel as you read this list and participate in these Self-Loving behaviors. When you have done any of these Acts of Self-Love, congratulate yourself! How did you feel during and after you completed any of these actions? Notice your thoughts, feelings and any resistance you might have felt.

- **Journal about how it felt to do these Self-Loving Acts. Open up the dialogue with yourself as to why you might feel that way. If you do feel resistance or guilt about doing anything Self-Loving for yourself, write down your feelings, and thoughts. We will work on this more later.**

Big changes can be difficult to make. Changing major behaviors such as eating habits, and addictions takes real commitment. These behaviors are deeply ingrained. Sometimes our self-esteem and the level of Self-Love that we are operating from are so low that to even suggest positive change seems like an impossible task. It is not impossible. Ask yourself, "what more is possible?" If you do not feel that you are at the place where you can commit to yourself to make the changes, look to see who are the loved ones in your life? Can you do this for them? For example, being Self-Loving sets a good example for your children, or eating healthfully can inspire your spouse to do the same. Use whatever you can to empower yourself to be committed. Trust this book and trust the process. Just *know*, that even when you feel you cannot do it, I know you can do it, and I hold the vision for your transformation.

Committing

Before you begin to delve in, let us examine your level of commitment. Let's face it, we probably all have books on our shelf that represent what we would *like to do or what we should do* for our self. I hope this is not one of those books for you. I really would like you to follow through on the exercises and do the interpersonal work and devote time to it. Your results will be a direct correlation to the amount of effort you commit. You must have the willingness to take a leap of faith that this can actually work. Believe that the change can really happen. Are you willing?

A Test for Willingness

Circle 1 2 3 4 5, 1 being the most willing, 5 being reluctant.

I am willing to get up early to meditate.	1 2 3 4 5
I am willing to journal my thoughts and feelings.	1 2 3 4 5
I am willing to do the work to define my heart's desire.	1 2 3 4 5
I am willing to forgive someone in my past.	1 2 3 4 5
I am willing to look deeply at my own childhood experiences.	1 2 3 4 5
I am willing to dream and have a new vision of my life.	1 2 3 4 5
I am willing to let go of people and things that do not support me.	1 2 3 4 5
I am willing to be honest with myself with what I need to change in my life.	1 2 3 4 5
I am willing to be open to new ways of looking at things.	1 2 3 4 5
I am willing to be more disciplined in certain areas.	1 2 3 4 5

I am willing to create a new story and let go of the old story.   1 2 3 4 5

I am willing to change my routines.   1 2 3 4 5

Willingness is directly tied to worthiness.

◆ **As you have just filled out your levels of willingness, journal about your attitudes towards those levels. If you found yourself unwilling to do some things in the list, did it stem from a knowing in your heart that you would not do that for yourself, or that you had failed to do that in the past? What if your best friend asked you to do it for them?**

Any resistance you feel here is a correlation to your worthiness and what you feel you deserve. Throughout this book, we will expand your feelings of worthiness and fill your life with more of the things you enjoy. You are making this effort for the most important person in the world... YOU!

Now that you have a better understanding of how this path will unfold and what are some of the areas we are working on, I will ask you here to commit to step onto the path with me.

Committing

I am committed to stepping on this path of Self-Love. I am willing to Clear, Connect and Create Self-Love in my life.

Signed:_____   Date:_____

I am committed to stepping on this path of Self-Love with you. I hold the vision of you manifesting your highest potential. I hold the vision of you embracing your journey of Self-Love and your highest expression.

Signed:_____ *Cindy Paine* _____

Now that you have committed to the path, there may be more than one area of your life that needs attention. My suggestion is to work with one area at a time and then you can always go back through the book and work with another area. Remember, we are working with the sub-conscious and it may not be obvious where to begin. Our Self-Love evaluation in Chapter 4 will help you reveal the primary wound and where you might want to step onto the path.

Self-Love Self Evaluation

ince the beginning of this book, we have outlined what it looks like to be loving to yourself. Let us look at the areas in your life that might need an adjustment or a complete overhaul. Below are some of the qualities and activities that people who are loving to themselves enjoy. Check off the statements that you find are absolutely true for you. Do this without judgment (really, no judgment).

Relationships:
- ☐ I tell the people in my life that I love them.
- ☐ I surround myself with caring loving people who support and empower me.
- ☐ I get along with my family members.
- ☐ I have released relationships that are toxic or unhealthy.
- ☐ I am able to fully express my feelings.
- ☐ I ask for what I need and want.
- ☐ I am comfortable setting and defining boundaries for myself.
- ☐ I do not hold on to past hurts or transgressions.
- ☐ I am able to communicate effectively when I have been hurt or have caused pain to another.
- ☐ I refrain from gossip, and being critical of others.

Career & Finance:

- ☐ I am passionate about my work.
- ☐ I work well with my co-workers.
- ☐ I take evenings, weekends, and holidays off. I use my vacation and sick days.
- ☐ My earnings are fair and commensurate with my experience and efforts.
- ☐ I pay myself first and save 10% of my income.
- ☐ I have a budget and a plan for financial security.
- ☐ I spend money responsibly.
- ☐ I am in financial and legal integrity: IRS, debts, tickets, car insurance, a will, alimony and/or child support.
- ☐ I am insured: health, life, and home insurance.

Health & Emotional and Mental Well-Being:

- ☐ I rest when I am tired.
- ☐ I am a healthy person with no ailments, disease or attention on my health.
- ☐ I have been to the doctor for a complete physical in the last year.
- ☐ I have seen a dentist in the last six months.
- ☐ I have had an eye exam in the last 2 years.
- ☐ My weight is in within ideal range.
- ☐ I exercise at least three times per week.
- ☐ I have a rewarding life beyond my work or profession.
- ☐ I do not have any behaviors that I consider addictive: alcohol, drugs, sex, tobacco, work, food, shopping or relationships.
- ☐ My environment reflects peace.
- ☐ I am able to remain calm in tense situations and do not respond with anger or irritation to myself or others.
- ☐ I allow myself to feel my feelings in the moment.
- ☐ I have had an AIDS test.

Spirituality

☐ I take the time to do personal growth work, either alone or with a facilitator or group.

☐ I have examined my core beliefs and remain open to growth and change.

☐ I hear and listen to that still small voice within.

☐ I have a clear vision to create my ideal life.

☐ I honor my truth and give it a voice.

☐ I meditate every day.

☐ I take the time for myself to be in nature daily.

☐ I take at least 15 minutes a day to journal, read inspirational material, or pray in order to connect with myself.

☐ I have an experience of something greater than myself to which I am connected.

☐ I have in place a practice of gratitude and thankfulness.

Look over your self-evaluation. Where you see the most checkmarks, are the areas in your life where you are being the most loving to yourself. The area that has the least amount of checkmarks (or none) is in some way being ignored or avoided. This is probably the area in your life that you want to work on first. Remember, this is a book about Self-Love. It is *not loving* to be mentally beating yourself up about the areas of your life that do not have many (or any) checkmarks. Now that we have identified what area you might want to start delving into first, let us begin to look at some of the stories we are telling ourselves.

> *Stories provide understandings which sharpen our sight,*
> *so that we can pick up the path... leading us deeper*
> *into our own knowing. – Clarissa Pinkola Estes*

Our Stories

Each one of these statements in the self evaluation represents the tip of the iceberg. The stories that we tell about a situation in our life can provide understandings which sharpen our insight leading us deeper to our knowing ourselves. The statements were designed to begin to paint a picture: showing you a piece of the situation at play. Not being able to place a checkmark in the box, means there is something going on there. There is a story to be told and released. Let us begin to make it personal by adding some specific circumstances that are happening in your life. If your area of challenge is financial, like our following example, your story of your challenge might look something like this:

☐　I am doing what I have a passion for.
　　I hate, hate, hate my job! I want to start my own Internet business but I have to work this job to pay the bills. But I'm not making any headway there. And at the end of the day of dealing with people, I'm just too tired to work on my stuff.

☐　I work well with my co-workers.
　　I like my co-workers, but I work in a service environment so all of our conversations revolve around how much we hate the customers.

☐　I take evenings, weekends, and holidays off. I use my vacation and sick days.
　　I haven't taken a vacation in 4 years. I work weekends most of the time.

☐　*My earnings are fair and commensurate with my experience and efforts.*
　　My wages are measly and a joke. I am college educated and working in customer service.

☐　I pay myself first and save 10% of my income.
　　Ha, I wish! I live pay check to pay check.

☐ I have a budget and a plan for financial security.
There's no plan. I worry about not finding the right relationship and am afraid of being alone. What will happen to me? I'll never have a home or be able to retire. I don't know how to do a budget when there's just not enough.

☐ I spend money responsibly.
I spend responsibly most of the time. Well, I had to have that new pair of leather boots because they were SUCH a deal! I would have regretted not picking them up, and don't I deserve a little something for putting up with this crummy job?

☐ I am in financial and legal integrity: IRS, debts, tickets, car insurance, a will, alimony or child support.
This is the killer. I'm in a ton of debt, my car could be booted because of unpaid tickets. I'm just waiting for that to happen. I sit and worry about my bills. I don't answer the phone because I'm afraid of collection calls.

☐ I am insured: health, life, and home insurance.
I don't own a home but I do have health insurance, which is one of the reasons I stay at my crummy job.

What IS?

What do you tell yourself? We all have a conversation going on in our heads that we tell our self about our current circumstances. We might tell a different story to our family and friends. Much can be learned by taking the story out of our heads and putting it on paper. The story is just a story, it is not happening in current time. It is not even real: it is a construct of our mind and our ego. It is a way of expressing who we think we are: it is a way of communicating that is not in our highest good. Every time we tell the story, we add mass to it and we make it real, more solid, and heavy. The more we keep telling the story, the more we create the story. Our lives are dictated by the stories that we tell ourselves. The story alone can be the most binding thing in our lives. If what we focus on we create, eventually, there is no room to move. The conversation that was continually being told in our example was an extreme, but in this case the message was, "*I am stuck.*" She looks at her pile of bills she cannot pay, she has no plan to get out of debt, and she stays at a job she hates. This is just WHAT IS, the now. For better or worse, this is where our example focuses her attention, and this is what she creates more of in her life.

We might keep from our loved ones the situations that we fear or feel ashamed. The secrets that we keep from our Self, however, can be downright damaging. Many times it is the story that we are hiding behind, so we do not have to take full responsibility for a situation. Why do we tell them? There is a payoff and a cost. We say our story over and over again for these core reasons:

- to make us right, to make the other person wrong
- to punish people
- to not take personal responsibility

We will begin to define the payoff and cost for our story.

From the Mental to the Emotional

Spock, the well-known character from Star Trek, had completely attained control over his emotions and only valued the logical approach to any situation. But time and again, it was the emotional or intuitive approach that got Captain Kirk and the crew out of harrowing situations. When a situation is uncomfortable, we often approach it with the mental fortitude of Spock, processing the mental without feeling it. Just the facts – reporting the details - or as I often say, "You are just a head." We cannot get to the essence of any situation without feeling it, and we cannot change any situation without feeling it. What do you feel about your story? It is only through really feeling the cost of continuing the behavior that you will be able to commit to change.

Writing Your Story

Write out your story about the area in your life you want to change. Add the details. Be honest with yourself. This is just for you, no one will read it or judge you. Write the story, even if it is embarrassing, or makes you uncomfortable. Write it all down, even if you think you should not think like that, or feel that way. I want your story to be very specific. Write down the amount of debt you have. Write about your relationship with God and religion. Write how you really feel about your boss. Write about the men who have left. The story you tell yourself, keeps you stuck. Since we do not live our lives in compartments, you might want to write your story for each of the areas because our challenges can bleed over into areas that are working perfectly fine. Write as much as you need to about every area, career and finance, relationships, spirituality and your health.

As you can see in our example, she not only has dissatisfaction around her finances, but she has fear around never finding a mate or having a home and security. We can only begin to change that which we accept about ourselves. Remember, our stories are not always bad. Sometimes we have empowered stories to tell, which will allow you to look differently at the areas that are not working so well. Maybe you expect great success with lots of money coming in. You expect to live well and have a nice home. You do not have a negative story in the finance area, but in another area you might.

As you are writing, what other feelings are coming up for you? Take note of where you feel the energy of your story in your body. When writing about your finances, you may get a pain in your lower intestine and feel like you have to go to the bathroom. When thinking about your career your shoulders might tense up. Call your attention to your body through this process and remember to breathe. Earlier I told you that thoughts and feelings have an energetic mass. When those thoughts and feelings are not expressed, it causes a wounding within us with its accompanying energetic thought pattern. So, in effect, by telling our stories, we are beginning to identify the thoughts that keep us stuck, and the places in our body and our life where the energy has stopped moving.

There are many ways to view the same set of circumstances. We will be going back again and again to fill in more pieces of our story. We will be releasing that story and create a new story for our lives. First, we need to take a moment and take three deep breaths because we are going deeper, and our path begins with Clearing.

CLEAR

CHAPTER 5

What Is Clearing and What Does It Do?

Clearing is...

* Releasing
* Letting go of the past
* Addressing and dissolving your wounds
* Erasing the history
* Freeing yourself
* Getting rid of tension, fear, anxiety, and stress
* Removing stuck patterns
* Making space for new growth and manifestation
* Experiencing yourself as part of the Universe
* Stopping the mind chatter
* Clearing is a way to be present
* Clearing is a way to demonstrate Self-Love

Why Clear?

We clear in order to create more peace and joy in our life. We clear to be present. We clear to release anything that is impeding our path to our own heart's desire. We clear to empower ourselves to face our fears. We clear to be free from the limitations that either we, or someone in our life, have placed upon us. We clear to call back the pieces of our soul that we have left along the path. Unfortunately, the consequences can be dire if you do not clear. Blocked "stuff" in the form of thoughts, feelings, and clutter can be the source of suffering, problems, and illness.

Recurring patterns are a motivating force; usually someone has to be really sick of something in order to change it. If a person is fed up and tired of a situation, he/she will seek answers somewhere. Some will call a psychic hotline, some will seek out a therapist, some will call a friend, some will meditate, and some will fall back on destructive patterns of denial. But when a person can no longer tolerate a situation, clearing gives hope for change.

Clearing the Past

The past can rule your life. It can be just as current for many people as the ticking hands on the face of a clock. We will begin with clearing the past. What do I mean by saying that the past can be current? For many, if something happened in the past that needs to be healed and has never been dealt with, the decisions and belief systems operating in the present can often be affected by that past event. Clearing is a technique that allows you to make new decisions and beliefs and change your present! There are many ways to clear, and I will give you a variety of techniques. In clearing the past, we will look back at the root cause or experience of an originating wound. There is no way to escape our woundedness, to whatever degree, we all have wounds. It is impossible to be human and not have wounds. Your wound could have occurred five minutes ago or 25 years ago, it does not matter. When you acknowledge and bring up to consciousness a past event that made you feel wounded, you become present to what is actually occurring in the now. We are about to learn when you clear it away with a technique, then there is room for you to be with the current experience of your life without the weight and energy drain of an incomplete, originating drama.

The Garden Analogy

Imagine that you decide to plant a garden. You plan to grow vegetables, fruits, flowers, or herbs. You have your plan for where things will be placed and you have your seeds. You have your plot of land in a nice sunny spot. But your land is full of weeds since nothing new has been planted in awhile. *Your life is like your garden!* You want to change some things and plant some new seeds, create new things in your life – a new loving relationship, a new job, or a new home. But the weeds are choking off the growth of your flowers. The weeds are your issues – anything from the past that has stopped you from creating this new growth. The roots of the weeds go deep down into the earth – or deep into your psyche. If you just pluck off the top of the weed – talk about it, pray about it, do affirmations around it - your plot of land is clear and you think you are ready to plant your seeds, but if you do, those pesky weeds will come back and choke off all your new growth. You need to dig all the way down to the beginning of the root, and dig underneath it and pull it out completely, so it will not come back. When you clear weeds out of your garden, you use a hoe or a shovel to get to the root. Likewise, to clear our past, we use the tools and techniques found in the next section to get to the root as well. Once you have done the Clearing, it is time to prepare the soil. This is the where we Connect; we do this by *connecting* with your Self, the Earth and Spirit. As related to the garden, Connecting is to prepare your soil, adding water and sun, fertilizer and anything which will nourish your garden and your new growth. When all three of these aspects of Self are aligned we move forth to Create the garden. When you are present and connected with yourself, supported by Mother Earth, and the Divine, you have the power to manifest and really bring forth your heart's desire. Seeds need to be planted to Create. We will be planting the seeds with our intention and we will be doing that in a way that will yield a beautiful bounty.

How Do We Clear?

When we are children and something happens that is traumatic, disturbing, or emotional and we do not have the words to express ourselves about it, we make a decision about what is happening and with those decisions we eventually form a belief about it. Those beliefs may dramatically affect our lives and our ability to manifest the life we want today. Clearing is a three-pronged process. The first part is to discover the original wound by considering the area in our life that is not working. We will then re-experience that experience, and analyze those feelings from the past (e.g., journaling). This process takes some of the "charge" off the emotional wound by facing it and releasing it. The second part is to uncover the decisions that were made as a result of that experience and discover how those decisions are affecting our life today. The third part of the clearing process is to reveal the beliefs that were formed from these decisions. When we re-examine these decisions and underlying beliefs, we can change them. You change your beliefs and you change your life!

I work with my clients to clear and get to the root cause of the patterns, issues, and wounds. Together, we discover what decisions and beliefs keep cropping up and impede the growth of their garden. The base or beginning of the root is called the *Point of Origin (POO)* of the wound.

> *Let's use an example to demonstrate how this works:*
> *POO: Your Father died of a heart attack at 50*
> *Decision made: I will die of a heart attack at 50 too.*
> *Belief: It does not matter what I do, I will die young.*
> *********
>
> *POO: Your parents got divorced*
> *Decision made: Marriage is a failed institution*
> *Belief: It is impossible to have a good relationship.*

The following table shows a glimpse into how some of my clients' original wounds continually re-manifested in their lives. Acting as their Psyche

Detective, I helped them to make the connection between where they were "stuck" in their life and the original wound they experienced. This is just the tip of iceberg. Our wounds can appear as disappointment, depression, fear, anger and addiction. They can also appear as patterns that evoke the same set of feelings. Wounds may appear as a type of person, a negative situation or experience that seems to re-occur. It may occur cyclically, like losing a job every three years, or finding yourself strapped for cash every spring. They can, and do, show up negatively in your career and finances, your relationships, and your health. Our wounds can affect us unconsciously through the choices made (or not made). By not going after what we really want, we hold ourselves back, "stuck" by our wounds. Sometimes a wound can bleed over into all areas of life and affect the growth of our garden. As you read through the following table, begin to think about your own situation and how you would fill in the table for yourself.

Make the Psyche Detective Connection		
Point of Origin/ Original Wound	Belief that was created	How it Manifests
Critical or perfectionist parents	"I'm never good enough," or "I'm fat, ugly, or stupid," or "I need to be the best."	Difficulty attracting a mate or a career. You are alone. You have difficulty losing weight. Poor self image. Eating disorders. You attract critical people in your life.
Emotionally inconsistent parents	"What is wrong with me?" "I'm in the way," or "I don't matter," or "I'm not loveable."	People that come in and out of your life with no explanation – inconsistent partners. People not being there for you.

Make the Psyche Detective Connection		
Point of Origin/ Original Wound	Belief that was created	How it Manifests
Verbal abuse	"I'm always wrong," or "If I stand up for myself I'll be in more trouble."	Fearfulness. Addiction. Unable to be with self. Overly critical of Self. No voice for Self.
Sexual abuse	"I must have caused it," or "I am sick, shameful, guilty or disgusting," or "No one will love me if they knew," or "I should be punished."	Fear around opposite sex. Promiscuity at a young age. Non-orgasmic. Hypercritical of body image. Overcompensate with body coverage. Issues with sexual relationships. Eating disorders. Self hatred.
Observing parents with a dysfunctional relationship with finances	"Money just slips out of my hands," or "I will never have enough," or "I have to always work hard."	Difficulty earning money. Irresponsibility with money. Fear of making money. Debts. Fear of poverty. Hoarding. Stinginess.
Divorced parents or a parent's death at a young age	"I caused my parent's divorce," or "I've done something wrong," or "I am not loveable."	Divorce or inability to create a relationship. Creating being abandoned. Leaving a relationship before they would be "abandoned" or when the going gets tough. Failed relationships.

Make the Psyche Detective Connection		
Point of Origin/ Original Wound	Belief that was created	How it Manifests
Observing parents' dysfunctional relationship with food	"I have always been overweight and always will be," or "I am big-boned."	Inability to lose weight. Low self-esteem, poor body image. Anorexia. Overeating.
Integrity issues or being lied to as a child	"I cannot trust anyone."	Lack of support. No support from others because you cannot trust anyone. No friends. Fear. Never trust yourself or your own intuition. General uncertainty.
Overprotective parents	"I cannot do anything right."	Inability to stand on your own. Failure in the world.
Parents' infidelity	"Vows of marriage do not matter," or "I lie and do not need to keep my word."	I cheat on my spouse also. Integrity issues.

Finding the Point of Origin from your Past

Your wound may be obvious. The belief system that you set up for yourself may also be obvious. For others, it might not be as clear because we have created stories to manage our pain. The mind protects itself when it wants to forget a traumatic or disturbing event. Notice what set of circumstances in your life you want to change, and see if you can identify the original experience and your underlying beliefs.

❖ **In your journal, answer these questions for yourself. Begin at the "How it Manifests" box, the last row. How is the wound manifesting in your life today? What has you stuck in your life? What do you want to change? Have you noticed a pattern of people or events that derail you? This is the area that you want to change or feel stuck. Now move over to the center row. Is there a belief system that you are holding about yourself, your behavior, or how the event is "controlling" you? Based upon this journaling so far, do you know your wound's Point of Origin? Describe it, write about it, and tell your story in your journal.**

A wound can manifest in many ways. Many people work extremely hard to avoid facing their woundedness. Part of your healing can be to practice Self-Love by slowing down, doing affirmations, and meditations, of which we will have many suggestions. But as mentioned, previously, if you *only* do these practices, on top of your woundedness, you may not find the ability to fully create your heart's desire. If you find you are working like a crazy person, never letting the mouse off the wheel, you are not present enough within yourself to connect with the right people or plan your next action.

What about when the Point of Origin is not obvious? When we are looking for the Point of Origin, there is a technique I use called Following the Signature Emotions. All of our emotions leave a signature within us, just as our senses cause us to recall similar situations from our past. For example, when we smell bread baking and remember that smell from grandma's house, a feeling of warmth and nurturing may come over us. When we hear a piece of music that reminds us of a happy time, memories are brought forth, and our soul makes a little leap. When you take a walk in the fall and the leaves crunch under your shoes, you may recall a time in the fall from childhood. When we uncover an emotional signature from a past event, we make the connection from the past to the way it is manifesting in the present. Just as a criminal leaves a fingerprint at the scene of a crime, our emotions leave a trace of evidence that lead us to our wound's Point of Origin. If the Point of Origin is not obvious to you, you will need to challenge your own story by asking yourself: "Is the story I have been telling myself really true?"

Remember, there is always a Point of Origin, and it is always related to what is currently happening in your life. Taking deep breaths, journaling, talking to a friend/therapist can help you discover, acknowledge, and release the *POO* (so to speak!).

How to Follow the Signature Emotion?

I want you here to go back to your journaling from the How it Manifests row, we are going to dig a little deeper to discover the Point of Origin. Answer these additional questions:

◆ **What is the current circumstance in your life that you want to change? How does the current circumstance that you want to change make you feel? It is very important to be extremely specific about your feelings. Attach as many words to them as you can. When was the last time you felt this way? What brought it up and made you feel that way? When was the time you felt like that before? When was the time before that? Can you trace your emotions to an event that changed your life or the way you viewed yourself? Do you see any patterns?**

If you were able to trace the signature emotion back to the Point of Origin, great. But if you are having difficulty tracing it back, go back as far as you can go, and allow yourself time and space for this technique. We are going to be calling in the "child within" to explore the Point of Origin.

The Point of Origin Adventure Visualization

 Get seated in a comfortable chair, turn off all the distractions, and settle into the silence for a few minutes. We are going to take an imaginary adventure in your mind. Notice if you feel any excitement or distress at this prospect. Calm yourself with a few deep breaths, and know this will occur in your mind only, and

you are safe. As you do this exercise, take your time with each step and allow yourself to feel whatever comes up for you.

Imagine a room with a table and two chairs facing each other. You walk in the room and sit down in one of the chairs. Call in the little boy or girl part of yourself. (For purposes of the written visualization we will use the female pronoun here) She represents the part of you that is your inner child and she remembers the Point of Origin. Notice her age, anything about her demeanor, how she is dressed, her facial expressions, etc. Let her know that you are taking her on an exploration. Tell her that you are doing this to make both of you feel better with more time and space for fun and play. Let her know that she is safe, that you will protect her no matter what she tells you. Share with her a little bit about your current situation and describe the feelings that are attached to it. Ask her if she can remember a time when she felt the same way and ask her to describe it. Listen without judgment. She might speak to you directly with words or images or thoughts may pop into your mind. If you start seeing yourself as a child, trust what you see. Whatever it is, accept it, do not analyze or judge it. Thank her for sharing and give her a hug. Ask her if there is anything that she would like from you, or anything she would like to do with you, maybe she wants to go outside to play, or eat some ice cream, (my little girl loves to play jacks). Let her know that you will do that for her. Put your arm around her and guide her out of the room. Open your eyes.

❖ **Write down any images, thoughts, and feelings that came up.**

This exercise should help you start unraveling the original experience. Do not worry if you cannot find it, it will eventually be clear. It may show up in your dreams or a memory might pop up out of nowhere. Whatever you promised your inner child, make sure you do it this week. Keeping this promise is Self-love for yourself and your inner child. You also need to trust what comes to you. You might disregard it and say to yourself, "oh, that was just my imagination." You will know if it feels true to you or not. This is called discernment. Discernment is deciding what is true for you by using all the tools you have available. Trusting your intuition is a big part of discernment.

If it feels right, it probably is right. Your inner child is that unconscious part of you that knows it all, and has all the answers.

It is great to find your wound's Point of Origin, but do not get hung up if you do not find it. Wounds may not always be available to our waking consciousness. For some, the original wound may have occurred while still in a crib, in the womb, or a past life. Whenever it originated, we can still work with it. When we see the dandelion in our garden, we do not have to dig down in the dirt to know there is a root below it. The original wounded experience has been keeping us stuck, choking off our growth. Just because you have not seen it until now does not mean it was not there. It has controlled us in ways we may not even be aware of. When you dig in the dirt, you begin to see that root. Whether we understand our Point of Origin of the root or not, we can still clear massive amounts of "stuff" without getting to the original wound. Finding the Point of Origin brings us to a deeper level of understanding into how our unconscious mind has managed up until now.

CHAPTER 6

Clearing the Past

Clearing Parental Relationships

As part of the Self-Love journey it is necessary to examine our relationship with our parents and our feelings about that relationship. We do this, not in an effort to assign blame to any person or event, but to begin to take responsibility for our feelings. When this relationship is not properly examined, or "investigated" per se, it can have a profound effect on our lives as adults. When our original wounds are created in childhood, as children we do not have the language or the ability to express our feelings. We unconsciously create belief systems that form our experience today. We have numerous belief systems that affect our lives. We operate on hundreds, maybe thousands, of beliefs that work unconsciously and form our life.

The great thing about beliefs is that at some point in your life, YOU decided to adopt them... and now YOU can change them and make a new decision and belief.

Often clients complain that the therapeutic process always seems to go back to the past or back to the parents. Likewise, if you are a parent you probably have been blamed at one time or another for everything your child finds wrong in his/her life. Regardless, working on your Self entails some delving into the childhood issues. Because this work can be painful and difficult to release and resolve, many clients will rebuff my attempts to go into their past childhood relationships, saying they have already done this work. If I know one thing for sure, there is always more.

Why is the parental relationship so important? It is important because *it is the foundation for all of your relationships, with yourself and others, for the rest of your life.* There are many reasons for this. As a child you were watching these adults, whatever your parental unit makeup. Whether you grew up with both parents or one parent you watched how they interacted with the same sex or the opposite sex, how they dealt with money, with career, with intimacy, with drugs and alcohol, how they handled fear, how they celebrated. As children we watched our parents. They were our role models. We made a decision to either emulate them or to do the opposite. These decisions impact all of our intimate relationships, dramatically! Life is the school of relationships from the womb to the grave; childhood is our primary education. We either embrace, mimic, or admire certain behaviors, or rebel, adopting the opposite behavior as a reaction – "I am going to be like that," or "I will never be like that." These are the two polarities to our parents' influence. Regardless of our opinions about how our parents parented, they became our role models. Consciously, or unconsciously, we do the dance of life around our parent models. No matter how much we have worked on this, we are still influenced by them. All of these experiences, beliefs, and perceptions impact our sense of Self and the way we relate with others.

To learn that your parental relationship lays the foundation for your decisions and your current state of relationship, may be both good and bad news. Watching your parents taught you how to be in relationship. It is good news because now you know what needs to happen to make space for yourself and a new way of being. It may be bad news because most people do not want to do it. Working on and clearing the parental relationship can sometimes be difficult, and a lifelong process. Life just keeps presenting new opportunities to go back and see if there is anything more that needs to be healed.

Decisions

A decision is a choice or judgment we make. As children we made a decision with regard to our parent's behavior. We decided to either emulate or rebel, we said yes or no to certain parent's behaviors. For instance, if you had a parent who was conservative with money, you made the decision to either turn out to be just like that, or the opposite. If you had a mother that was remote, your response might be, "I am not going to be like that with my children," so, then, you become a mother that is very hands on, loving, and nurturing. It is neither a good or bad response. It is a *reaction to* and not always a conscious decision. Sometimes, we realize that our spouse or even a friend might have many of the same character traits or behaviors as our mother or father. When someone gets married and their spouse is just like their parent, they are unconsciously working out unfinished business with that parent.

As an adult we begin to examine and clear the decisions and beliefs that were made in childhood that have a negative effect on life in present time. Sometimes people experience a breakdown or loss before they are ready to examine some of these decisions and beliefs from which they were operating. This is the process of transformation, breakdown to breakthrough. When I am acting as the Psyche Detective for my clients, I sometimes use the chart below as an easy way to see what emotions are evident. I have used an example from one of my clients, Suzanne, to demonstrate how the chart works. The visual display makes it easier to follow the string of events that led to the current manifestation, and ultimately the changes that will lead to healing. The column headers are the guided questions that I ask my clients. For now just read through the process, I will be guiding you through this in the next chapter.

Decisions Made in Childhood

What parental behavior did you see that had an impact?	What decision was made as a result of the parental behavior you witnessed?	How has this decision affected or shown up in your life?	Why are you still making this decision?
Father would emotionally retreat on occasion.	Something is wrong with me. I must have done something. I am not loveable enough. Do I need to change something about me to be loveable?	Rejection from men. No lasting committed relationships. Strong feelings of abandonment or rejection in relationships. Feelings of unworthiness. Continual need to fix myself, to make me "good enough, attractive enough, loveable enough."	Stuck in my little girl part of myself. It has been an unconscious decision. It has not been fully healed or acknowledged.

It is important to be aware that what we observed of our parent's or anyone else's behavior was our interpretation. We have no idea what others were thinking or feeling at the time. We spend our lives observing how people act and we make up stories about it. We then form decisions and beliefs, which, in turn, form our life patterns. In the past, you made a decision based on those interpretations, and you can now create a new interpretation and make a new decision.

Why is it important for us to get clear about our unconscious decisions and be committed to making new ones? Many times, a pattern will emerge, a family pathology. This means that there is in a dynamic between the individual family members that is generational - family violence, sexual abuse, drugs and alcohol abuse; all of these problems are commonly passed onto the next generation unless there is a disruption in the pattern. In order to heal certain aspects of childhood, we unconsciously recreate the same dysfunctional relationships that we observed as a child. The "aha" moment occurs when we realize that we have the power to make new decisions and form new beliefs that allow a better possibility in the future. We do not have to be the product of our childhoods. We can choose to make a new decision.

To create a new decision we will work on releasing the power the decision had over our lives. The decision in this case is like an affirmation. It is a statement that we are making to our self that supports the outcome that we want to produce. We will use this statement as an affirmation until it becomes firmly anchored in your consciousness. Make this statement positive and life affirming. The new decision from our example is: *I am loveable. I deserve to have a consistent loving relationship. I am perfect as I am. I am worthy.*

Beliefs

The decisions that we made as a child formed the beliefs we have today. A belief is defined as accepting that something is true without positive knowledge; it is also having a conviction and feeling; and to expect a specific outcome. Beliefs are the next layer of the issue. The belief can take deep root in our psyche and affect what we believe is possible for us to create in our life. One of the reasons why beliefs get so deeply rooted is because they are adopted with such great feeling. The feeling is the glue that keeps them stuck. When we challenge our beliefs, just like we challenged the decisions we made; and create a new belief with a tremendous amount of emotion or feeling behind it; then real, lasting change becomes more of a possibility. We will be using the following statement to discover the belief that we want to change.

"Based upon the parental behavior I experienced, I made the decision that _____. This decision has held me back in the following ways because I believe: _____."

In the case of our example: "Based upon the parental behavior I experienced (my father's emotional retreat), I made the decision that something was wrong with me and I was un-loveable. This decision has held me back in the following ways because I believe: I will never have a good relationship; all men will leave or are not available; I have to pursue men because they do not pursue me."

If you change the decision and you do not change the beliefs, it makes it much more difficult to create a different outcome. Many people try several alternatives like counseling or healers before even realizing that it is their beliefs that are keeping them stuck in the same patterns. In my experience, I have seen that if you do not change your beliefs, things will generally stay the same or get worse.

How do we change beliefs?

We first need to get clear and identify our beliefs. In the next chapter we will be doing this together. We will use the Socratic Method to arrive at the truth by asking questions. In our continuing example with Suzanne, we took a look at her old belief, the one that was not serving her, and discovered what the opposite affirming belief would be. State it in the positive, using the words "I am," as if the behavior is already occurring in the present. The words "I am" bring with them a tremendous power and feeling of support from the Universe (we will be working more with this statement in later chapters). Make sure your affirmative statement really resonates with you.

The belief I am changing: I will never have a good relationship. All men will leave or not be available. I have to pursue men because they don't pursue me.

My new belief: I easily and effortlessly create a wonderful, loving and consistent relationship. I am pursued. My partner is present and loving.

Suzanne's Transforming Beliefs Process

Old Belief: *I will never have a good relationship. All men will leave or not be available. I have to pursue men because they don't pursue me.*

Question #1: Can you guarantee that that statement is absolutely true? No, of course not. So, therefore, it is possible that the statement is not true and may even be something that she made up. She could meet someone who is an exception to what she has always created in the past, especially if she does the work.

Question #2: How did you form these beliefs? Look at the decision that formed the belief. In our example, Suzanne observed her father's emotional withdrawal, she created decisions and beliefs that formed her perceived current reality.

Questions #3: Who are you still blaming? In this case, Suzanne still has not forgiven her father. The key to this shift would be for Suzanne to release and forgive her parent, and own and take 100% responsibility for her part in creating this scenario. Taking responsibility does not mean to judge or blame ourselves. Total responsibility means to question, "where am I responsible in forming this outcome?" You were there, you were present, and you made certain choices (or didn't voice your choice or opinion) which has led to the relationship pattern you are experiencing now.

Question #4: What is the payoff? Even after changing our beliefs, if you are still getting something out of this old behavior, it will be difficult to change. The payoff is the negative, unconscious benefit one receives from staying stuck. In this example, Suzanne gets to be right. She can make her father and men wrong. She gets sympathy and attention from girlfriends who are more than willing to identify with this scenario. Suzanne gets to continue in her old behavior and not work on herself. She gets to be the victim. Once we identify the payoffs in our beliefs, they lose much of their power. Out of the shadows and into the light, we now can do something about changing our ways of being.

Question #5: What is the cost? Now that we have discovered the payoff in our example with Suzanne, we can look at what the cost has been in her life for holding onto this way of being. The cost has been not attracting a sustained happy healthy relationship; being alone; lack of joy and aliveness; feeling incomplete; not fully sharing herself with another. Once we really get the cost of our attachment to our history and beliefs, we realize in many cases that this attachment has cost us our lives in a certain area. By going through this process it can awaken our commitment for real change.

Changing the decisions, beliefs and even becoming aware of the payoffs and costs are not enough in some cases to deeply root out the brain grooves that have been formed by the repetitive behaviors. A belief is nothing more than a thought that we keep repeating. Instead of speaking to yourself or thinking these negative messages daily, tape record your new decisions and beliefs and listen to them. Read them every day, feeding the subconscious the new beliefs, especially using the 30 day rule of repetition without interruption. Eventually, our new beliefs will become our reality. When working with decisions and beliefs, it is also helpful to use our recording, possibly while you sleep or find subliminal cds or computer programs that have similar empowering words and affirmations that can support changing these grooves in your brain to begin feeding your subconscious a new program.

The final piece of this process is to look at the following question: **What could your life look like when you make these changes?** This is the fun part! This is the vision that we will be creating for ourselves that we regularly go to in meditation or quiet times. This includes the possibilities for your life with your new beliefs. Looking at our example, Suzanne would have a new confidence and relationship with Self that includes feeling worthy and deserving of a wonderful partner. Her Self-Love work would manifest a committed loving man who pursues her, easily attracts someone who is consistently there, who really sees who she is and loves her for herself. Get ready... it's your turn!

CHAPTER 7

Decisions & Beliefs

N ow the ball is in your court. We will be clearing our childhood history, much like we did with Suzanne, our example in the last chapter. Read these questions about your family of origin and begin to act as the Psyche Detective for yourself. This will help illuminate the decisions you made as a child while observing your parents.

Were you raised by both parents or a single parent? How would you describe your relationship with your mother; with your father, and how did it change over the years? What was the climate of the family; tense and guarded, or loving and free, or something in between? Recall any events that changed your family or had a traumatic effect on you; a death, a divorce, abuse, addiction, unwanted sexual attention or any other circumstances that affected you negatively. Identify any feelings of abandonment or not feeling heard or acknowledged.

Now look at an area of your life currently that needs work. Re-read your answers and begin thinking about the total picture of how it was for you as a child. Begin to write a story with as much detail as you can recall as the pictures come into your mind. Really allow yourself to feel these emotions as they arise. These are the areas that in your childhood could have gotten stuck and may be holding you back in your present story or blocking you on your journey to create the life you want. Are any of the feelings that came up for you from your childhood similar to how you are feeling now about the current circumstance that is giving you trouble?

Discovering and Changing Your Decisions

Start thinking about any decisions that you made from having this childhood. Write down some of the decisions you made as a child - where you decided to either emulate or rebel, where you said yes or no to certain parent's behaviors. Pay attention to the words you use to describe these decisions and the emotions that come up for you. Remember that the decisions that you made as a child are neither good, nor bad, they are just a reaction to what you observed and experienced. These may not have even been conscious decisions.

Parents Behavior

Decision Made as a Child

Once you have written your own observations of your parent's behavior and the resulting decisions you made, look at how it has affected your life. Go back to each decision and see what area was affected most. What I hope you will find is a direct connection between the parental behavior, those decisions you made as a child, and the place where this is negatively affecting your life currently. Believe me, there is always a connection. This is your motivation for clearing out the past.

Parents Behavior	Decision Made as a Child	How it has affected or shown up

+ **How has your decision shown up in your life?**

Were you able to see that any of the decisions you made as a child are currently affecting you in your life now? Evaluate whether the decisions you made as a child have been beneficial for you or not, has it been detrimental or empowering to your life? If it has been detrimental, why are you continuing to make the same decision? The answer to this question may just be that you never were conscious you were making a decision with your behavior. If you have never known there was another way of being, you have never had the freedom to make a different choice. But now that you are examining your thoughts and belief systems you can begin to change them. And once you have the knowledge, you cannot go back to not having the knowledge.

Why are you still making this decision?
Are you ready to make a new decision? Do you want things to be different? Evaluate your circumstances around the decisions that you have made. Ask yourself why it is important for you to make a new decision in your life. You originally made this decision and operated your life from it, once you bring it to consciousness, acknowledge it and clear it, you can make a new and conscious decision.

You made the decision... YOU can make a new decision!

Let your new decision for your life become an affirmation. An affirmation *affirms* your new statement and positive way of being. Use *I am* or *I choose* as the beginning. The Universe will give you whatever you ask for, even if it is what you do not want. By saying, "I am not going to... or I do not want ..." – that is what you will get, you will produce the opposite result. By putting your request to the Universe as "I am" or "I choose," crafts your request in a way that will produce the result you are looking for. Write down the new decision that will support your empowerment.

Say your affirmation out loud to yourself every morning when you wake up, and every night before you go to bed. Say it with feeling! Our goal here is to make this new decision part of your regular thought process. We are replacing your old thoughts that you have decided no longer serve you. We will be saying our affirming decisions often, out loud, and with feeling. Be committed and say your affirmation for 30 days (I mean 30 days - if you do 28 days and you miss a day, you have to start the 30 days over again)! After 30 days, look around and see whether you are producing the result that you want.

> We always attract into our lives whatever we think about
> most, believe in most strongly, expect on the deepest
> level, and imagine most vividly. – Shakti Gawain

Techniques for Keeping our New Decision Prevalent in our Thoughts:

- Write it on a post-it note and place it all over your house.
- Laminate it and put in the shower. For many of us shower time is wasted time, our mind wanders, to all the worries and self-deprecating thoughts we have about our selves. This is a perfect place to stay conscious and repeat your new decision.
- Subliminally put it on your computer.
- Speak it into a recording device (most phones have this option) and play it back to yourself when you are at home or driving in the car.
- Come up with your own ideas how to best anchor this new decision.

30 day rule: It takes 30 days to a behavior.
If you miss the 30 day mark, you have to start all over again.

Your Beliefs

When we begin to examine our beliefs we can see that our long held beliefs, many of which may have been unconscious, have literally shaped our experience. This is why it is so important to examine the beliefs you hold and choose which of them support your current vision. An example of how a belief may manifest is someone who has come from a family background of financial struggle. The decision they made as a child is that life is a struggle because that is what they observed. The belief they adopted was, I will never have enough money. But their vision is to be a millionaire. If you are holding the belief that to get ahead you have to struggle, then no matter how hard you work, or what ideas you might have for financial abundance will not come to pass because you will always sabotage the result. Your deep seeded belief is I will never have enough. One of the keys to clearing this challenge would be to fully acknowledge and own your experience of being a child in a family struggling financially, without judgment.

Discovering and Changing Your Beliefs

"Based upon the parental behavior I experienced, I made the decision that _____. This decision has held me back in the following ways because I believe: _____."

Now that you understand what your belief is and where you have been coming from, write the opposite of the belief that will lead you to your intended outcome.

"My old belief was not serving me. My new belief is _____."

Transforming Your Beliefs

Look at the belief that is not serving you and in your journal answer the following questions:

* **Can you guarantee that your belief is 100% true?** Examining your beliefs may be a foreign concept. For most of us our beliefs are the repetitious thoughts that randomly run through our mind that we unconditionally accept as truth.

* When we put these beliefs to the test : *Can you guarantee that that statement is absolutely true,* our beliefs almost always collapse. So in looking at our example: If your belief is, I will always struggle financially, under scrutiny of this question the answer is no, I could win the lottery. I could overcome my financial past and be successful. I could get an unexpected inheritance. There are so many reasons why you cannot guarantee you will always be financially challenged. Answer for yourself.

* Proceed with your examination of your belief against this question. **Who are you still blaming?** Blaming always keeps us stuck. If you are still blaming another person for your past, or your current situation then you are not taking full responsibility for where you are. If you are unwilling to take responsibility then it is nearly impossible to move forward and change your situation. This is the one aspect of the process that most people miss and without it, permanent change is unlikely. This is the glue that is holding the belief in place. It is important to express the anger or even the blame for our past. Even if you just showed up, there is a part that you played. Therefore by taking responsibility, and acknowledging what happened, will help release the situation and allow you to move forward.

* **What is your payoff?** What are you getting out of staying stuck in your behavior? It may not be readily apparent to you, but if you really probe, there is some payoff you are getting, even if it is just that you get to be *right!* The payoff is the negative benefit of staying stuck. Who in

their right mind would want to stay in these painful situations, jobs, relationships, or whatever? People sometimes think it is easier to remain in the behavior that is not working because they do not know what is on the other side - that real change is possible. What is the reason we do it? For every area that is not working in your life, examine why you have not changed the situation? Obviously, this may not be as easy as it sounds. Our payoff is an unconscious thing, so it may take a while for you to uncover this for yourself. The payoff is something you get for staying stuck. Look at your own beliefs and examine what you get out of staying in your old way of being.

The Payoff

In the following examples, the first sentence is the possible payoff one would receive for staying entrenched in beliefs. The second sentence is how that payoff might appear in your thoughts.

- You get to be right. *This might look like, "I told you so, men just leave me." Or "I was never good with money.*
- You get to be a victim and people feel sorry for you. *She is so miserable at that job," or "Poor me."*
- You get attention. *"He cheated on you again? How terrible!"*
- You get to not take responsibility. *"My ex-husband robbed me of my good years, I'm too old now to have a vital, loving relationship."*
- You do not have to move, or change the status quo. *"At least if I stay at this job, I don't have to risk failure."*
- You do not have to work on yourself. *"I get to buffer myself from any possible painful thoughts. I do not have to feel."*
- You get to be lazy. *"I'll start my diet tomorrow."*
- You get to stay in the comfort zone. *"At least I know I am a great writer, so what if I never have the courage to send my novel to a publisher. It is too scary to put myself out there, I might be rejected!"*

* **Write a paragraph, or pages, what is the payoff for your story? Pinpointing the payoff for your story makes it very real and impossible to ignore any longer.**

The Cost

What is the cost? What has it cost you to stay entrenched in this limiting belief? What are you doing or not doing for yourself and why and how can you change it? What has it cost you to have that belief and continue to repeat it to yourself and others like a mantra? How has your belief hindered or hurt you in your life? Look at your current situation as if it were to never change or get better. What would that cost be to your life overall? Truthfully, by staying stuck in your belief it will cost you your life. I know that sounds dramatic, but think of the precious moments your belief has already robbed you of, how it keeps you in your head, in your fear, in your blaming, in your victimhood and away from pursuing your life's true purpose.

Possible Costs

Look at your life and the people close to you. How do your limiting beliefs affect them? How will it affect you long term? These are some common costs of staying stuck:

* Your aliveness
* Being present in your life
* Relationships
* Your health
* The cost to your family
* Joy
* Peace
* It means failure v. success.

Imagine yourself looking back at your life from your deathbed and review what it is you had wanted to achieve. Would you be disappointed? Is there regret that you had not achieved your goals? When thinking from this place, one can bring forth their willingness and commitment to change, to grow, to transform!

♦   **Answer the questions for yourself and write down some of the possible costs of holding this belief.**

Your New Vision

Now that you are very consciously aware of the payoff and cost that this limiting belief has had in your life, you are ready to make permanent changes. You have now gotten clear about what the stuck behavior was. We have looked at what decisions were made in the past. We looked at what beliefs were adopted and you created a new positive belief in that area. We have begun to utilize subliminal tools to anchor the new behavior and now we are ready to see ourselves as having moved through this process and come to a place of our new affirming lifestyle.

Begin to form a vision of the new you in your mind. Create a detailed picture of yourself in your mind; being, doing, and having, all that you desire. See yourself, in this new body, in that new relationship, having total abundance - whatever your heart's desire. Do this technique once a week for at least six weeks to firmly anchor this vision in your subconscious. We will do much more work on visioning in later chapters, but this is just a "taste" to get you started in a positive direction on our journey!

There came a time when the risk to remain tight in the bud was more painful than the risk it took to blossom. – Anais Nin

CHAPTER 8

. . . .

Releasing Techniques

To acknowledge your decisions and beliefs is all very "heady," mental work. It is also important to honor your feelings. Remembering your past, examining your wounds, patterns, and the pieces of ourselves that can seem "broken" are difficult steps along this journey. They are signals that tell us what needs our attention. Even the so-called negative feelings such as anger and fear serve to alert us to the "obstacles" in our life. Throughout this book, I will talk about "releasing your feelings" and giving your feelings "room." This is a very self-loving technique. As you decide to change things going forward, know that this is a process and will not be magically transformed overnight. Your feelings are your feelings and sometimes they need time and space to expand and be released. I also often tell my clients to let their feelings "percolate" or "simmer." Some releasing techniques like burning rituals are the final step, whereas sometimes a burning might be a setting of an intention to begin a process. Use your discernment and decide if you are ready for the next step and what that step may be. In this chapter, we will explore some Releasing Techniques to be used along the journey. The key to releasing is to have a strong intention to let go of the circumstance or emotion that is holding you back.

Evaluate What Needs to Be Released

Take your time and answer these questions for yourself. Look at something that is a recurring upset. We all have something in our lives that feels like a nagging emotion that keeps rearing its ugly head. Remember the first time this issue appeared in your life. Take your journal and answer the following questions. As you sit with each of these questions you will know whether it applies to you. This is an issue in which you feel stuck.

- With whom are you still angry?
- With whom are you incomplete? This might be someone you have unspoken communication or unfinished business.
- Are you still blaming someone else for the circumstances in your life?
- Where have you been betrayed?
- Who have you not forgiven?
- For what have you not forgiven yourself?
- What are you willing to release to create freedom, energy, and abundance in your life?
- To what secret or lie, or withheld communication are you holding on?
- What is out of integrity in your life?
- What situation or circumstance (past or present) has you upset that you are still carrying?

If any of these questions bring up stress or sadness or anger, choose the one that brings up the strongest emotion. This story is not going to be just about you, other people will be involved, your parents, spouse, teachers, siblings, and friends. Write down the story and be as specific as you need and then proceed to the next step.

Preparing to Release Visualization

 For the purpose of releasing your issue, we will be going to the Screening Room. Get comfortable and close your eyes and take three slow, conscious breaths. Breathe in light and breathe out any distractions. You are now the director of this movie. You are also the actor and you will play out the scene of this circumstance. When you feel ready, bring into your awareness the specific situation or person that you want to work with from your story. Take a moment, take a breath and allow yourself to experience this moment again. "Lights... camera... action!" See all of the participants playing out this experience on the big screen. What are you observing? What are you feeling as you watch this play out. What did you smell, taste, and hear? Continue to allow yourself to feel the feelings as the scenes play out before your eyes. In this original experience, some emotions became trapped, preventing you from letting this situation go. What was it? Feel the feelings of what holding onto this experience has brought into your life. Take a moment now, with your eyes still closed, to observe if there is any place in your body that feels sore or tight or a feeling of restriction. This is where the trapped energy from that experience resides. Your movie is coming to a close, and the Director shouts "Cut!" Slowly open your eyes and bring your awareness back to the moment.

The decision to not let go of these feelings and circumstances have caused you to punish yourself. By not letting go of a circumstance we are not hurting another we are hurting ourselves. See if you have made the decision to let it go and release this experience once and for all! If the answer is yes, proceed. If not, come back to this group of releasing exercises at a later time. Either decision is important for you and your process. Read through the following releasing exercises, see which one resonates with you and choose to complete the releasing by following through with the action indicated. These releasing techniques are designed to break up and move the trapped energy through vibration, physical movement, and breath.

Releasing Exercises

 With all of the following exercises you will be taking the images of the circumstance off the screen and moving those feelings into your heart and body to feel it on all levels. Breathe it into your DNA, cells, and consciousness. Allow your emotions to be present for you as you do any of the techniques below. Your intention is to RELEASE!

Journal and Speak Out Loud

Whatever your wound and however it appears in your life, it is important for you to give it a voice, put words around it, and begin to express it. If you are not ready to engage another person in this process yet, read it out loud to yourself and journal about it extensively. As you continue to speak it out loud, you will begin to release some of the pain, or "charge" around the wound.

Look at the questions you answered earlier about all the players in your story and notice with whom you are incomplete. If you were able to say *anything* to this person, what would you say? When I say, *anything*, I mean anything. We are trained to be good little girls and boys and we were taught to not yell, or be angry, especially with a parent or authority figure. If something wrong happens, we have to push it down, turn the other cheek, and "take the high road." I am now telling you that nothing is against the rules with regard to this expression. When you are "re-creating" this experience you have "permission" to say or write anything! This is your opportunity to "unstick" what you feel and express that which is feeding the wound. You are doing this for yourself! You do not actually have to contact the perpetrators of your wounds, you may want to one day as part of your healing process, but we are not there yet. For right now, we will contact them in our consciousness. You have identified with whom you have unfinished business, and you are clear about what part they played in your wounding. We are going to write them a letter.

Letter Writing for Releasing

Pick the person you feel you have the most "charge" with and write them a letter. You will not send the letter. This is a process to get out all of the unexpressed emotions that you feel. These unexpressed emotions can act like a cancer in the body, which feeds our wounds and keeps us stuck. Think of this process like it is your last opportunity to express to this person, either your last moment on earth or theirs, and you know your life depends on making this communication. Think about what took place with this person and have yourself feel all the blocked emotions. Express fully and with abandon! All your training of being a good child goes out the window. Be as angry as you want. Use "I" language, fully owning your feelings and experience, "I was hurt when you said this," or "I felt my heart was broken when you did that." Continue to express and write your letter until you feel complete. It is not acceptable in society to say words with that much force to full out blasting someone in a letter. It is very cathartic and beneficial to get all that rage out, so you can release it completely. If possible, read it to someone who can hear it objectively. Utilize the structure around the Re-Creation Exercise in Chapter 2. When you say it out loud, cry and re-experience the experience, accelerating the releasing. Later, we will burn the letter with the intention of releasing the stored emotions.

Vocal Therapy

Feel the emotions as they come up for you. Allow your feelings to build as you begin to express through sound and your voice. You may start with anything from a low growl to a full blown scream. The more you let go and make sound to let it all out, the better! Let whatever comes, come out until the emotion has transmuted or transformed. Fully experience these emotions, shout it out and move the emotion. Cry it out if you want to, or shout about it. Making noise breaks up the emotion's energy. Give yourself permission to let it rip! Another good technique is to add movement, stomping around or beating a pillow (see below).

Re-Creation Exercise

Do the Re-Creation Exercise (located in Chapter 2) with a partner describing your experience. If the negative feelings you are experiencing involve another person who you are not ready to (or are unable to) confront, you can use the Re-Creation Exercise as another person. For example, if you have unexpressed emotion for your father, and actually confronting your father is impossible because he is deceased, or confronting him will cause him or yourself too much pain, do the Re-Creation process speaking to the person as if your partner was actually your father. This "dumping" of feelings is a powerful way to change the relationship or your perception of it. You will be surprised at how effective it is to use a "surrogate" for the person you need to express to.

Free Form Dance

Put on a powerful piece of music. This is where you move your body. Let your body and your feelings move you. Dance out the emotions until you feel that all of the energy has been danced into Mother Earth. Let the energy move from your head all the way down to your feet and send it down into the Earth. Let yourself go until you are exhausted. Dance it out until you are complete. When you are done dancing, sit on the floor and take a couple deep breaths. Scan your body from head to toe, and send any residual dense energy into the core of the earth.

There are short-cuts to happiness, and dancing is one of them. – Vicki Baum

Drumming

Drumming is great for clearing out the energy that gets stuck in your body from emotions. Drumming is also an excellent tool to pound out grief and loss. Locate the place in your being that has experienced the loss – is it in your heart, stomach or solar plexus? Breathe into that area to create more space there. Relax and give yourself permission to feel the loss fully. Let any images come up that are associated with this circumstance. Accept whatever you are feeling. Begin a slow rhythmic beat on your drum. Continue to be present with your feelings and allow them to build, traveling down your shoulders, arms and hands and out through your fingertips, directing your rhythm. Beat your feelings into the drum. Do it until you feel a release and the emotion is transmuted (changed form). The vibration emitted from the drum is cleansing to the emotions, aura, and energetic field.

Breathing

Breathing is the simplest and the most profound tool you can use to clear experiences. Many of the great spiritual teachers speak of this phenomenon. But on a purely physical level deep breathing brings in 20% more oxygen to your brain, oxygen shifts your brain waves from short and staggered to long, which causes stress to immediately be released. If you just mastered your breath, you would be on your way to a more relaxed and calm state of being. The key is slow and conscious breathing. Put your full attention on your inhalations. Slowly count to ten while inhaling, and slowly count to ten on your exhalation. Allow your abdomen to expand. Conscious breathing means being one pointed in your focus. The beauty of this is that when you are completely with your breath, you cannot be anywhere else. You cannot be in your mind, with your thoughts, past, future, or fears. You can be one place at one time and that is in the present moment with your breath!

Breathe. Let go. And remind yourself that this very moment is the only one you know you have for sure. – Oprah Winfrey

Breathing to Clear

Set yourself up with a clear intention, such as I am releasing this anger (or whatever emotion) with my breath. With the inhalation, breathe in love and light and visualize the light filling your body. On the exhalation, consciously release and visualize the feeling, thought, experience or circumstance leaving your body. Do this ten times, until you feel a lightness of being and your thoughts begin to shift.

Going into the Pain

This is a technique used to release physical or emotional pain. Bring your attention to your physical body. Locate in your body where you feel the pain or the uncomfortable emotion. Pinpoint exactly how you are feeling, sadness, grief, frustration. What emotion is present and where does it exist? Take your time with each step of this process. Continue breathing and observing the pain in your body. What does it look like? What is the color or shape - A circle, square, blob, or the shape of something familiar? What is the size, two inches in diameter, bigger than your body? Keep watching it to see if the size, color, or shape of the pain changes. Breathe into the area. Keep identifying the size, shape and color until it disappears. Continue this process until the pain either dissipates or disappears all together. This is a powerful exercise that one can use any time you are feeling a stuck emotion in your body.

Bodywork

Have a massage or a bodywork session with an intention of releasing. Let your bodyworker know that you are working on a particular issue and are consciously intending to release it during the session. Your practitioner may be able to help you find where the energy is stored in your body and facilitate its release.

Dialoguing with your Self

When you realize you are upset about an incident or experience, ask yourself what you are feeling or thinking. Get in touch with it and be as specific as you can. Wait for your body to respond, what is your body telling you? For example, if you are not feeling well, you can close your eyes, go within, take a few deep breaths and ask your body why it is manifesting a cold. Ask and listen to what it is telling you? You can use this process for unconscious emotions or thoughts that are coming up to be released. This is a way to communicate with your inner self and enhance the connection between you and your feelings.

Write about it

Journaling about what you are thinking and feeling is expression and a form of releasing all that is going on in your head. You can journal or write unedited for two or three pages about a particular issue. This releases the conversations that occupy your mind.

Release to the Earth Visualization

 Bring to mind what you are ready to release and imagine that it resides as a specific energy within your body. See it move down from the top of your head through your eyes, cheeks, nose, neck, mouth, down to your shoulders, arms, hands and chest... this energy gathers up like a ball, all those stresses and worries you are ready to release. They are traveling down the body through your heart, solar plexus, stomach, and pelvic area. As it travels, gather all the wounds and hurts wherever they reside in the body flowing down the legs, knees, and into the feet and out the toes. All that you wish to release is sent into Mother Earth and transmuted into light. Imagine a shaft of white light coming from the heavens down into the top of your head all

the way to your toes. See this light surround, purify and cleanse your aura bringing in beautiful spiritual light to uplift you!

Walk with Intention

Walking on the Earth with the intention of clearing out any negativity is a powerful way to move that energy. Do the Release to the Earth exercise while out for a walk. With every step imagine that the negative feelings are draining from your feet into the earth.

It's quite possible to leave your home for a walk in the early morning air and return a different person – beguiled, enchanted. – Mary Chase

Burning Ritual

 I first understood the burning ritual within the tradition of Peruvian Shamanism. It can be described as energy medicine. As a doctor cauterizes a wound, so does a burning ritual cauterize or heal a pattern or situation. It is a powerful way to release the wound's energetic part or pattern. Whether you have worked on this issue for many years, or just started, there is, from the perspective of the shamanic work, an energetic component that exists in your energy field and that attracts these energy patterns. This energetic piece is still sending out the message to the Universe to bring you more of the same. Our Native American elders have taught us that all ceremonies, tribal or private, must be entered into with a good heart so that we can pray, sing, and walk in a sacred manner, and be helped by the Spirits to enter the sacred realm.

Perhaps you have just completed some of the other interactive releasing techniques. The Burning ritual is a wonderful way to complete the process. If you did any of the writing exercises, a journaling or a letter, you brought your thoughts and emotions up to consciousness in order to clear the energy around them. It is a powerful statement to the Universe. *I am done with this! I am ready to let this go!* Your intention throughout the burning process is to release the feelings from the letter. Choose a time that you will not be interrupted. Pray, meditate, and approach this technique with reverence and clear intention. Use a fireplace, a fire pit, a metal container, an abalone shell, a ceramic bowl or ironstone dish. As you build your fire, focus your thoughts on your feelings, where are you feeling tension, pain or "stuck" in your body?

Intention, intention, intention – we put forth our powerful intention to release. We call upon our angels and guides. Once your fire is burning powerfully, you can add sage, cedar or sweetgrass. This is an ancient practice to accelerate the clearing. The smoke is the agent that cleanses and purifies.

Take out your letter/story and read it out loud for the last time, really feel all the places in your body where those feelings and beliefs still reside. Place the letter, your old story into the fire. Take out another blank piece of paper. This blank sheet represents that which is still hidden from you in your subconscious about your story. Put that piece of paper in the fire as well. Sit in silence and watch it burn with the intention that you are letting go and letting God release any part of the pattern that is left, out into the Universe.

Observe the fire. Shamans would read the fire, and notice if it was smoldering, or difficult to light or keep burning. This shows if you have further attachment to your story. Is there any resistance to how it is burning? When your letter is completely burnt, ask God to bring to you that which you need at this point on your path - courage, clarity, peace, whatever it is for you that comes into your mind when you are sitting and watching your story burn. Thank your celestial team for assisting you in this ritual.

You are complete with any of the techniques when you begin to feel lighter and more clear. Continue to work with the Releasing exercises until the charge around any negative experiences dissipate. Pick whichever ones resonate most with you and make them part of your regular practice. Be loving to yourself. More emotions may come up in the following weeks as you do these releasing exercises. You may have dreams or memories that reveal more to you. I acknowledge that at times releasing work is challenging. Releasing is also a very Self-Loving act that will propel you on your healing journey.

....

CHAPTER 9

Clearing Self

Those who love others grandly are those who love themselves grandly.
Those who have a high toleration and acceptance of others are
those who have a high toleration and acceptance of themselves. You
cannot show another a part of you that you cannot show yourself.
Therefore, begin where all growth, where all evolution, where all love
must begin: with the person in the mirror. - Neale Donald Walsh

This chapter includes a myriad of Tools and Techniques for you to practice to begin to develop a personal, close, loving relationship with the most important person in your life... YOU! Choose to do the ones that speak to you the loudest, that you think might be fun. Then, make a commitment to yourself to do the one that that you think would make you the most uncomfortable. Very likely, that is the one that you will get the most out of.

Mirror Work

Mirror work is near and dear to my heart. For me, the real start to my Self-Love journey began in front of the mirror. As I shared earlier, the mirror exercise that I did for myself while going through a breakup opened up my awareness to the sacredness of Self-Love. I would like to share with you how you can do this exercise for yourself. Mirror work can be used in a number of ways. For our purposes, we will be clearing to be present. We will be releasing negative thoughts and feelings about ourselves to align with who we really are.

Mirror Exercise

 Pick a time when you can spend a few minutes by yourself and will not be interrupted. Ideally, I would like you to use a full-length mirror where you can see your whole body from head to toe, but a bathroom mirror will do. Stand in front of the mirror. Close your eyes and take a few deep breaths. Bring yourself into this moment now with your eyes closed. When you feel ready, slowly open your eyes and look into the mirror. At first glance, you will notice your body, your hair; like most people, this is when we become fairly self-critical. For women, the voice in your head might zone in on a wrinkle or a grey hair. For men, they might go to the spare tire around their abdomen or a receding hair line. Begin to observe your thoughts and notice how you criticize yourself. Do not latch onto any thought; just watch as your thoughts go by. Which ones are loudest and most predominant? What are the feelings that you are having as you look at yourself in the mirror? Is there sadness, anger, frustration? Look into your eyes and see what is there. Begin to let all of that loud conversation in your head and those feelings that are bubbling up, go! Now close your eyes for a moment again and bring to mind someone that you feel tremendous love for, and that love for that person is unconditional and without judgment. Imagine yourself giving that person a big hug and letting them know how much you love them. Take a moment to notice how that makes you feel. Now let that person go out of your awareness, take another breath to anchor those feelings you are having in your body and gently and slowly open your eyes. This time, gaze directly into your eyes (the seat of your soul), allow the rest of your body to fade into the background as you focus on seeing your soul within your eyes. Imagine that you are looking at someone you unconditionally love. Tell yourself out loud how much you love yourself, how wonderful you are, what a great job you are doing and that you love and accept yourself exactly the way you are now! Practice this technique in the mirror everyday for thirty days, it will make a huge difference in your life. Going forward, when you pass a mirror, look into your eyes and say, "I love you." This simple exercise may bring up some emotion for you. This exercise can be a good indicator of how much Self-Love you feel.

Allowing Expression of Self

Many come from families where it is not o.k. to express strong emotions. When we suppress these feelings they come out in aberrant ways. For example, we might experience sudden outbursts of anger or project our own feelings onto others because there has never been any outlet to express them. If you, as a child, were told to put a smile on your face when you were angry, or told not to cry, the feelings got pushed down and tend to erupt at inappropriate times. That energy of suppressed emotion needs to go somewhere. A way to handle suppressed emotions is to release the judgment that was learned as a child and give the experience a lot of space. First, realize that all emotions are neither good nor bad. We are taught in this culture that being happy is better than being sad, or that it is not o.k. to feel anger, etc. We have value judgments on emotions, some are good, and some are bad. On top of being told to not express them, if we do not express the negative emotions, they get stuck. It may feel as if there is always a backdrop of sadness or anger, and your current feelings exist on top. By giving ourselves the permission to express all the emotions present, like sadness, fear, and grief, it opens up that bottled up energy that has been pushed down. When you give yourself permission, all the trapped energy becomes available to you, creating an opening for the full expression of your joy and aliveness!

The Weather Analogy

Just like weather systems, emotions are free to move in and out. By taking the value judgment off of different emotions and treating each of them equally, it gives us much more room and permission to express the full range of emotion instead of just the "good" ones. This creates a new freedom to allow yourself to enjoy exactly who you are, all of the time. When we do have untapped emotions bubble up to the surface, see these emotions as weather fronts. The joy is like a warm sunny day. When you feel impending sadness or grief, it can be held as if clouds are rolling in and rolling out. If you are feeling a lot of anger coming up, instead of judging or changing it, notice and tell yourself a storm is coming. Just like the weather passes through, know the clouds roll out, you will feel that sunshine again, and you will feel that lightness of being. Nothing gets stuck.

Stompie

I call this technique Stompie, and the name implies the action. It is allowing expression of your feelings and moving any pent up energy through raw, physical activity. It includes stomping around, beating on pillows, allowing whatever noise you have churning to come forth, waving your arms or doing whatever other physical expression you can think of until that energy gets dissipated. I believe we all have a child part of ourselves that exists in all of us, even as adults. This is an integral part of who we are and this child part sometimes needs expression. When we are young and told "don't cry," "be happy," then there is no space to fully express all of these feelings and they in turn get stuck. When you see kids kicking and screaming and throwing tantrums in the mall, it is because there is so much repressed anger and upset that finally it just explodes. Many times, teenagers will begin to express some of those pent up feelings and behaviors through their own rebellious ways. When we accept this child part of ourselves, knowing intuitively that we have repressed, to whatever degree, childhood emotions, then we begin to understand the great need we all have to express our feelings. By giving these emotions space and room to be and breathe, the explosive behaviors are few and far between.

Be With – Accepting/Forgiving and Granting Space for "Unacceptable" Behaviors

 I believe it is important to give people permission to have different moods, to have different behaviors and emotions. But as we mentioned in the previous section, to the degree that we repress, suppress or have judgments about them, they can actually stay stuck, at all times lurking in the background and for many of us, come out in inappropriate ways. You may be living with this emotional background of negativity, or judgment or depression and not even be conscious of it.

One exercise I do in all of my workshops is to give people full permission to know that being happy is no better than being sad. To be negative is no better than to be positive. They are all equal... it is just the judgment we put on our feelings. In workshops, I have participants express any of their behaviors they may be embarrassed about or have a judgment on. You can do this for yourself with a partner by expressing to your partner which of your re-occurring behaviors you have a judgment about, think are negative, or feel uncomfortable with. Use the parameters of the Re-Creation Process located on page 23. These simple steps can free you from stuck emotions.

- Take the value judgment off of "sad is bad, and happy is good."
- Give yourself some way to express it, whether you write about it, use the Stompie technique, or any of the Releasing Techniques in the last chapter, whatever works for you.
- Be self-loving to yourself, and give yourself the time and space to feel what you are feeling.

Express Your Personality and Style

A friend of mine recently commented that she liked a long flowing skirt that I was wearing. She said that she and her sisters loved the "idea" of dressing that way, a sort of Bohemian style with bangles. I asked her why she doesn't dress that way. She said, "Oh, I could never!" I walked away from that communication feeling a little sad. Why not? If that is the style and personality your soul longs to embrace, why say no?

Examine your own style and personality, does it truly reflect who you are? Is there any place in your past where you wanted to express yourself more fully by pursuing a style, a dream, a passion or a goal, but got told no, or something along the lines of, "we just don't do/act that way." See if it needs to be cleared, and set an intention for yourself to discover and embrace more fully a new side of yourself. Give yourself an assignment for this week to wear the color that you might think is too flashy, or to eat a food you have never tried before, or even something more daring. You may want to continue this practice once a week to expand your sense of Self. It is Self-Loving to allow yourself to release any pre-conceived sensors and express your true authentic self!

Express Yourself with Another

Allowing expression of Self is not just allowing yourself to verbally clobber another in the hopes of getting it all off your chest. I am not condoning bad behavior here. It is Self-Loving to know what feelings are operating, discern how you want to communicate them in a responsible way, and understand what does not need to be spoken if it might be hurtful or not progress the communication. It is important that we begin to communicate with respect, with an intention to hear and honor the other person. I will often ask another during a communication, "Are you complete?" I am asking the other if they feel they have said all that needs to be said on that topic. It is also important for us to communicate until we ourselves, "are complete." When you are in communication with another person and you are expressing, get in the habit of silently asking yourself these questions:

- Am I complete?
- Have I expressed all my feelings on this topic?
- Have I achieved the positive intention or result that I wanted to create?

Getting Stuck in a Position

There are some situations in life that we feel "stuck" about. Something has happened, and we have our own point of view, we do not feel heard, or maybe we feel wronged. We may have made a decision about something, we feel righteous indignation, and the outcome is that we get to be right in our own mind. That is the problem. To be attached to a position of being right, you are the sufferer. Many times we may find that we have locked ourselves in a fixed position when there are deeper issues underneath. There may be some history in the relationship where you did not speak up, so whatever is occurring now has more charge. Scan the history, look at the dynamic that is operating, and take responsibility for where you have not spoken up for yourself in the past. See if there is some other dysfunctional dynamic going on that should be addressed and/or communicated. Forgive yourself and the other person for creating this situation, and be willing to let it go now. This creates tremendous space to move forward. Just imagine letting go of all these stuck positions in your life, how free you would be?

Unfulfilled Expectations

In the 1970's, I went through a very powerful transformational course called EST Training which was the forerunner of Landmark Education. The creator was Werner Erhardt who I find myself regularly quoting thirty years later.

Unfulfilled expectations are the source of suffering in life. – Werner Erhardt

What that quotation means to me is that we have many pictures of how things should be, anywhere from the "perfect holiday celebration," to how our husband should treat us on our anniversary and how people should respond to our birthday. We have these visions in our mind of how everything should look. Many of my clients get very attached to the holidays turning out a particular way. These pictures generally come from childhood. Some people want it to be like their mother did it, or the opposite of what they experienced as a child. For some, when they do not meet their childhood expectations, some people will go over the top and drive themselves and everyone around them crazy in the process, which of course, is why the holidays are perceived as so stressful. Nothing in life turns out exactly like our pictures. More than likely, one will always be disappointed and suffer from these attachments to our expectations. Knowing that our pictures in our mind are just that, pictures; can we put forth our best effort and just let it go? That is the challenge! This year it may not be "perfect" but it can be fulfilling and wonderful, nonetheless.

If you aren't good at loving yourself, you will have a difficult time loving anyone, since you'll resent the time and energy you give another person that you aren't even giving to yourself. ~ Barbara DeAngelis

Releasing Expectations

 First release the picture of the event from your mind and get clarity about your intention. Let us use the Christmas holiday as an example to walk through this process. This is a good one because we have our own childhood pictures and expectations as well as every year being bombarded by the media and the retail industry's vision of what our holiday should look like; everything from finding the perfect gift to having the classiest table decoration. Say you are having a holiday dinner with friends and family, instead of everything looking perfect, think about how you would like your home and the environment that you are creating to *feel* – a warm, inviting, nurturing, joyful atmosphere can be a lot more rewarding than *perfect decorations*. An intention might be, "Everyone that walks through my home during the holiday season feels loved and nurtured and joyful, celebrating with our family." This takes your attention off those "Martha Stewart details" and puts your attention on what is important. There is nothing wrong with having the intention to have it be beautiful and festive, but one needs to prioritize expectations.

Make a list of your expectations for the season, these might look like:

- The best decorations
- My table looks like it was on a Martha Stewart show
- My food is perfect
- Everybody gets along and no fights break out

Now, pose these questions for everything on your list:

- Is it possible or is the bar set too high?
- Is it really important?
- Will it be fulfilling?
- Is this expectation something that is even within my power to control?

Now we are going to create your vision. You can include some of the things that were on your list of expectations, but you have to know where to go and ALLOW. Cross off the ones that really are not do-able. Circle the things that are still important to you, even if you have crossed them off. Prioritize them. From the list write a vision: in present tense, as if it is already occurring, using I AM where appropriate to invoke that Universal support (more about this later). Write about what is important to you and your ideal picture based on having worked through the list. Start your vision with the intention you created. An example of your vision might be:

> Everyone that walks through my home during the holiday season feels loved and nurtured and joyful, celebrating with our family. I am seeing all the people involved being harmonious and loving to one another. The food is hot and delicious and beautiful and everyone loves it. My house is sparkly and lovely and is a reflection of the best of my family traditions. Everyone experiences the true meaning of the holiday, love and generosity.

You do want to reach for the best, and it is important to eliminate that which you cannot control. This exercise can be used for any event, such as your dream wedding, a first date, a job interview, a speech or a public performance – anything you have going on that you have a lot of expectations around. This exercise goes a long way to eliminate the suffering that is caused by unfulfilled expectations and supports you to create a vision that really aligns with your essence!

CHAPTER 10

Clearing Relationships

The most loving thing we can do is to surround ourselves with a circle of people who honor who we are and treat us with respect. It is not self-loving to put up with relationships that are unhealthy, toxic, or abusive. To be Self-Loving in relationship means to communicate responsibly with the people in your life; put up boundaries; clear any energy drains; and eliminate relationships that are not working. Acting responsibly with others is a way we honor ourselves and treat ourselves with respect. We tell ourselves that we put up with bad behavior because, "they are family," or because the person is a friend you have had for 25 years, or because you are married to that person. But upon further examination, we see that we are not being treated in a way we would treat others, nor how we expect to be treated. Many times we "put up with", or we feel obliged or guilty, so we stay in toxic or negative relationships. By clearing these relationships, you are saying to yourself, the Universe, and the other person involved that I deserve respect and I love myself.

Every relationship in our lives reflects our relationship with ourselves. When we truly love ourselves, we attract loving, harmonious relationships with others. – Arnold Patent

Who Are You In Your Relationships?

First we need to be clear about who *you* are in your relationships. It is much easier to look outside ourselves and find how people are not meeting our expectations, but more difficult to analyze ourselves and determine how people really see us. Answer the following questions.

* *Are you nurturing, loving, and empowering to others?*
* *Are you honest and in integrity?*
* *Would you call yourself a good friend, sister/brother, daughter/ son, or mother/father?*
* *How do you handle having your buttons pushed in a relationship? Are you quick to attack or defend or do you retreat?*
* *Do you speak up for yourself, or do you withhold communication to make things ok for others?*
* *Do you have siblings, where categorically the oldest takes responsibility for everything, the middle child feels overlooked or taken for granted, and the youngest child gets spoiled or left on their own?*
* *Do you feel seen for who you are?*
* *Are you treated with respect in your family?*

Some of these questions may have triggered you. If you saw some aspects of yourself that you do not consider positive characteristics, the purpose is not to make yourself to feel wrong or bad. Many of the traits that we do not want to own started out as a coping mechanism. For instance lying starts as a child. We lie to get what we want, to get out of trouble, to make the other person wrong. We also lie when we do not want to experience another person's reactions. When we get away with lying, we justify it to make it ok, and this continues through adulthood. It becomes a pattern and a habit that still does not work. As an adult, we take responsibility for situations and do not lie to get out of something or to avoid consequences or hurting someone's feelings. This may be a level of self-responsibility and maturity you never learned. See if you can be willing to make a commitment and try this adult-like behavior going forward.

The degree to which you love yourself will determine your ability to love the other person, who will be reflecting back to you many of your own personality traits and qualities. ~ Sanaya Roman

Looking at Relationships

Now, let us look at the relationships in our lives. Answer these questions to begin to analyze your relationships.

- *Are the relationships in your life loving?*
- *Are you putting up with being treated worse than you feel you deserve?*
- *Is there give and take?*
- *Is there a lot of strife, fighting, and hard feelings?*
- *Are there any relationships that have become very difficult or unfulfilling?*
- *Do you make everything ok for the other person?*
- *Do you occasionally say, "no" or do you feel a yes is always expected?*
- *Are you doing things in relationships that you really do not want to do out of obligation?*

Energy Drains

"Energy drains" are the people in our life, who, when we are around them or talk to them, we literally feel drained or exhausted. An energy drain can also be a problem, subject, or circumstance that is perceived as negative, and zaps us of our vitality. It may feel like we are constantly defending a position, or desiring to be heard or seen. When we are around these people or dealing with this situation, we feel small or not empowered. We have all had people in our life that we just do not get along with, and most times we can just choose to limit our time with these people. In close relationships, we form bonds of energy between us. Energy can easily be sent back and forth and our energy can also be drained by others who have less energy. It is better for them to learn to receive energy from the universal supply rather than taking your vital energy. Some bonds, the love bonds between us, we want to remain and grow stronger. If a relationship ends and you still feel an energy drain, that misuse of energy is inappropriate. If the person is an, or has been, an authority figure, our mind can sometimes make these people and circumstances larger than life, and more important than they actually are.

⬥ **Write about the energy drains in your life and how they make you feel.**

How do we manage these types of people and/or situations? The first thing to do is not to think about it, dwell on it, or get upset about this person or situation. When we obsess about the "energy drain" we are putting more emotional energy into it, and "adding mass." We need to learn to manage our thoughts around this person and situation, so they do not drain us more. See where you can limit your exposure and pare down your participation with this person, place, or thing. Given that it takes laser-like focus and energy to manifest our heart's desires, if a lot of our energy is being drained, you may find that you do not have the energy to create. It is Self-Loving to notice when any person or situation is pulling vital aliveness and joy from your being. Is there something you can do to diffuse the situation? The following techniques help you manage or get rid of energy drains.

Cartooning Your Drain

To begin to release some of the energy around your energy drain, turn the person or situation into a cartoon character. You can imagine or draw the person, exaggerating all of the characteristics that put you off. As we imagine the caricature, we begin to throw these energy drains off their proverbial pedestals. For example, turn your menacing brother into Brutus from Popeye, to diffuse the charge.

Cutting Bonds Visualization

 When your energy is being drained by another, the nature of the relationship is out of balance - one person is constantly pulling more energy from the other. You may be able to feel your energy pulled when the other feels they need extra energy from you. In most cases, this is unconscious behavior. You may not feel it at the time, but later may feel exhausted and cannot figure out why. We all receive our energy from the Universal supply and it is not in their integrity to be zapping yours. Do not allow it. Minimize your exposure to this person if necessary and examine what is out of balance in the relationship. Here is an energy technique you can use to help you maintain your own energy if you feel drained by another. The key here, again, is your intention.

As with all energy work, be sure to be completely grounded. Send your energy into the earth, and pull earth energy up through your roots and into your body from your feet to the top of your head. Take several deep breaths. Do this for several minutes. Visualize yourself sitting across from the person who is your energy drain. Imagine a rose in front of their solar plexus region and another rose in front of yours. Ask your guides to help pull the energy that is yours from the others' rose into your rose. Watch until your rose becomes very full, plump, and vibrant. Then give back, gift wrapped in a box, all the fears, problems, and energies they unconsciously projected and sent to you. Notice the energy bonds between you, they may look like ropes or tubes. There might be a few or several.

Become aware of them in your mind's eye. Take a scissors (or even a machete if you need to) and cut the inappropriate bonds between you. Your guides will make sure that only the dysfunctional energy bonds will be cut. The healthy bonds will remain intact. Ask their guides to fill them up with gold light. Ask your guide to fill you with gold light. Then, put a bubble up around yourself. No one, nothing can penetrate this bubble without your permission. Do this several times until all your residual energy is returned. This is a very powerful tool to maintain your own energy.

Bubbles and Shelves

 In the last visualization, we put ourselves in an imaginary, impenetrable bubble. This technique can be done on its own, without the Cutting Bonds aspect, as well. When you have a concern or problem or someone is invading your energy field, you want to place them outside of your aura so you can be clearer in your own space.

Get grounded by taking several deep breaths. Close your eyes and imagine the source of your energy drain. If there is a conversation you are having in your mind, or if it is a situation or a person that is bothering you, place it in a bubble outside of your being until you are ready to deal with it. Or, visualize putting the person or situation "energetically" in a box, jar or container of your choice. Close or wrap the container and literally "put it on the shelf" to be taken down when you are ready to interact with it. With most energy drains, there is a pull to go there, to interact with the drain, even if only in your mind. Designate specific times you will allow yourself to address it. Be clear and specific about the shielding and the boundaries around it so the energy does not seep into your day and pull your vitality. Through the day if you find yourself drifting back to your drain, tell yourself, "it is on the shelf."

Energetic Shield

 *Get into a quiet sacred space, take several deep breaths. In your mind imagine yourself just as you are in the clothes you are wearing. Now imagine a shield of the strongest material you can imagine coming up around you. You have contained yourself in this shield, and nothing anyone can say or do can penetrate your shield. All of the people or situations that are your energy drains are outside of your shield. Nothing can get in without your permission. If you know that you will have interaction with someone who is an energy drain for you, or before having a difficult conversation with someone, put up your shield. I especially like to put mirrors on the outside of my shield so any unwanted energy is reflected back to the person. Especially if you are sensitive, it is a good idea to dress every morning and don your energy shield.*

Seeing the Good in the Relationship

When you want to heal a relationship, you can do it on the energetic level first, paving the way for it to be healed in actuality.

In your mind, visualize yourself and the other person. Think of the relationship healing. Imagine the relationship in harmony, with laughter, good feelings, joy and peace around this person and yourself. Do this whenever you think of the person. Do it when you are angry with them, and do it when you appreciate them. End your session with a prayer that this or something better may occur between you and the other person. Continue to do this for as long as it takes. You will see a shift occur.

Clearing Relationships from the Past

There are many different kinds of relationships over a lifetime. Of course, the first and as we said, primary relationship is parental. But other relationships, siblings, cousins, first boyfriend/girlfriends, best friends, bosses, teachers, have a tremendous impact on our being. Certain events or circumstances occur that can get stuck, and create recurring patterns effecting our decisions and beliefs in the same way as the parental relationship. These are just as important to clear to change the patterns. Given most of us have placed importance on looking for love, this is often a place where suffering can occur. Look at your personal intimate relationships, i.e. spouse, boyfriend/girlfriend from the past. Remember from kindergarten forward. Look at your relationship history. Has it gone smoothly? Are you currently in a wonderful relationship? There will be some of you that married your high school sweetheart and all has gone well, but that is not the case for most people. How has your relationship history been? Is there anything from the past that you feel needs to be released, something that still bothers you? Also, if there is anything within your current personal relationships that you feel could be enhanced, this is a process that can help. Ask yourself what memories still linger from any of your encounters with the opposite sex that bother you or feel unfinished. Write down the names of the people that pop into your mind. See if you can write something next to each name of what happened. If it is still in your awareness in any negative way, then it is incomplete and is could be affecting the present time. Take your time with this process, and any of your encounters that have a large "charge" meaning you have bad feelings around a particular one, circle it. My suggestion would be to write a letter to that person, fully expressing all of your feelings about what happened and saying to them whatever you need to say in order to be fully complete. You do not have to mail it. There is power in writing it with an intention to let it go forever. Go through the list and write letters to any of your former relationships that are still affecting you in any way or are in your mind. This process can open up the space to release the past and create a new future.

Managing Difficult Relationships

When we look at how we operate in relationships, and define how we want to be treated, we may begin to see the imbalance in some of our relationships. Many of us have been brought up in dysfunctional family dynamics. Throughout the Clearing process, we have discovered that it is Self-Loving to raise the bar in our relationships. As you change, the people around you may need to change as well. You may need to retrain the people with whom you are in relationship to communicate more clearly and to be more loving. In the rest of this chapter, we will look at ways to communicate our needs, set boundaries, and as a last resort, ways to consciously eliminate the toxic relationship.

Relationship Standards

A relationship standard allows you to decide for yourself how you want and should be treated by everyone in your life. Allow yourself to consider setting the bar higher than you ever have before. I want you to stretch your own self-loving awareness here. For instance, my own personal Relationship Standard is:

> *I choose relationships that are loving, supportive, honest, have integrity, are nurturing and empowering.*

Have all my relationships always met this standard? Are all of my relationships always, 100% meeting this set level of expectation? Of course not, this takes work!

◆ **Write down five things for yourself that are non-negotiable in your relationships.**

Now think about the close relationships in your life. Do they meet your criteria? If they do not, I will give you some tools to bring them more into alignment with your relationship standard. In the following paragraphs about relationships, begin to think about the individuals who do not meet your relationship standard and determine for yourself what actions you might take to make them more harmonious and loving.

Communication

There is a tendency for family members or old friends to "hold each other" in a certain way, sometimes not seeing the real character and personality of the other person. For example, the youngest sister in a family may always be looked upon as a child, even after she has grown up to be an accomplished and powerful woman. These adult attributes are overlooked and the old image is superimposed over the woman that is. The youngest sister, not being seen as she is, finds herself continually acting in a defensive mode and never feels like she can be herself when around her family. As we have said, it is not Self-Loving to who you really are to be seen and treated this way. Rather than engaging in old behaviors, such as defending or attacking, a healthier and more powerful way to address the situation is to make a clear request of what it is you want. Prior to your communicating with your family members, write out your request so you are clear about your intention. The objective here is to not make them wrong, which would put them in a defensive mode. Clearly state your request, saying something like, "I would love for you to be able to hold me as the adult, accomplished woman that I am." This simple request will open up a dialogue that will change the dynamic of the relationship. Even though your intention is positive, you cannot predict how it will be received. This communication is for you! It is you stating to your family, friends and the Universe, your truth, regardless of how it is received.

Steps for a Clear Communication

* Be clear about your intention and the reason for the communication. Know what it is you want to see change and grow in the relationship. Write about it until you feel you are complete, then succinctly make a statement of intention.
* Acknowledge the importance of the relationship to you, and remember specific instances where you were not treated in the way you desired.

- Set up a time to speak when neither of you will be interrupted. Let the person you are communicating with know there is something you would like to discuss about your relationship, so they are not "blind-sided."
- Start the communication on a positive note, saying something along the lines of, "I really care about you and you are important to me, so I want to discuss something that has bothered me for a while so we can get past it." Beginning your communication this way, opens up their listening so they can really "hear" you.
- Set some ground rules for the communication. Ask them to hear you without interrupting. Tell them they will get an opportunity to respond when you are complete. When they are speaking, you do the same. When everyone is interrupting each other, no one can be heard.
- Read your communication to the other person. Let them know what your intention was for the communication in the first place.
- Use "I statements" to take full responsibility for your feelings. For example, "when you do this, I feel…" or "I felt hurt when…"
- Be open for their response. You have opened this door, and you have to hear them also. Listen without getting stuck in your position, there cannot be any growth when either one of you digs in your heels. You need to be willing to be wrong.
- You both need to agree on the next steps. In the example of the youngest child not being truly seen, this might look like her older sister agreeing to try to see the younger sister in a new light or for them both to attempt to work on their relationship going forward by bringing up ways they have felt overlooked or undervalued in the past.

To communicate your feelings clearly is the first step and can change the dynamic of the relationship. The real work then follows with maintaining the open dialogue, setting and enforcing boundaries, and continuing to listen to each other.

Finding Your Voice

It is very dis-empowering when you want something and realize you do not have the courage or words to speak up for it. In those moments you lower your personal value and decide you are not worth the effort. You decide that you will put up with the terms as they are. You do not make waves. Communication will always change the dynamic. Is there a communication to this person that you need to make or do you need to deliver a request in order to get your needs met? Sometimes we realize we are not even comfortable speaking to the person, perhaps they constantly interrupt or get defensive, making the communication even more difficult. In these situations you may want to consider sending the communication in a letter or email form. It is still important to follow all the steps for Clear Communication listed previously. If you find yourself afraid to speak up, there may be a long history from your past when you have communicated and not been heard. If you find that to be true, go back to Clearing Your Decisions and Beliefs (Clearing, Chapter 3). It is never easy to have a difficult conversation with someone, but it is so worth it, because you are worth it! In these difficult conversations it is Self-Loving to come from a place of calm strength, taking control of your emotional state. By coming from this empowered place you are being more loving to the other person as well. Communicating consciously is always better than communicating in a reactionary way.

Communicating in a Tense Situation

Plan to follow all the Steps for a Clear Communication listed previously. If the communication pops up and you are not ready for it, see whether you should put off the conversation and come back to it when you are clearer. Ideally, you might want to first run it by a friend or write down your thoughts. You absolutely have the right to say that you do not want to discuss this topic right now and set a time when you can be better prepared. If you do decide to discuss it now, before you speak, take a few deep breaths, and try to calm yourself as much as possible. The calmer you are, the less charge you will deliver in your communication.

Boundary Making

When we look at making boundaries, we are taking a fresh look at a current relationship and deciding to change the old way of doing things. Boundaries are a line of protection we draw around ourselves. Whether you have consciously or unconsciously defined your boundaries, they are your unwritten rules you have about yourself at an emotional level. Boundaries need to be implemented for people that invade your space in certain ways. There are boundaries in business where you do not share personal information. Boundaries are about respect and clarify appropriate and non-appropriate behaviors. The discussion around boundaries comes up when you feel trampled by the behavior of another person, or when your own energetic or emotional space has been compromised. It is healthy to be clear and conscious of your boundaries with relating to others. Know your own boundaries. For example, I have a boundary about not being spoken to abusively by anyone. Some of you may have a boundary around others living up to their obligations. Another person may not have as defined a boundary in this area which can lead to strife in the relationship.

Someone has stepped over your boundaries, what do you do? Maybe you have not defined your boundaries to the person, but now you feel violated in one way or another, so now is the time. If it is a relationship that is important to you, look at the situation and clarify for yourself what boundaries you need to define in order to feel comfortable. Write out the situation for yourself, so you are clear. How did the trespass or encroachment make you feel? What would support you in this situation? What boundary would hopefully prevent this from happening again? A simple boundary setting example could be used when someone always interrupts you when you speak. You can request each person take their turn without interruption. This is setting a boundary. In an intimate relationship, boundaries are important to support you and the relationship. For example, if in the heat of an argument you both begin name calling, you can create a boundary that there will be no name calling, and you will each attempt to treat each other with respect. Do not try to engage in boundary work when in the middle of an argument, wait for a time when things are calm and harmonious and use the communication tools to present your new boundaries.

"You teach people how to treat you." – Dr. Phil McGraw

Go back to your relationship standards and see which relationships may need some boundary work. What boundaries might you need to establish? If you have tried all of these techniques and the relationship is important to you, you may need to seek professional help to support the process of healing.

Eliminating the Relationship

Eliminating the relationship is a last resort. These relationships are unhealthy, toxic or abusive. We do not have to be in relationship with people that make us feel bad, even if they have been in our lives for a long time. It is not Self-Loving to continue in this relationship. No relationship, no matter how close or how long it has been in our life, should hurt our spirit. What does it mean when a relationship hurts your spirit? When your well-being and health are negatively affected; when you feel your spirit is dying; when you continually are not speaking up for yourself and are under stress or feel you are being controlled or abused by another person. These parameters should be non-negotiable! After you have tried the preceding techniques to manage the difficult relationship in your life, you may realize that the most loving thing you can do for yourself is to let the relationship go. Are you willing to let go of the relationship?

How do you eliminate a relationship? The best way to do it is with integrity. This is usually a difficult conversation, so you will want to utilize all the tools previously mentioned. If you do not feel it would be constructive to do this in person, let the person know through a letter or email. Be clear about your intention. Write all your feelings and thoughts about what happened, and let them know you are ending it. Describe the behavior that you no longer condone or find acceptable. Tell them that you choose to no longer be in relationship with them. Tell them not to contact you and put up specific boundaries. Use the "I" statements, not pointing fingers or placing blame. Your communication might look something like this: "I feel that I have tried to repair this relationship and everything has failed. At this point, I need to step away and take care of myself. Please do not contact me." Is any of this easy? No, ending a relationship is one of the most difficult things we do, but in extreme cases, it is the most Self-Loving thing to do.

Once you have communicated your feelings, the ball is now in your court – so, do not throw the ball back! If they cross your boundaries and contact you again, ignore the communication. If they continue to disregard your request, reiterate your request of no contact.

The main thing I want to express here is that it is a very Self-Loving act to manage your relationships on a day to day basis. Many people have lowered their standards, some even to the point that they are miserable. It is not ok to have abusive situations around you that are hurting you. It goes back to how do you want to live your life? You have a choice! Look at all of your relationships, even the ones you consider "good." Determine if there are any relationships that can be brought to new heights of Self-Love for you!

CHAPTER 11

Clearing Career & Finance

Clearing Career

Work is fundamentally a series of relationships: your bosses, clients, employees, or co-workers – it is all connections! Sometimes these have less of a charge than our family and friends because they tend to not be these deep, long-term associations. Regardless, they still have an impact in your life. Your ability to co-create and manifest your heart's desire in the area of career and finances comes down to the value you place on yourself... your self-worth. I have worked with many people who have challenges in their career area: some cannot figure out what their passion is; others have difficulty keeping a job; and others have settled in a position where they are unhappy. Underneath it all, there is generally something going on from their past. Perhaps there is a significant event from the past, like being fired, that has never been fully expressed. Maybe there are relationships from your career history that are dictating your actions and reactions in your current work environment. Maybe there were decisions or beliefs that were unconsciously made about your career that need to be brought to light. By clearing out these blockages and/or patterns, whether in career history or current time, it opens up the possibility of having a career you love.

Clearing Career Exercise

In your journal, begin to tell the story from your childhood dreams to the present state of your career. Remember when you were a little child and you would dream about what you wanted to be when you grew up... the excitement and the passion you pictured yourself doing with your career; or when you were in college and deciding where to focus your energies, all of the options seemed open and available. Do you feel that same thrill and enthusiasm about your current work situation? If you are not eager to jump out of bed in the morning and get to work, examining any past or current stuckness can open up the path to a fulfilling expression of yourself in career. Answer these specific questions about your work:

* *What is your current story of your career?*
* *Are you satisfied, fulfilled?*
* *Do you feel you are making a difference?*
* *Does your compensation feel adequate?*
* *Are you happy in your work environment and the people you work with and your supervisor?*
* *Do you feel excited to jump out of bed and go to work?*

We will be especially focusing on any area that will need clearing, like any significant or traumatic events in the area of career – having been fired, or a fear of that happening; looking at the history and getting clear of what really happened. With firings, many times we point fingers or blame our perpetrator. Where are you responsible? Until you take 100% responsibility, owning your own part in the scenario, it remains incomplete. That in turn can cause you to bring that history into your next job situation.

- Make a list of your career history, starting with your first job to the present. Write down every position, every boss and any outstanding experiences with fellow employees, with any important memories that stand out. Acting as the Psyche Detective, try to find the piece of the puzzle that will illuminate your current situation. Circle the ones that really stand out, that you have the most emotional charge on. How do you know if you have a charge on a memory or a person from your past?

If you can remember the incident like it was yesterday and it actually happened five years ago, you have a charge. If recalling the memory makes you feel bad about yourself, you have a charge. If you feel physically uncomfortable while recalling these memories, you have a charge.

Podium Exercise

 In order to move forward and clear this charge from your past, I will be guiding you through an exercise called the Podium. In this visualization you, your conscious self, will be entering a room and going behind a podium, acting as the CEO of your life addressing the workforce of your career past (this will also work, and have transformational results on anyone that you may be having a problem with in present time).

Get into a comfortable position with your feet flat on the ground. Close your eyes and take several deep breaths, centering your attention and focus on the center of your forehead. When you feel relaxed, picture yourself standing center stage of a large room, the lights are dimmed but there is a spotlight on you. You are standing behind a podium that comes up to mid-chest height. You speak in the microphone, calling out the name of the first person on your list that with whom you need to clear. You, your conscious highest self, is calling on the conscious highest self of the person from your past. You invite them to please step forward. There is nothing to be afraid of, they no longer hold any power over you. You are two souls meeting on the astral plane, a plane of light and energy only. Begin to speak to the person from your past, telling them how they transgressed you in the

*past, how it made you feel, how you think they affected you. Speak until you feel
complete with your communication. Ask them if they have anything to say to you
in return. See if you can find your culpability in the situation, and if you need to ask
for forgiveness for your own behavior. When you feel you are complete, pulling
everyone you need to speak up to the podium, thank them for their participation,
and release your audience. When you feel complete, open your eyes.*

Doing this exercise helps you release the stuck energy on people
from your past, and it miraculously helps the energy move for a situation
happening in current time. You might be surprised by some of the effects of
doing this exercise. Communicating at the podium with a co-worker you are
having problems with at work, can cause them to show up tomorrow with
transformed feelings for you. Once you do the Podium Exercise above, you
will begin to feel lighter. This exercise can clear out a heavy history. Look
and see if there are any other people that you need to do this exercise with.

When you finish with everyone on your list in doing the Podium Exercise,
start to take personal responsibility by beginning to look at the role you
played in all of these situations. There are always two sides to the story and
the old saying, "it takes two to tango," is true. It is very important to first
clear out your perception of what happened, but without the other part of
taking ownership, there is something left incomplete. Let us go through a
process of owning your part in the situation which I had you begin to think
about in the last meditation. In looking at the situation you had the most
charge on again, in your journal answer the following questions:

Taking Personal Responsibility

- What could you possibility have done differently in
  each job situation?
- Did you not honor your own internal values but acted as a
  "good soldier" in order to keep your job?

- Write about any transgressions against yourself, so you are clear of how your own actions impacted you.
- Could you have communicated differently?
- Did you take action inappropriately or refuse to take action?
- Give the people around you credit for being able to read your body language and any unexpressed resentments. Did this play a part in the unfolding of your firing or conflict at work?
- If you see any character flaws, how can you improve yourself in the future to change those behaviors?

The purpose for this exercise is not to have you feel judged or bad about your actions, but to see that there were two sides to the story. Taking 100% ownership of your part in the story will go a long way to clear out the past and create a new position or a better situation in your current job. When you take personal responsibility, you are able to actually let the experience go!

Forgiveness Exercise

 Before we move into forgiveness, check in with how you are feeling now about your situation. As you look back at your history again, are you feeling lighter with more space around you to move on? Are the emotions as charged as before? At this point, you have spoken with the other participants in this situation at the podium and you are now ready to take full responsibility and forgive yourself.

Take a moment and find a place where you will be undisturbed, close your eyes and take a few conscious breaths. Breathe in energy and light and breathe out all the work that you have done in clearing your career history. With each breath become more and more relaxed. Think once again about the part that you played in this scenario. No matter how much you felt it was someone else's

fault, true freedom comes when we own our part in any challenge. From this perspective, you have already taken responsibility and now it is time to forgive yourself. Imagine yourself walking into a room and sitting down in a chair. Ask that your higher consciousness come into the room and sit in front of you. Relate to your higher Self the experience of taking responsibility where needed. Tell your higher Self all the times when you could have done something differently. Own your feelings: shame, sorrow, sadness, fear, anger, resentments and pettiness. Own your own inadequacies. Imagine your highest Self saying anything it needs to be complete, and then saying, "We do the best we can. When we know better, we do better. I forgive you. I love you. Now YOU forgive you. Let go and let God, all is for your highest good." Keep doing this process until you have 100% owned your part in this situation and forgiven yourself. As your higher Self is speaking, allow yourself to open to the forgiveness. Breathe into your heart and say, "I am ready to let go, now! I forgive myself. This situation taught me... (fill in for yourself what you learned as a result of this challenging situation). As I go forth, I will know better and I will do better! And so it is!" Do this process until you feel complete.

The Shoulda – Woulda - Couldas

Many times we look back at our lives and the decisions we have made in the past with remorse. Maybe you "shoulda" stayed in college. Maybe you "woulda" had 15 years at a now hugely successful corporation if you had not left for perceived greener pastures. Perhaps you "coulda" tried harder at being an actress instead of taking a job in administration. These decisions can play in our mind especially at times when we are dissatisfied with our current situation. This is the proverbial road not traveled. From my perspective, this thinking does not support our moving forward to an empowered position. Another way of looking at our past decisions is what I call *It's A Wonderful Life Review*. What would your life look like if you had chosen a different path?

It's A Wonderful Life

If from time to time you regret decisions made in the past, try on this exercise as a way of re-perceiving the road not traveled. Hindsight is 20/20. With all the information you had at the time, could you have made a different decision? I truly believe that people do the best they can with the information they have. It is best for us to come from our heart in making all these big life decisions. If you are not familiar with the 1940's classic movie, *It's a Wonderful Life*, it is about George Bailey, who throughout his life has lived self-lessly, making most of his life decisions for the betterment of his family and his home town. Facing a crisis, he is visited by an angel, Clarence, who shows him what the lives of the people around him would have been like without him.

❖   **For yourself, take on the role of George Bailey, and review the decisions that you are regretting. Journal your responses.**

Imagine if you had made a different decision, what would your life look like today? What would you not have in your life that you currently have? How would things be different? By not being where you were, you may have missed out on meeting friends, having loving and fun experiences and many of the joys you did experience. List some of the things that were benefits from choosing the path you took. Acknowledge and forgive yourself. By doing so, you loosen the grip of regret and give yourself the freedom to acknowledge and appreciate the wonderful life you have created. With a deep breath, release once and for all, those shoulda, woulda, couldas, and know that you truly have had a Wonderful Life!

Clearing Financial

No one can deny you anything.
Only you deny it through your vibrational contradiction.

124 · CLEAR · CONNECT · CREATE

Finance, Money and Abundance

There are common messages and misconceptions about money that we all carry around with us and from which we operate. These messages set up our relationship with money. Unless we consciously assess and clear our relationship with money, the unconscious relationship will be the blueprint from which we are working. See if any of the following beliefs are true for you. Journal any additional beliefs you hold about money and abundance not on this list.

Common thoughts/beliefs about money:
Money comes and goes.
You have to work really hard to make money.
Money is the root of all evil.
Buying things makes me happy.
Money burns a hole in my pocket.
Money just slips through my fingers.
I have bad luck with money.
You can never be too rich or too thin.

Changing Our Beliefs About Money

* **Take a few minutes to write a positive affirmation next to your current beliefs about money.**

These affirmations will help you begin to change your attitudes towards money, abundance and flow. Put your new affirmations where you can see them to read them regularly. These new thought forms will begin to take root and grow in our subconscious.

Current Belief:	*New Affirmation:*
Money comes and goes.	I am experiencing a consistent flow of money now.

CLEARING CAREER & FINANCE · 125

You have to work really hard to make money.
Money is the root of all evil.

I effortlessly produce a large income and am financially independent.
I do good works with the abundance I am afforded now.

Clearing Our Finances from the Past

Answer the following questions to determine if you have more to clear with regard to abundance and finances from your childhood.

* What was your parents' relationship to money?
* Did both your parents work?
* Did they have a satisfying work experience or did they come home frustrated and complaining?
* When you were a child, was your family financially secure or was there a sense of fear when the bills came?
* What were some of the spending habits of your parents, were they frugal or extravagant spenders, or somewhere in between?
* What were you taught (or not taught) about money, either from your own observation or from an actual lesson learned?
* Recall any events from your past that changed your family or had a traumatic effect on you related to finance.
* What is your current relationship to money, include any fears and beliefs.

When prompted by these questions what came up for you? Were any emotions charged for you? Go back to Clearing Chapter 3 to clear out your Decisions and Beliefs regarding career and finance.

Tackling Worry & Fear

Many of us have worry and fear in the area of finance. There are many places one can be at emotionally on the financial spectrum, but there is no doubt that this is one of those subjects people find challenging. People who have a lot of money have fear about hanging onto it, and people who feel they do not have enough money worry about handling their obligations. For some, it is literally a thought addiction. There are those who spend all of their time to amass more, more, more, and those who feel it is not even spiritual to have it. Some may feel jealousy of another who has much, and others live into the idea of being the "starving artist." What is valuable is to bring any fear, worry, or anxiety up to consciousness and acknowledge it. This can allow you to clear the underlying fears and prepare you for creation.

Meditation Exercise to Release Financial Fear

When you feel the fear, worry or lack...:

* *List your fears or write about what is bothering you and read over what you wrote.*
* *Find a quiet place where you will not be disturbed and lie down and close your eyes.*
* *Take three deep, slow conscious breaths and breathe them out forcefully, pushing the breath out of your body, making a noise on the exhalation if you would like to and return to normal breathing.*
* *Scan your body from head to toe and try to locate where the fear resides in your physical body. It may show up as a tightness or pain somewhere, or a discomfort in an organ or bowels, or you may even see it in your mind's eye as a shape, form or darkness.*
* *Look at the fear without judgment, not analyzing it but noticing what is coming up, whether it be a memory, a picture or thought. Give it space to be, honoring that this is what you are feeling in the moment.*

- Watch it, observe it and notice if it changes to a different emotion or location in your body.
- Allow yourself to be with the fear in whatever expression it has chosen. Send it love and light and thank the fear for teaching you. It has served its purpose.
- Now it is time to let the fear go, merging back to the Source.
- Taking a few more deep, slow conscious breaths and breathe out forcefully, pushing the breath and the fear out of your body.
- Fill in the void that is left where the fear used to reside with Self-Love and light from the Universe.
- Repeat this exercise as often as needed with any other fear on your list and any that may come up for you.

Deserving and Integrity

Deserving is the foundation that the house of Self-Love is built on.

Without feeling deserving and worthy of abundance, it is very difficult to be open to receive what the Universe has for us and create what we are trying to achieve in the area of finance. We can put out our intentions, but if we have a guilty conscience, do not feel we deserve good things, or feel we have transgressed another, it will be much more challenging to create consistent financial flow. Clearing our area of finance includes a large dose of getting in integrity. When we feel we have done something "bad" in our lives that has not been cleared: taken money out of your parent's wallet when you were a kid; not paid someone you owed; not paid your taxes, etc.; all of the many things that we could list that we perceive as "bad"; then why would we feel we deserve good things? When our perception of our Self is negative regarding money, this can be a deeply ingrained belief we may not be conscious of. Most people's lives are a reflection of their deepest feelings and beliefs about Self. When we feel we are "bad", we punish ourselves by not having money, have it come and go, overspend, or some other manifestation of the belief.

Financial Integrity Exercise

Acknowledge and write down all the things that you have done, or feel are bad, or out of integrity about money. Shine the light on all the things related to money that we would prefer to not look at. List out your debt. Pull your credit report (I know that may be a tough one!) On your list, are any of these things occurring in present time? For example, taking money out of your father's wallet is not in present time, it is from the past. However, having not paid taxes in the last five years, is being currently out of financial integrity. Make the distinction between what is past and what is current. Review your list and put a circle around anything that is happening in current time and a star by those things that have happened in the past.

For the financial issues from the past, admit your transgression, apologize or utilize the podium exercise. You are being 100% responsible. Once you have done that, let yourself off the hook. Stop sending yourself the message that you are "bad." That is no longer true for you. Look upon yourself now without judgment. Do the Forgiveness Exercise to release.

For the things that are happening in current time, see if you are willing to clean them up. Are you ready to contact an accountant about the tax issue, for example? Even if you are not ready to do it today, just by putting it in your planner to handle a month from now, you will open up the energy and restore your integrity with yourself. By setting the appointment, you will feel more financially responsible and more deserving of financial flow. If there is someone you owe money that you have not felt you could pay back, set up a payment plan to begin to resolve this issue. Acknowledge your culpability, apologize and restore your integrity. You will be amazed at the opening for flow! Clearing in the area of finance allows you to begin to really experience deserving and that you are worthy of having more and more good. When you are living and acting at your highest potential, your path is clear. It opens the doorway to all that you desire, whether it is a relationship, health, money or career. It is a Self-Loving act to clear.

CHAPTER 12

Clearing Health & Wellness from the Past

What you believe is reflected back at you like a mirror, just look at your life.

mentioned in the first chapter that one of my big "aha" moments in this life was when I realized that my body was a temple that housed this soul. Health and wellness can be seen as the physical manifestation of everything we have going on, acting as a check and balance system. What this means is, if we are out of balance in any area of our life, many times the telltale sign may first crop up as an outcry from our bodies. If we are working too hard and not getting enough rest, our immune system becomes compromised and we get sick. Our body will make sure we are now absolutely going to get the rest we need. For practical purposes if we do not have our health, we do not have much else. The rest of our life pretty much goes on the back burner until we are healthy again. Aside from the flu, or something debilitating like a broken bone, we can pretty much *coast* until things get really bad. We need to make our health and our bodies a priority. But, as we all know, we can really be remarkable creatures at denial and avoidance. In this chapter, we will focus on rooting out and facing any fears that may be working against us unconsciously. We will also look at what decisions and beliefs we have made about our health in the past.

In the area of health and wellness, more than in any other area of our lives, our physical self is molded by our beliefs and decisions. These are usually unconscious and we may not realize that our own health and wellness is related to what we saw and accepted as a child. We need to bring up these decisions and beliefs, as well as any fears, to consciousness, so that we can either clear them and/or choose to keep the ones that support our well-being. Without examination they lay dormant in our subconscious and mold our physical body.

My experience has been that our decisions and beliefs or fears are often associated with an underlying cause of aberrant behaviors. Below are some of my clients' health and wellness blocks, see if any of them are true for you, or if you have similar beliefs:

- Your father died of a heart attack at 50, as you approach 50, you fear you are going to die.
- You had cancer in the past, and worry about re-occurrence.
- You or a family member were sick at a young age which changed the family dynamic and changed your own feelings around health.
- You watched your parents' unhealthy (e.g., addictive behaviors) and fell into those patterns yourself.
- You had an accident as a child and were not fully cared for by a parent or guardian.

Fear is a place that has not yet discovered love. – Sanaya Roman

The way a person treats his/her body almost always is an indicator of the amount of love they feel for him/herself. We may wonder, why can't I lose this weight, or why do I keep putting off this doctor's appointment? Why am I not working out 3-5 times a week like I promised myself? Why haven't I gotten a mammogram? It is not that you are lazy or consciously self-abusive. There may be many underlying causes that manifest in these decisions to not act. We have beliefs and decisions, blocks and patterns, fears and concerns, keeping us from living to our fullest potential. As we have learned, because of the distractions of the world, many of us are living the proverbial "unexamined life," we do not know what we believe... until now!

In the Self-Love Test you may have answered some of these questions. Now, let us enlist our Psyche Detective to help us get a clear picture of where we are in the area of health and well-being. Do your best to answer the following questions. We need to be *real* with ourselves about what is happening.

Evaluating Our Health and Wellness

- Do I make healthy food choices?
- Do I rest when I need to?
- Do I exercise regularly at least three times per week?
- Do I schedule a physical every year?
- Have I seen a dentist in the last six months?
- Have I had an eye exam in the last 2 years?
- Have I had a mammogram every year since I turned 40?
- Is my weight within ideal range?
- Do I have a rewarding life beyond my work or profession?
- Am I responsible in areas that can be considered addictive: alcohol, drugs, sex, tobacco, food, shopping, and relationships?
- Have I had an AIDS test?
- Do I meditate?
- Does my environment reflect peace?
- Am I able to remain calm in tense situations? Do I respond with anger or irritation to myself or others in tense situations?
- Do I allow myself to feel my feelings in the moment?

Someone who is loving to themselves takes all of these steps. You can do it too!

Owning it with Honesty

If you are not able to affirm these questions for yourself, the question is WHY? Why haven't you done these things that give you the peace of mind that comes with taking care of yourself? Have you not made yourself a priority? Is there something deeper going on? Are you afraid of something? Acknowledge the ways in which you *do* take care of yourself, and for the rest, I invite you to take a deep breath, pause here, and examine if there is more going on in the areas that you are not taking responsibility for your health and wellness.

For example, you may not have had that mammogram because your aunt had breast cancer, or you have not gotten that mole looked at because you fear a bad diagnosis. You made that decision to not think about it, fearing that you would be diagnosed with cancer. You may have even forgotten the original decision; you just know that if anyone brings up mammograms, there is an uncomfortable feeling, and then you avoid it again for another year. If this is the case, then we need to clear out these fears. Write about those feelings and fully express your emotions. Allow all those deeper emotions to come up to the surface. Start to be your own Psyche Detective and reveal to yourself those underlying motivations. The following will illustrate three examples how blocked emotions can cause you to exhibit less than loving behaviors to yourself.

Fears

There are many types of fears. Fear of that which goes bump in the night causes our heart to thump and our palms to sweat and creates a fight or flight response. This bodily reaction is a survival instinct. Another type of fear is phobias. Fearing something specific will happen if... if I get on the plane, it will crash; if I walk too close to the edge, I will fall; if I swim, I will drown. All fears present us with a challenge to face it or live with it. Fear of any type, if experienced over any length of time, causes stress and wears our body down. The type of fear we are talking about here is the worrying type of fear, dread, a general feeling of disquiet, having apprehension. We are going to use the Psyche Detective to uncover what the fear is, where it came from, and then root it out because with this type of fear, if you change your thoughts, you can change your life.

When you were reading the health and wellness list of loving inquiries, were there any behaviors of which you would like to let go? What were your feelings when you thought about actually changing those behaviors, did you feel the worrying type of fear I described in the paragraph above? When you think of going to the doctor and you feel discomfort, some part of yourself says, "I do not want to feel that way." So, we do what we can to avoid that feeling of discomfort. The avoidance neural pathway is set. It is easier next time when we think we should go to the doctor, to avoid and not make that appointment; the anxious thoughts and feelings are reinforced. These particular thoughts, feelings, sensations and behaviors get stored in our memory and become a stronger habit. Here we need to zone in on that initial feeling of discomfort, apprehension, or disquiet that started the avoidance pattern.

Tackling Our Fears

If the reason you have not taken responsibility for your health and wellness is because of worry and fear, it is time to take back your power. When you make the new decision to face your fear, with your new belief that getting tested regularly is your best defense, you are confronting your fears and practicing Self-Love in the area of health and wellness.

Worry is negative planning for the future. Many of us are addicted to worry. It zaps our energy and prevents us from changing our circumstances. What problems are you worried about? Be specific. Is it an event that could occur in the future, or an event from the past that has its grips on you? Talk about it with a Re-creation partner or journal about it. Acknowledging these feelings and not ignoring, stuffing, or succumbing to them, is self-loving.

Think of this situation and assign the worst case scenario. Our mind is happy to go there. Fear is almost always based on a lack of information. Not knowing how something will work out causes us to immediately go to the worst case scenario anyway, so in this exercise we will let our mind go there one last time to shine the light on how ridiculous it is to let our fear control our actions. The mind dreams up all of the terrible things that could go wrong... "and then what if...," "and then what if...?" Your scenario might look something like this: *I am avoiding getting that mole checked, because I am sure that it is cancer, then I will have to get chemo, I will be sick, I will probably lose my job, I will be homeless, I won't have health insurance, so I will die anyway and my kids will be motherless.* I know this is an extreme example, but this is how our mind works. All of that gets avoided if we never get the mole checked. See how our fears control us?

Examine your worst case scenario and ask yourself these questions. Does it change your feelings about your fears?

- What information do you need that could put you at ease?
- How could you get that information?
- What resources do you have?
- What is the likelihood that the worst will happen?
- Is it not more likely that a less severe version will occur, or nothing at all?
- How much is your mind controlling your view of things?
- Is it better in this scenario to act or to not act?

> *In order for us all to learn the important lessons in life, we must each day surmount a fear. – Ralph Waldo Emerson*

What do you do when the fear comes in? When we acknowledge that we have fear or worry over some situation, we have a choice. We can wallow and hide, or transform it. Some people will avoid the fear destructively: take a pill (dull it); or eat (bury it); or have drinks (drown it), have sex (avoid it). Others will avoid the fear in what are considered constructive ways: work, watching TV, reading a book, or a million other pleasurable distractions. Some of these ways of avoiding our fears do not seem that horrible, after all, reading a book engages the mind, sex is pleasurable, work is productive. There is nothing wrong with those activities, *unless* we are doing them to avoid our fear. Fear needs to be met head on, faced with courage. Being in the fear and avoiding the fear is the same thing, we are still in fear. Avoiding the fear is worse because we are not allowing the fearful emotions to surface. By using any coping tools to push our feelings away, we are alienating our true emotions. When you do this, it is harder to get back to the place where we acknowledge the fear and transcend it. The worst part is that the avoiding does not even work. When the binge is over, the meal is eaten, the sex is done, and the work is complete, we still have the fear, worry, anxiety, and despair.

Don't give into the fear. Not giving into the fear, not going where the mind wants to go, holding in your mind's eye a perfect vision of the best possible scenario, remaining focused on the desired end result... these are the ways you can stay conscious. By meeting the fear head-on, you change your energy.

Clearing Health & Wellness From the Past

Answer these questions for yourself:

- What was your parent's relationship to health/wellness?
- Were your parents active or couch potatoes?
- What kind of food was served in your home?
- Did you eat at least one meal a day together as a family?
- Did your parents encourage you to exercise or do sports?
- What is your relationship with food and exercise?
- What are your beliefs around your own wellness?
- What negative or challenging behaviors have your created for yourself based on what you witnessed in your childhood?
- What beliefs have you taken on from what you witnessed.
- How have those beliefs manifested in your life?

Food and Health

Obesity is a huge concern in this country right now. We are eating over processed foods, and we are eating too much of it. Most of us are not getting enough exercise. For many people, food is a control issue. Overweight individuals are not exerting enough control and overeating. Anorexics and bulimics are exerting too much control by exercising too much and not eating enough. There are also "stuffers," those who do not want to feel the emotion they are experiencing, so they distract themselves with food, stuffing their feelings. The relationship between our emotions and our eating habits are, for many, closely linked. Food in some homes is a celebration, representing love, nurture, family. Food in another home can be a way to abuse our bodies. It is no wonder there is the full spectrum from eating yourself to death and starving yourself to death. The following case study is another example of how decisions and beliefs made in childhood can affect health and wellness in the present.

Emotional Eating: Case Study – Julie's Story:

When Julie came to me for coaching to help her lose weight she was an attractive woman, about fifty pounds overweight. I asked her if she remembered the first time her weight became an issue. She had been a chubby child, and when she was ten years old, she had undergone a growth spurt and gained some weight. Her baby fat, once seen as cute, seemed not so cute anymore and her clothes were not fitting properly. During a dinner party, she asked her mother for a second dessert. Her mother told her she didn't *need* a second dessert, and then proceeded to tell her friends how she was putting her daughter on a diet. Julie felt embarrassment, shame, and guilt. She felt like crying, which made her more upset because, in her mind it was just a dessert, but it had been the first time she was told, "No." In that moment, Julie decided she would never again ask for dessert. Sweets and candy became the enemy. She still wanted them, but decided she would not eat them in front of anyone. That was the first night she began to sneak sweets. She decided she was not going to be told no again; she was in control. Her desire was wrong or "bad." She expressed to me how in that in that moment, she felt her life had changed. From that point forward, when she looked in the mirror, she saw a fat kid who was weak, ugly, and full of shame. Julie's Decision Table looked like this:

Julie's Decision Table

Parental Behavior	Decision Made	How it's affected or showed up in your life	Why are you still making this decision?	New Decision
Mother is not loving or accepting of my weight as a child	Rebelliousness. "I will eat whatever I want." I am in control!	I am overweight and unhealthy.	1. When I sit down to the table, my mother's voice is still in my head.	I am committed to being healthy and fit.
			2. By eating the way I want, I get to make her wrong.	I eat healthy and delicious foods that support my weight loss goals now.
			3. I felt so judged as a child, I nurture myself with food.	I only eat when I am hungry, not based on my emotions.

In the case of our example, why would a 40 year old woman still make the decision to rebel against her mother and her weight problem when the original wound occurred 30 years earlier? The answer is because she has never challenged those decisions made, and she may not have been conscious that she had made those decisions.

Your Decisions About Health and Wellness

Create a decision table and fill it in for yourself. Do you remember a decision you made as a child that is affecting your current health and wellness? Evaluate whether that decision has been beneficial for you or not. Has it been detrimental or empowering to your life? If it is detrimental, are you ready to make a new decision? Do you want things to be different? Why is it important to you to lose the weight and be healthy – could it be that you are looking for a mate, having health issues, you want to be around for your kids in 20 years, or is it something else? Evaluate your circumstances around the decisions that you have made. Ask yourself, "why it is important for you to make a new decision in your life?" You might be asking yourself, "How can I possibly change this?" You originally made the unhealthy decision and operated your life from it. Once you bring that decision to consciousness, acknowledge it and clear it, you can make a new and conscious decision.

Now that we have seen what we have been doing and the affect it has had on our lives, it is important to remember that YOU observed something that happened in your life, YOU interpreted it a certain way, and then YOU made the decision. Therefore, YOU can make a new decision, now!

What is the new decision that will support your empowerment? Look at the decision you made realizing the negative effects it has had in your life. In looking at the new decision, write the opposite, something that will empower your life. The decision is an affirmation, a statement that you are making to yourself that supports the outcome that you want to produce. Use this affirmation until it becomes anchored in your consciousness. Make this statement positive and life affirming. Use your affirmation for 30 days before you even make a commitment to change your behaviors. See if just my adopting a new decision, if your health and wellness habits begin to change on their own.

Beliefs

The decisions made as a child form the beliefs of today. Here is Julie's Belief Table:

Julie's Belief Table

Parental Behavior	Decision Made	How it's affected or showed up in your life	New Decision	My Belief	My New Belief
Mother not loving or accepting of my weight as a child	I'm rebelling. I'm going to eat whatever I want.	I'm overweight and unhealthy.	I am committed to being healthy and fit. I eat healthy and delicious foods that support my new weight loss goals now.	No matter what I do I can't lose weight.	I effortlessly maintain my ideal weight now.

Changing the decision without tackling the core belief system makes it much more difficult to change the behavior. You can diet, and do all the right things, but if you do not change the beliefs, the desired outcome is difficult to achieve and maintain.

Transforming Your Beliefs About Health and Wellness

First get clear on what your beliefs are, and then, if need be, challenge them. Here is what the challenge looked like for Julie. Read through the process and do this for yourself.

Belief: *No matter what I do I can't lose weight.* The first question to ask is: **Can you guarantee that the statement is absolutely true?** Have you used every diet/method that has ever been created on the planet throughout time? Have you really been 100% committed with full discipline, following a plan exactly as written? By answering these questions, we can clearly see that there is no way that one can say with complete accuracy that the belief statement is 100% true. Therefore, if it is possible that the statement is not true, then it may be an inaccurate belief and that this person *could* lose weight. There is a possibility here, so go for it!

How did you form these beliefs? Look back at your graph and look at the decision that formed the belief. In our example, *I'm rebelling. I'm going to eat whatever I want.*

Who are you still blaming? In this case, Julie is still blaming her mother and making her responsible, not herself. The key to this shift is to release and forgive, own and take 100% responsibility for the decisions and beliefs created. When this is done, you have taken your power back, so you can make a change!

What is the payoff? Even after changing our beliefs if you are still getting something out of this old behavior, it will be difficult to change. The payoff is the negative, unconscious benefit one receives from staying stuck. In our example, by not being able to lose weight, Julie gets to be right and make her mother wrong, and not take responsibility for herself. "Because my mother always judged my appearance, no matter what I do, I cannot lose weight." What is your payoff? What are you getting out of staying stuck in your behavior? It may not be readily apparent to you, but if you really probe, there is some payoff you are getting, even if it is just that you get to be *right!* Look back at the Decisions and Beliefs Chapter and see if any of those payoff listed apply to you in the situation. What is the benefit you are getting out of staying in your old way of being? Once you have identified your payoff, it loses much of its power.

What is the cost? Now that you have discovered the payoff, we will look at what the cost has been in your life for holding onto this way of being. The cost for Julie is having extra weight for all these years, possibly having health issues that are related to carrying those extra pounds; feeling uncomfortable and less confident than she might have otherwise felt. Perhaps she is more tired or unable to fully engage in life. Being committed to being right and making someone else wrong, and being stuck in that place, could, literally, cost Julie her life. Is it worth it? This is where you really need to take a good look at whether you are ready to make the change. Write down what it has it cost you to stay entrenched in this limiting belief.

Visioning the New You

Visioning will be handled more in the Create section but begin to form a picture of yourself being, doing, and having all it takes to change your health and wellness. See yourself making a commitment to change. Create a picture of yourself doing all of these new actions. You are now going to be someone who pays attention to his/her weight, exercise, and water intake. You are going to be someone who gets physicals from healthcare professionals, eye exams, and dental exams. You are someone who examines and creates positive thoughts and beliefs about your body temple!

CHAPTER 13

Clearing Religion & Spirituality

W hen writing this chapter I realized what a potentially touchy subject it is to clear our views on God. I kept remembering the old saying, "never discuss politics or religion." It is not my intention to, in any way, impose my beliefs on you, but I would be remiss if I ignored this subject. Religion and spirituality, just like we have been talking about in the past chapters, is another relationship; it is with God. Like any relationship, if it is toxic or dysfunctional, it can get in the way of your manifestation, and block your experience. This chapter may not apply to all of you. You might have total clarity when it comes to this area. If there is no clearing to do, if there is none of the proverbial "baggage" we have discussed, if there is no "charge" and "no weeds" to pull... just read through and move onto the next section.

It is important to clear spirituality, God and religion. When your relationship with God is blocked it can obstruct your access to the extraordinary or miraculous. That is our goal: to transform and create miracles! When we are open to the belief that there is something outside of our ordinary human existence, we feel we are not alone, that there is some force working with us. When we feel there is something bigger than our self, bigger than our ego, some part of us that is transcendent, inspired, and sees the bigger picture ~ a soul, that grows and blossoms~ then that force offers us a larger sense of purpose, support, and nurturing. This does not have to come in the form of something outside of us. This can be an energy that we feel within, a power that can be accessed, an awareness of our own strength. Ultimately, accessing the power within ~ that "force" we use for manifestation and creation is our Highest Self. It does not have to be a form, it just has to be a "connection." For some people it *is* in a form: an image of the Virgin Mary, the Tabernacle, Buddha; or maybe it is a symbol, like the OM, a crucifix, or the Star of David. Maybe that connection comes to you when you feel the sunlight on your face and the wind in your hair, or when you feel a part of nature. Maybe it comes to you through a piece of music, a poem, meditation or viewing a piece of artwork. Whatever part of you which speaks to your transcendent Self, I want that connection to be clear. My experience and my beliefs suggest to me a "bigger plan." This energy, force, God, feels like my partner illuminating my path. For me, Spirit feels like an energy behind me that wants me to succeed. When I get stuck in my rigid thinking of having to do it all alone, I have closed myself off to the Source that is God acting in my life. I can feel the blocked energy within my body. My constant prayer is to stay open without any blocks to this force for good that stands ready and willing to assist me.

I will approach clearing religion and spirituality from a "re-interpretation" perspective to see if you do have issues around this subject. The purpose is to see whether there is an alternative view you can adopt from the way you saw all things religious and spiritual as a child. I will bring up scenarios where your views on religion and spirituality may have gotten blocked, and invite you to examine that for yourself. And lastly, I will offer up opportunities for clearing these out. This chapter makes sure that there is nothing more stuck from the past, memories or emotions, beliefs or experiences that are in your way of using whatever Source or Force you believe empowers you, nurtures, and supports you. Even if you are an atheist and believe in no power outside yourself, I invite you to check that you are clear so you are ready to connect with the Universe within yourself and create.

The Spiritual Connection to Self-Love

What is the spiritual connection to Self-love? As I wrote in the forward, if God is everywhere, remember that God is also within you. Therefore, if you have difficulty loving yourself, in effect, you are cutting yourself off from your connection with the Divine. A Course in Miracles says, "Do you not recognize, a war against yourself would be a war on God?" (Chap. 23) In judging our self harshly, we separate from the spiritual aspect of our being. In our self-critical thoughts, words, and actions, we are judging God and separating from God. By not doing every possible act that would bring fullness, happiness, love and all we desire, we are no longer in the flow. There is a block between our essence and the Divine; from the wisdom and love available to us. Therefore, we cannot receive the Universe's spiritual backing. By clearing our judgments, negative feelings about our self, and embracing all aspects of our self, the doorway to that Divine connection is opened.

These are some of the areas where religion or spirituality can get stuck from the past, block our development, and our ability to create. Below are a series of questions for you to answer for yourself. See if these specific questions, beliefs/experiences/thoughts ring any truth for you.

Clearing Your Story of Religion and Spirituality

- Do you feel angry at God for something that happened to you? Do you feel punished, or judged?
- Were your prayers answered as a child? Did you feel forsaken, disillusioned, or not heard as a child?
- Do you believe in a supernatural being? Can you accept what seems illogical?
- What, if any, religious or spiritual upbringing were you raised?

- Have you experienced a loved one's untimely death or a child's death?
- Have you been abused by a clergy person/ Do you feel you have given your power away to a priest or authority figure in the church?
- When you look around and see senseless suffering and death, do you look to God and ask, "why?"
- Do you ponder the hypocrisy of religion?
- Were you told you would be punished for certain behaviors?
- Were you frightened by an experience as a child that centered around God, religion, or ritual?
- What prejudices or misconceptions about words like God, New Age, your Higher Self, or the Universe, do you have?
- What is your relationship with God like? Do you have a story of one specific incident?
- Describe your relationship with God, even if are you an atheist or agnostic. Do you have a strong religious or spiritual background? Did you attend a religious service regularly as a child? Did you ever pray as a child? What were your parents' beliefs about God, religion, or spirituality? What is your interpretation of a higher power and soul? Do these ideas bring you joy, nurturing, and empowerment or do they bring up feelings of betrayal, fear, or sadness?

Whatever your story is around God, spirituality, and religion, I want you to use the clearing techniques of writing and talking about it to bring it up to consciousness and examine it for lingering emotions. Is it somehow getting in your way?

The following is a case study from one of my clients. It describes how we can re-interpret our story to move forward and heal our relationship with our Self and Spirit.

Case Study: Sally's Re-interpretation of a Master/Teacher

One of my clients, Sally, was working with me to manifest her ideal career. She had always been very successful in a technical field, and wanted to change her career to utilize her artistic talents. When we began working on the manifestation process, I shared with her about connecting with some Source that was bigger than herself, for support. I inquired about her religious/spiritual beliefs. She shared with me that she had just come upon a guru from India who was teaching meditation techniques. While practicing these techniques, she described feeling some sort of energy or force that made her feel inspired, connected with herself, and empowered. She also said that she did not think she was going to return to the group because many followers in this group believed that the guru was a manifestation of God in physical form. Being from a religious background where the commandment of "Thou shalt not hold false idols before me," created a conflict for Sally. She felt confused about this concept of the guru as God. She did not experience this teacher as God, and she was unclear as to who, or what, was God. I suggested that this was an opportunity to clarify her thoughts and beliefs, and to discover this powerful new energy she had experienced. Being pragmatic, she admitted that throughout her upbringing she had never had any spiritual experiences. The closest she had felt to any type of "awakened energy" was the feelings she had experienced doing those guru's techniques. I suggested that if this new technique gives her power and supports her, it should be re-interpreted and re-contextualized, and not dismissed. I asked her several questions to see if she could possibly see him in a new way, a way that did not make her uncomfortable. For example, is he a great teacher? She answered, "yes." I asked if her feelings experienced with the guru's techniques could be an experience of her own power within which felt greater than normal waking consciousness? Again, "yes." Do you feel you can learn more from him and learn more about yourself? Yes. How does the term master/teacher work for you instead of God or even guru? She could see what I was trying to do. I explained that by re-interpreting this guru from God to a master/ teacher, she did not have to push away the whole experience. I asked her if it would be possible for her to use the parts that "worked" for her and supported her? This was an "Aha" moment for Sally. She could keep her teacher by seeing him in a different light and begin to explore the new energy and empowerment she was feeling. She could possibly use this experience in our work on manifestation.

I suggest that you use Re-interpretation to change the context of the beliefs you have been holding onto, that no longer work for you, or that block your development in some way. When we interpret something, we explain it, clarify it, and form beliefs around it for ourselves. To re-interpret is to change your explanation or re-contextualize that belief. One way of re-interpreting is to ask yourself questions around the topic, fully examining how you hold your beliefs. In Sally's example she needed to:

* examine her beliefs from childhood
* pinpoint where the discomfort was coming from
* decide if her old beliefs were currently serving her
* weigh her old beliefs against the value that she was getting from the guru

Clearing Religion and Spirituality Exercise

If you were charged by any of the religious/spiritual blocks from the writing exercise, after you have written your story, begin to question yourself.

* Are your old childhood beliefs serving you?
* What value do you get from the religion you practice? What, specifically, is the value that you are receiving?
* Is it time to re-evaluate your religious or spiritual practices?
* Where could you re-interpret your beliefs?

So now we will practice Re-interpretation on some of the other points listed above, to further shed light on how you may need to challenge your beliefs. For example, one of my clients had an issue around the hypocrisy of religion. As a child she watched the head of her church, the supposed pillar of the community, go out and treat people with different lifestyle choices with disdain. She felt that this person of distinction should, at least, be following the basic laws of the religion – treat another as you want to be treated. To re-interpret her disconnection with the religion, I asked her questions: Does the law have value? She said, "yes, being kind and just to others is a worthy law." Second, just as we uncovered with Sally... does the whole teaching have to be thrown out because of one aspect she witnessed with one community leader? In this example, does the whole religion need to be abandoned because of "one bad apple?"

Turning the Mirror on Our Selves Exercise

Humans are fallible, and we learn from making mistakes and growing. Can you re-interpret the person in our last example as human and fallible? Maybe, at some point during his/her life, someone will point out the error of their ways, but you are not responsible for this person. Who knows what is going on in their lives? Since it has such a strong charge for you, turn it back on yourself. Where are you possibly being ruthless or unkind? Where is the hypocrisy in your life? Oftentimes, we may find that the one thing that we are railing against another person, may be just the thing that we are railing upon ourselves in another area of our lives. Maybe we have not admitted to ourselves the similarity and/or the severity of the behavior. The reason we find no mercy for another, and the reason we judge them so harshly is exactly the reason we can find no mercy for ourselves and cannot admit our own behavior. Holding up the mirror can release the charge you feel for another person or situation. Where are you judging someone and not having compassion? By Re-interpreting a person or situation one of the gifts you receive is to clarify where you may have a charge, and use the opportunity to do some cleaning up of your own. The next step on this path is to forgive and release.

Forgiving and Releasing

Forgiveness is the gift you give to yourself.

One of the techniques that really helps to clear blocks and get movement in any area of our lives is to work with forgiveness, whether it is forgiveness of our self or of someone who transgressed us. Forgiveness is one of the most important spiritual principles. Forgiveness allows us to be free and open up the channel between ourselves and the Divine. By forgiving, letting go of the resentment, and the desire to punish, we begin to let go of the pain and anger that keeps us stuck. To pardon another is for you, not for the person who transgressed you. To forgive is not to condone one's behavior. When we acknowledge what happened, and our willingness to let it go, this in itself can release the energy that has blocked us, holding the pain from the past in place. Forgiveness is a choice that is made for ourselves. Through forgiveness, we can expect to move forward and release the pain of the past event.

Even if it seems like it would be impossible to forgive another, we will be exploring techniques that will move us closer to the possibility of forgiveness. If this topic feels too difficult, and you feel you need professional support, especially in the cases of childhood molestation or abuse, you may need to work with a facilitator or counselor. These are extremely painful memories and can trigger deep emotional responses. If you feel you are ready to explore this area, I suggest working with forgiveness and releasing.

Forgiveness does not change the past, but it
does enlarge the future. - Les Brown

If you have someone close to you that you totally feel safe with and trust, you may want to begin this process by sharing your feelings, experiences, and memories to begin to get clear about the event and start putting words around it. Getting it out and up from the darkness of the subconscious starts the process of letting it go. Take three deep conscious breaths, breathing in light and breathing out anxiety or tension. This allows you to begin to relax and see more clearly what actually happened. Think of it this way, although you have been hurt, which has caused you pain and misery, whether you choose to stay in the pain now, is up to you. You need to decide whether you are willing to let it go.

Guided Visualization: Letting Go of the Burden

 You have brought the story up to consciousness. Put yourself in a bubble of protection. See yourself and the others involved and feel the willingness to release it and forgive whoever needs to be forgiven. Call in your guides, masters, and teachers and ask them to help you put down the burden of the pictures in your head and the story you have repeated so many times before. See if you are ready to let it go. Can you give up the resentment and the desire to punish your perpetrators? Can you stop being angry? If all the answers to these questions are yes, then continue. If you want to, ask your guides to help you. Visualize the look, color and shape of your experience you are forgiving, shrinking down the scene. Hold it in your hands, seeing it for the last time. Put the whole experience in a plain, white box. Archangel Michael carries a mighty sword of fire and assists in clearing away any negativity and fear. Ask Archangel Michael to help you cut all the cords; you have connections to this story because you keep repeating it in your mind, that repetition forms energetic bonds. Ask Michael to take out his sword and cut all the bonds you have to this experience. Any lingering energy also goes into the box. Let Archangel Michael go. Now call in Archangel Raphael, the master healer, to come in. With the help of Raphael heal your heart around this experience. Imagine a big white funnel or tornado. Ask your guides and angels to take this box and put it in the white tornado. You have now "put the burden down." As the box is sucked up into the tornado, you have transmuted the darkness into light. If you are still feeling emotion in your heart around this, ask Raphael to put his hand on your heart and send emerald green energy to your heart area. To heal the wounds that you have been carrying about this experience, forgive yourself for any part you played. Be willing to stop judging

yourself. Move forward on your journey knowing that you have put the past in the past and you are now holding a positive vision for yourself to be in the present. You are opening to your clear connection with the Divine.

Apology Visualization

Another technique to move you closer to forgiveness is the Apology Visualization. When someone apologizes to us, even if we are not ready to accept an apology, the process opens your heart a little bit towards the person who transgressed you. Apologies can be extremely powerful. Close your eyes and imagine you are in a safe place of your choosing. Realize that no one can hurt you and that what happened to you, happened in the past. Imagine your transgressor entering the room and sitting down in the chair in front of you. Notice your feelings and calm yourself if need be. There is nothing to be afraid of. Speak from your heart to your transgressor about how their actions affected you. Describe your feelings and what that experience has cost you in your life. Tell what you lost. Once you are complete, imagine your transgressor asking you for forgiveness. You may not understand their pain or feelings; see if you can be open to receive their apology. If you feel you are ready, agree to forgive him or her. Even if you are not ready to forgive the other person, expressing your feelings creates room for your healing. Commit to release this past experience and forgive.

True forgiveness includes total acceptance – Catherine Marshall

Re-interpretation of God's Will

When I talk with my clients about God and His/Her will in their lives, I think I have heard it all. Most people's view of God's will in their lives is experienced on a broad spectrum from being rewarded, punished and ignored – none of which are healthy or supportive. What if we could re-interpret our view of God's will as, "*expressing that which is highest and good in my life.*" Now God's will is our own growth, our own expansion, a spiritual presence in our physical lives, helping us do the hard things, and stepping out of our comfort zones.

*What if God's will is the Light of Spirit showing us who we are
meant to become – Spirit's constant call to "Go higher!"*

When God's will is the absolute good for me, the biblical directive of surrender "thy will be done," takes on a new depth of meaning. When we turn off our ego and turn our will over to a Higher Power, we surrender to the highest good in our life. What different choices would we make? How much more strength is available to us?

Technique to Unconditionally Love Yourself

We have cleared judgments of our Self and others but we still have a mind and an ego. So, from time to time the small mind will say, "you are stupid, you are too fat, you are not good enough, you are not smart enough" ... the ego seems to find whatever you feel is the vulnerable part of your being. I call it, "cookies for the mind." These thoughts pop up in unexpected moments for the mind to gnaw upon. In these moments, we have to connect back to our Divine Self and look for ways to unconditionally love ourselves and realign with the best parts of our Self. One of the ways that you can experience Self-Love is by giving ourselves the love and acceptance that we are seeking from the outside. Here is an exercise to deepen that awareness.

Love Yourself Exercise

Find a comfortable spot to lie down and close your eyes. Take a few deep conscious breaths focusing the energy into your heart. Imagine, instead of air, you are breathing in the light and it is traveling to your heart center. Do this until your whole heart center looks like a shining sun, with rays beaming out, filling every inch of your body. Bring your total awareness into your heart center now. Place your hands on the heart and tell yourself how much you love YOU. Say, "I love you, _____ (state your name), I unconditionally love you. I accept everything about you and I know that you are a Divine Spirit having a human

experience. I know who you are!" Breathe into that space for a moment. Now say, "I receive unconditional love now!"

Divine Mother and Unconditional Love Meditation

 From my point of view, there are both male and female aspects of the Universe that embody the masculine and feminine attributes. By bringing in the feminine aspect, one can use this to nurture and deepen a feeling of Self-Love and connection with Spirit. The feminine aspect of God has been called the Divine Mother. She is the unconditionally nurturing, feminine aspect of God. By doing this exercise we can "mother" ourselves and anchor the feeling of unconditional love. Maybe you did not have a mother who was as healing, nurturing, and validating as you may have needed. When we access this force of the feminine aspect of the Universe, we heal this piece from our childhood. We now are going to meet the Divine Mother and embrace Her for our healing. (In this meditation and in several other meditations throughout this book, we will be accessing the chakra system. Feel free to access the internet for a visual display of the chakras.)

Sit quietly and take a few deep breaths. Imagine a grounding cord at the base of your spine as wide as your hips. This cord goes all the way down into the Earth; deep, deep, deeper than you have ever gone before. Go to the center or heart of the Earth. The Divine Mother is represented in the heart of the Earth as a big blue star. You want to tie your cord around the blue star. You will be connecting with, and pulling into you the blue energy from the Divine Mother. You pull this blue energy up the cord, up through the Earth, to the base of your spine into your first chakra where it forms a pool of Divine Love energy. It is blessing and dissipating any blocks. Dissipating is clearing and dissolving any energy that is blocked in these chakras. The blue energy moves up through the second chakra, third chakra, all the way up, stopping and pooling, blessing and dissipating at each chakra. We move all the way up to the crown. The crown is very important because this is where you make the connection with the Divine. You bless and dissipate the crown chakra and the blue energy spills out from the

top of your head out all around you in your aura or energy field, blessing and dissipating your aura. You sit for a moment in this Divine Mother energy filling your being to the brim with a feeling of Divine Love. Now we will call in the Divine Mother and she appears to give you an embrace. Your job is to be receptive of this unconditional love. Embrace and feel Her love, nurturing you beyond any type of mother love you have ever experienced. This will begin to help you melt away any of your own personal judgments. In the reflection of the Divine Mother, you begin to unconditionally love yourself! Do this meditation regularly to clear your chakras and bring in the deep, nurturing love of the Divine Mother.

Now that you are experiencing a new perspective on religion and spirituality, you are ready for the next step on our journey... Connect!

CONNECT

CHAPTER 14

What is Connecting and Why Do It?

Congratulations! You have completed Clearing! Most people live the unexamined life, and you had the courage to go in and rustle around in your Psyche and begin to clear it out. After all the work you have done, I am sure there are certain aspects of yourself that you have uncovered. You can say that you know yourself better. You know your triggers. You know more of what you want to create in your life. You have a clearer understanding of what you do not want in your life. If you have completed some of the exercises, you have a better understanding on how to manage your stress and take better care of yourself. In clearing the past and present in all of the areas of your life, here are some of the things you may have accomplished:

- Examined and cleared out the past (the first layer of the onion, this work is never done).
- Healed the wounds that were stuck, and wounds from your family of origin.
- Increased emotional awareness and recognized how they physically manifest.
- Improved your boundaries and communication with the people in your life.

* Examined your beliefs and learned techniques to change false beliefs.
* Utilized techniques to be more loving to yourself.

Acknowledge your work by taking in all that you have accomplished. This is not easy work. You have done an amazing job that most people never undertake in their lives. Think about it, our culture does not support taking time at any point in our lives to build a deep sense of Self. If people do this, it is usually as a response to a crisis, a death or an illness. This is a sacred opportunity you have created for yourself. By giving yourself permission to work on yourself, you have begun to create a more loving relationship with the most important person in your life – YOU!

Now it is time to begin forging and anchoring that deep connection with Self. This is a three-fold process:

Connecting with Self

Connecting with Earth

Connecting with Spirit

Clear – Connect – Create this is how we express love for Self. Connecting is the bridge between Clearing and Creating. In order to create, it is necessary to first Connect. One cannot go from clearing to creating without connecting. Without connecting you will not have that center, that strength or alignment from which to create. Alignment, grounding, connection to Self, connecting to Earth and connecting to Spirit is the fundamental way to create, to be "at cause" in your Universe. For myself it is impossible to create a workshop when I am not in alignment with myself and Source. I can spend a lot of time spinning my wheels, going through all the correct motions, doing what worked in the past, but if I am not grounded, in alignment and connected, all of my efforts will seem to go nowhere. Our Source is a power that is within us. This is our compass, our guidance system to operate in the Universe.

We have already begun using words like "alignment," "flow," and "Source." This is the language of connecting. This, as with clearing, is all an internal process. The alignment is within you. The current of your creative flow, the Source, is within you.

What It Looks Like To Be "Connected"

As you read through the following, see if you can remember a time when you felt fully connected. Remember, being connected is a feeling of being centered and grounded. It is a feeling of comfort with your surroundings, and your relationship with yourself and others. It is a feeling of empowerment.

- When we are connected, life experiences and opportunities flow. As a comparison, when we have a chiropractic adjustment, our spine is in alignment and we feel better. When we are connected, we feel aligned with the Universe.
- Information downloads; we have a deeper connection with our intuition – our own knowing. We are open to the Universe, God, and our guides for any communication that is there for us, for our empowerment or support, and for our Soul's growth. This could come in the form of dreams, intuitive hunches, automatic writing, flashes of inspiration, imagination, and other forms. Some people may even see visions, or hear things.
- Life is easier. New business comes easily, great new ideas emerge, we effortlessly create new relationships, and communication in existing relationships becomes easier. Everything seems to run smoother. We are in the flow.
- We feel expansive, unreserved, and unrestrained.
- We feel positive, joyful, alive, awake, and conscious.
- When we are connected, we can re-contextualize what our circumstances are; we feel positive. There is a feeling that whatever comes our way, we can manage it.
- We see in more detail, we notice the cardinal in the tree, we are more present with people and our senses are awakened.

These are all ways that we may experience connectedness. All of these attributes need not be present at all times.

◆ **Describe for yourself how you feel when you are connected.**

What It Looks Like When You Are Not "Connected"
◆ Irritable, cranky, grumpy.
◆ We are not creative and do not feel inspired.
◆ Lethargic, not motivated.
◆ We are out of touch with our feelings.
◆ We do not see our surroundings; we operate from our heads, not our hearts. We find we are in a state of constantly judging and evaluating ourselves and others.
◆ Negative perspective; pessimistic; closed off; contracted, inflexible.
◆ Impatient.
◆ Overly vulnerable and sensitive.

How Do We Get Out of Our Connectedness?

Really, any sudden unexpected issue from the smallest detail to a crisis can throw us out of alignment. Your car can break down, you can feel fear about an issue, you can have a fight with someone close to you, you can get out of alignment with a sudden medical diagnosis, and sometimes, we just wake up out of alignment. It could depend on your temperament, circumstances, hormones, and body rhythms as to what and how you can be thrown off course.

It is easy to get out of alignment; the trick is catching ourselves as quickly as possible, clearing as needed, and then taking the path to connectedness. Everyone is either connected or not connected – either in alignment or out of alignment. When we are not connected, sometimes we do not even realize it until it gets really, really bad. Days, weeks, months can go by and we begin to be aware that something feels off and we do not even want to get out of bed. Some may realize that something is off fairly quickly and do something about it to begin the journey back to connection; others will ignore it. There is a whole range in taking the steps to get connected.

Asking yourself the question, "Am I in alignment or
not?" begins the process of being in alignment.

For some, it happens in the moment. Just as quickly as one realizes that one is out of alignment one can begin the process to be aligned. What if you, too, had the ability to be so conscious that you knew immediately when something was off and had the tools to bring yourself back? That is empowerment! Connection is not necessarily a state that you get in and stay in, but it is a process that moment by moment, you move in and out of, throughout the day. It is important not to judge yourself or make yourself "good" or "bad" by being in or out of alignment. This is a process of noticing, acknowledging and allowing. Your preference should be to be in alignment, so this section is about moving towards that state of being. This section is about seeing when you get out of alignment, and, when it happens, using the tools to bring yourself back into connection.

Using the garden analogy, connecting strengthens and empowers you. If you hold yourself like a tree, the roots are the connected part and the blooms are your creative parts. When you strengthen your roots, when you are truly connected with your Self, Earth and Spirit, you are ready when the storms come, and you will not be uprooted.

How Do We Make This Connection?

Sometimes when we are really in a bad place it is baby steps forward to move into connection.

Acknowledge your feelings. When you are angry, or anxious, or frustrated, there is nothing wrong with those feelings. By acknowledging your feelings, they are able to flow through. Honor those feelings and recognize that you are out of that true highest connection with yourself and Source. If you are wanting to get connected, what do you do? As always, begin with Self-Love. Engaging in a Self-Loving act will begin the connection process. This is how we begin connecting with our love of Self!

CHAPTER 15

Connecting with Self

Know Thyself.
– written on the Temple of Apollo at Delphi

The Unexamined Life

Connecting with Self, what does that even mean? After all, we have had these bodies, these personalities our whole lives. We know our own history and the people who played a part in our lives, intimately, better than anyone! What we are talking about here is the unexamined life. It is commonplace for most people to sail the stream of life without thinking of consequences and without taking responsibility for their choices. Growing up, our parents may choose our food, our friends, our schools, our clothes, activities, the way we wear our hair, how we act in public... the list goes on. In a "normal" coming of age scenario, the children begin to make some decisions for themselves and begin to chart the course of their lives. When we experience overbearing parents, we may not have had that opportunity. Our choices define us. Our thoughts, behaviors, personality, relationships, and Spirit define us. In this section, you will begin to create a relationship with yourself. There will be tools and exercises to experience connectedness with our Selves, and stay in connection!

Your Connection With Self Exercise

Close your eyes, take a few deep breaths and take a moment and think about a time in your life when you felt connected with yourself and empowered. It is important to remember this time, so we can use it as a point of reference. We will return to this experience and spend more time feeling this way going forward. What were you doing when you did feel connected and loving with yourself?

Co-author Margaret answers this for herself: When I was in my early 20's I started attending a meditation class. It woke me up! I fully understood the term *co-creator*. I saw the big picture of my soul's growth and I felt like I was conscious and making decisions in my life for the first time. I was alive! I was grateful! I was taking responsibility for everything, for my choices in the present, for my choices in the past. I was in control of my body. I was eating healthy, I was exercising a lot. I stopped my heavy partying. I was doing a daily practice. I was meditating daily. I prayed. I read spiritual books. I was awake!

❖ **Journal about this time in your life when you felt really connected with yourself.**

Describe your thoughts, feelings and practices. Recall the circumstances that were occurring at the time of this experience. Do you remember how long it lasted, or why it stopped? Not everyone has had this kind of experience, but even if you had more of a sense of connection with Self at one point in your life, journal about that. Our lives can be looked at as a journey; as an ongoing process of "waking up" and falling back to sleep. Once you have written about this time of alignment, as you go forward in this section, use this writing as a point of reference for your connection with Self.

Connecting with Self Physically

How do we expect to know ourselves without knowing our own bodies? I am sure we could immediately conjure up an image of our beloved, our parents or our children, with utmost precision. The beauty we would find in their faces! We would not be judging and criticizing, ticking off the flaws as many of us do to ourselves. Our critical self, the thoughts that tell us we are not pretty enough, thin enough, young enough, tone or tan enough, in most cases, rule our thoughts of our bodies, causing us, as individuals to disengage. Most of us are disconnected from our physical being and in judgment of ourselves because we do not look like the images we see on TV or in magazines. When we do not accept our bodies in a loving way, this launches our first "out of body experience," and is an example of us not living in the present moment. We cast aside our image of our self, and in our minds we replace it with a body we want to have... 6 weeks down the line... after I join the gym... after I buy some more makeup... after I buy a new outfit to help me feel better... after I starve myself. Change cannot come from self-deprecation. Creating a new you can only come from loving yourself, beginning with loving your body.

Beginning to Love Our Self

Can you conjure up the image of your own body and look at it in the way a lover would? Notice the curves, the small hairs on your face, the play of light on your skin. Have a sensual experience with yourself, just accepting everything you see. Take some time when you know you will not be disturbed to look in the mirror. Look at your hair, your face. Repeat a mantra of love and acceptance. Say to yourself, "I love and accept this body as it is. I love the curves of this body. I love the tone of this body. I love the feel of this body. I am home." Depending on your level of critical judgment for your Self this exercise may cause a degree of discomfort. Acknowledge and accept it. Find the part of your body that you do like. You might be able to say, "I like my eyes and lips," or "I have pretty feet." Talk it up; say to yourself, again a mantra of love and acceptance, "My feet are REALLY exquisite! Who wouldn't fall in love with these feet?" Then begin to be loving to the parts you do not like. Find something positive you can say about those parts that you do not find beautiful. This might take time before you feel comfortable, but this exercise will start your journey of connection with Self. Your body is your vehicle and the more you love it and are at peace with it, the more you can move closer to the vision you have for it. When the critical voice says, "I never saw THAT wrinkle before," acknowledge it and let it go. Replace it with a loving affirmation and thought, such as, "My wrinkles are my wisdom, and I love my wrinkles." Some people may not even be able to look below the shoulders due to negative thoughts and self-condemnation. Be gentle and patient with yourself. Take your time. Do this exercise repeatedly until you are more comfortable with looking at your body from head to toe, front and back, with acceptance and eventually Self-Love.

Falling in Love with Your Self

I use this practice with my clients who are having a hard time creating a relationship or are not feeling good about themselves within a relationship. This exercise can also be used in business, like when you are going after a new job, or in selling a product or service. It will help you to feel your own power and confidence. Begin by making a list of your gifts, talents, attributes and abilities. Include your physical, emotional, and spiritual attributes. List everything you can think of. You may, for instance, not think you are good in relationships with men, but you are a really good girlfriend, a great listener, and fun to be with. What are your special gifts? Make a list of everything that you consider positive about yourself. Read your list every day; it will inspire you. Feeling good about yourself is an inside job. Feeling that you are deserving of money, a career you love, a healthy relationship, and supportive friends is worthiness. You are worthy of having a beautiful life, but it is you who must accept, believe, and know this at a deep, deep level. The changes that can occur by doing this exercise can be dramatic! It is especially empowering for women, who traditionally do not have a core built on strength and self confidence. This technique will raise your awareness of your core beliefs about yourself and begin to build a strong sense of Self. When you have a strong sense of self-worth, you do not look to others to validate yourself. A strong sense of Self comes from within.

I celebrate myself, and sing myself. ~ Walt Whitman

Falling in Love with Your Life

Some people walk around like the character Eeyore from the Winnie the Pooh books. He was the grey stuffed pessimistic donkey whose tail continually fell off. Even when his tail would be reattached, he would claim, "it will just fall off again." Notice for yourself where you are pessimistic in your life. Where do you assume that when things are going well, that they will just fall off again? Falling in love with your life is not just a list of what you are grateful for in your life that is good, there is a distinction. Falling in love with your life is more active.

Falling in Love with Your Life Exercise

Make a list of the things that you love in your life, and for what you are grateful for: friendships; an intimate relationship; your job; home; garden; car; something you are doing that you feel is making a difference in the world; your health; vitality; neighborhood. There is so much to see as good! Take a day and dedicate it to falling in love with your life – actively acknowledge and interact with the good in your life. Notice the beauty in your garden or home. Interact with nature. If you have a good friend or a person you appreciate, call that person or take them out for lunch. Acknowledge them and let them know how much you value the relationship and their support. Take a walk and notice your vitality and your working body. The practice is to take in the joy of the small things that make your life a miracle. Find the beauty in whatever you are looking at and send that appreciation out. What you focus on expands, so as you do this exercise and make that appreciation last longer and longer, you will find yourself in a state of gratitude and bliss.

Connecting with the Child Part of You

We all have a child within us. We are all in some ways little kids in larger, older bodies. Most of us carry wounds from our childhood. These can appear in our lives as withheld communication, unexpressed emotion, a need for an inordinate amount of attention. You may have healed some of these issues in the Clearing section. Now let us move onto focusing on this area again using it as a pathway to connect with your Self. Learning how to communicate with your inner child is to acknowledge, to validate and to allow that inner child to, at times, have a voice. Metaphysically, the inner child has been known to be in charge of the creative part of us. When that child part of us is not noticed, it sometimes will express itself in tantrums, or acting out in other aberrant ways. At the very least, an inner child starving for attention can dampen your creativity and full self expression, affecting your joy, aliveness, and your playfulness. By opening up the communication with your inner child, you begin to access the many gifts that this child within brings to you. The following are techniques to help you make this journey to your little Self. Once you have an established relationship, feel free to create your own techniques to strengthen this bond.

Developing a Relationship with the Child Within Exercise

 Sometimes this whole idea of loving yourself is more difficult to do as an adult because we have been conditioned that it is silly or selfish. If you cannot nurture, love and support your adult Self, maybe you will be able to do so with your child self. To begin the relationship with the child part of you, find two or more pictures of yourself. The first picture should be of you as far back as you can find, an infant between the ages of 1 month to 6 months old; the second picture should be you at the age of 3 or 4 years old. If you have any other pictures you would like to work with from up to age 10, feel free to gather them as well. It can be very powerful to see yourself at these ages and begin to make the connection through looking into the eyes of yourself as a child.

First, take the picture of the baby and really look into those eyes. See the essence of that being, the light and energy with which you entered into this world. Take your time and allow yourself to feel the connection to who that being is, because that is who you really are, now, just in a larger body. What I suggest is to leave the picture out in a place where you can easily and regularly see it. Start to interact with that being. It is obvious when you see yourself at 1 to 6 months that you are not yet formed, you are not yet conditioned, you are just pure being - light that has come from another place and entered into this realm – a pure essence of being. Talk with that baby and looking into his/her eyes speak in very loving ways. "I love you. I am willing to honor and nurture you and accept who you are." During this process, open your heart to this being that is you. Love and let your inner child know that you are there and you want to validate and connect with this being that is you!

Look at the picture of the older child. Do you see a difference behind the eyes? Are you truly joyful? Look beyond the smile if it is there. Do you see the same light that you saw in the first picture? What conditioning has transpired at that point? What have you been told? What behaviors have you already adopted? What has happened to you since you were that pure essence to the time you were 3-5 years old? What emotion are you not expressing? What are you not saying? You might even want to write something about what changes have occurred and what memories you have of what took place between these ages. The five year old needs even more of your love, nurturing and attention because she has begun to live in the world. Write about what you have already begun to suppress. If a lot of repressed feelings or memories come up for you and you want to use this as a clearing exercise, go with it. But this exercise here is more about being fully aware that something has happened and that this child part of you still needs your love and compassion. By directing our love and nurturing to ourselves through the picture, we return to that essence of *pure light. What is great about that child, and what aspects of that child do you want to honor and bring forth into yourself? Continue to interact daily with these pictures and love and nurture these children. Have compassion for yourself and let all of yourself know that you are loved and perfect just the way you are. Say "I love you, I really love you," to the picture. Begin to notice the difference it makes in your life. Say to the picture, "I know you did not get what you needed, and I am here for you now. I unconditionally love and accept you just the way you are." After you have worked with the pictures and you have had some realizations about your big Self and little Self, then I like to take my clients on a visualization with their child within.*

Re-parenting the Child Within

Re-Parenting the child within is taking the time and making the effort to treat your inner child with the nurturing and love that you may not have received in the way that you needed as a child. Many of us, because of circumstances in our families, were forced to become an adult way too early. We somehow missed the space to have the full expression of being a child, allowing ourselves to play, and to feel joy with abandon. There are many adults in the world who had no childhood at all and therefore have no access to this part of themselves. I believe that the child within rules our emotions and our creativity. By working with this child, we enhance our connection with our Self by fully expressing our emotions and accessing the Creative. This is a great exercise to heal that child part of you that deserves Self-Love.

Re-parenting the Child Within Visualization

Sit down in a quiet place, close your eyes, and take a few deep breaths. You are breathing in light, energy and breathing out fear. Imagine yourself in a room seated at a table. See that 3 or 4 year old little you coming into the room and sitting down across from you. Ask your little self if there is anything that he or she wants to express or say. Welcome her and ask if there is anything that you can do for her. Be silent and watch for body language, listen for any words, and be aware of any impressions that you feel. Let her know that you are there for her or him. Then take the child in your arms and hug and nurture the child. You are rocking and loving the child. Look into the child's eyes with complete love and acceptance. Ask yourself if there is anything you want to share with the child, and open yourself up to see if the child has anything more to say to you. Is there anything that the child needs from you? Take whatever you get. My inner child loves to play jacks and eat ice cream cones. Again, accept whatever comes. Say "thank you, I love you," and at this point, let the child go. Open up your eyes.

Once the visualization is over, the instruction now is to do whatever the child has asked. I literally sit on the floor and play jacks. Do not disappoint her/him. Does your child want a special food? Maybe your child wants to pull out some old toys or stuffed animals you may have stored. I recommend doing this exercise once a week, nurturing the inner child and keeping this dialogue open with this part of yourself. It may take some time to develop good communication and a solid relationship, after all, he/she has probably been silent for a long time. Once your inner child starts talking, you may be surprised at how profound the requests from your inner child may be. At the time I began doing this exercise, I did not have a lot of play in my life. My inner child realized this and showed me the imbalance.

Taking Responsibility – Negative Self Talk

Our words are powerful. Whether they are actual words coming out of our mouths or thoughts that float through our heads. Our thoughts define us as readily as our choices. Begin to notice all the times your words about your self are negative. As a coach, I often hear my clients speaking of their dark sides, also known as the shadow self. This is the part of our self that we generally do not let others know about. We may not even acknowledge it for ourselves. Out in the world, you might be a high-powered executive, confident and commanding, but the shadow side expresses, "I'm so stupid," or "I'm so fat," or "I'm so bad at this or that." Begin to notice for yourself your negative thoughts and words.

Negative Self Talk Exercise

Listening to all that negativity is like listening to a piano that is out of tune. It does not resonate. It does not serve you. When you speak about yourself, speak how you want to be perceived. Speak in a loving way to yourself. But if you, like many of us, slip and speak negatively about yourself, simply say, "Cancel that," and change your thoughts to something positive. For example, if I were to say "I'm so stupid," stop and say, "Cancel that," and then say, "I'm doing this to the best of my ability," or, "I am just a student at this," or "I am just learning." Whatever comes to your mind, put in a correction. For one whole day, focus on your spoken words and thoughts Use more accepting and loving words and thoughts and put in the correction when you slip up.

The Journey Back to Connection

When we are not connected, we feel disconnected from a sense of Self. It is difficult to come up with good ideas. You might feel scattered, and it is difficult to think clearly. You might feel overwhelmed or resentful. The path back to connection starts by being willing to admit that we are not connected. Sometimes we just need to scream out, "I am a mess." Acknowledging that we cannot always be super-humans, and that we have some work to do is the first step on the path back to peace, contentment, and getting grounded.

Acknowledge, allow, and commit is our recipe for connection with Self. You need to take responsibility for the choices you make and focus on what you can direct. Even if you are at a time of your life when you feel you are at the effect of circumstances out of your control, you *can* put back in place some of these practices that connect you with Self. Your healthier choices build on one another until you produce a different result that you are proud of. Allow yourself the room to change by not judging yourself so harshly. See what behaviors are not in alignment with the You, you want to be and make a plan of action. Commit to beginning the day with a new practice. Set a goal for yourself of doing four or more of the practices in this Connect chapter a day. You will find yourself in a much better place.

Taking Responsibility For What Is Yours and What Is Not

Taking responsibility means owning your part in any situation that you find yourself in. To clarify, taking responsibility is not judging yourself and not blaming yourself. Ask yourself the following questions to determine your responsibility in a given situation:

* *How did I get in this situation?*
* *What have been my thoughts and feelings around this situation?*
* *How have I contributed to this scenario?*
* *Where am I at cause, or how am I responsible? (Remember, answer with no self-judgment or self-blame)*

This is not an easy exercise. We can feel safer when we are caught up in the blame game, but when we are blaming someone else for the circumstances we are in, we are placing ourselves in the role of the victim. Victimhood is not a place of empowerment. Asking and answering these questions will allow you to be complete with the scenario and to see what needs to change. By examining these questions and taking ownership of your part of it, you will more quickly connect with yourself and return to alignment. So if things are not working in your job, ask yourself, "How am I responsible?" Do not to judge yourself or blame another. Define for yourself the facts. See yourself objectively, as if you were someone else looking at you at your job. Maybe you can now see how you are being perceived by others. For example, if you have a bad attitude, this may be causing friction in the workplace. You may think you are hiding your negative thoughts, yet, chances are someone has noticed. Whatever the scenario, you are a part of it, and when you own your responsibility, it is much easier to be complete, and come into connection and alignment.

Taking Responsibility Versus Not Taking it Personally

I have counseled you here to take responsibility for your situation where you can, but that is not to say that it is yours to take responsibility for another. Not everything that happens to you is yours to own. When others lash out at you in anger with words or actions, more than likely, the battle is not with you, but within themselves. If you do not take their behavior personally, understanding it is their personal battle, in time, they will leave you out of it. Even when they do not leave you out of it, by having the ability to stay separate and not emotionally attached to the situation, you can learn to stay connected to yourself and move more quickly back into alignment. When your feelings are hurt by another's mistreatment of you, take a little walk in their shoes. Imagine what could have had them feeling so bad, that they would want others to feel as bad as they do. When you can see they are hurting themselves, and not trying to hurt you, then you no longer feel bad about yourself. You may need to take a break from the relationship for re-evaluation, to take care of yourself. This process allows you to have genuine feelings of compassion for another, and that is self-loving!

Integrity

The dictionary definition of integrity is "strict personal honesty and unity." Being in integrity with your beliefs, speech, and the way you walk in the world is a very important part of feeling worthy of loving yourself. When you feel "out of integrity" with yourself it is hard to feel in alignment or good about yourself. Examples of being out of integrity range from not keeping your word to harming another. We all have our own beliefs and values about right and wrong. When we cross over our own lines we are stepping over our own integrity. We spoke about integrity in Clearing mainly with regard to finances. If you have unresolved issues related to finances that need clearing, it can stop the flow of abundance in your life. That is why it is so important to be clear about your own values, standards of behavior, and recognize when you are denying or when you are not being in your conceived integrity.

Most of us have nagging thoughts about what we have not gotten done, items we said we would do, or other issues that we feel badly about. These perpetual conversations in your head ABSOLUTELY keep you from being in the present moment. These are self-punishing thoughts because you are probably berating yourself every time the thoughts come up. Being out of integrity can be one of the main causes of disconnection with Self.

Integrity of Your Word

Moving towards integrity in all areas of your life will create connection with yourself. We will begin to examine integrity in your life through your word. In the Book of Genesis, God began the creative process with the word, "First there was the word." So too, with us, out of our words, we create our lives. There is great power in keeping your word to yourself and others. There are lots of things we say we are going to do, from the simple and mundane, like committing to making a dental appointment to serious life and death situations, like vowing to change your health, or I am no longer going to lie to my friends about my life. Many people break their word and they think, "oh well, it doesn't matter." This can become a habit. Little white lies become the norm. On some level, breaking your word begins to erode the fabric of your sense of self, and affects your connection with Self. You may not even be conscious of your own dissatisfaction with yourself; you may just feel less powerful. When you have broken your word enough times, neither you, nor others believe you when you commit to something. When you keep your word, it strengthens you, it is a way to honor yourself and it honors the other people involved.

One of the areas that gets in the way of people being in a loving relationship with themselves are the events in their lives they cannot forgive themselves for, like those times when their actions did not match their own integrity. That pesky mind will hang onto the ways they have been out of integrity, their laundry list of things that are not ok, and therefore they do not deserve to be loved or be "loving" to themselves. This is one of the areas that I work with people on, getting in touch with those things that are out of integrity in their life. When we take a look at them, do some work on them and then release them, you can create more space for yourself and see that you are deserving of love.

When you break your word, you need to acknowledge it and clean it up, instead of blowing it off. So if I say I am going to walk five days a week and I only get out three times, own it, take responsibility for your action or non-action. Simply state, I said I was going to walk five times, I walked three times... without judgment, the operative word. Once you bring judgment into the process of integrity, it is easy to now make yourself wrong, or bad, and you stay stuck in not keeping your word going forward. The next step is to look and see if you really want to commit to your original intention. Do you really want to walk five times a week? Is it feasible? If the answer is yes, then give your word again. The same is true with giving your word to others. If I say I am going to meet a friend at 12pm and I'm always ten minutes late, I need to own that, and acknowledge that to my friend, without a story or an excuse. The most powerful way to reconnect quickly with your word is to simply state to your friend, "I was ten minutes late for our lunch, and I would like to give you my word that next time I will be on time." Next time you meet, be on time.

Integrity In All Areas Exercise

Answer for yourself, where in your life you are out of integrity? Here are some examples to get you started:

Physical - You haven't started that exercise program you told yourself you were going to begin. You have not gotten a mammogram in two years.

Emotional - You have a friendship that ended badly because you stole her boyfriend when you were 17.

Career - You consistently fudge your expense reports.

Finances - You haven't paid your taxes or you haven't admitted to your husband about a large expense.

Write down anything that crosses your mind from the simplest to the most horrifying. Allow yourself to let these thoughts and feelings come through. Make a list of all those things until you feel like you are completely cleared out. For some people it might be a page for another it might be a whole notebook. When you feel complete, look and see if you are willing to take action on any of those things that you wrote down. Do you feel ready to make that doctor's appointment? Are you willing to call an accountant? Are you willing to speak to that person you may have hurt or face them in a visualization. Take each item line-by-line and address it by taking these action steps:

- Circle anything that you do actually want to do something about. (For example, you do want to make that doctor's appointment. Get out your organizer or computer and put in your schedule to make that appointment. It is now out of your head and in process of being handled.)
- Put a star next to any item that you do want to take action on... not necessarily now, but in the future. Make a list of those things and put next to each item when this will be taken care of by setting a date. (For example, you have been thinking you want to write a book but you just had a baby and you know it is not going to work for you this year. Put a date next to that item that works for you, even if it is a year or more out.)

- ❖ Anything that is left may still be in your awareness. You have not let it go, but it may no longer be appropriate. At one time it felt important to you, and it is still rattling around in your mind. Cross off or amend the things left on your list and release them. (For example, you may have set a goal for yourself to run 3x a week. It is something you would really like to do, but in reality you have bad knees and it is not the best exercise for you now. Your self-critic is continuing to say "you are lazy." But this goal really no longer fits. Maybe you decide to walk instead.)
- ❖ Make peace and forgive your Self with the things you have crossed off and put forth an intention to let them go now.

Be In Integrity For A Day Exercise

To strengthen your integrity, keep your word for one day. Do everything you say you are going to do. See for yourself how empowering this can be. At the end of the day, how do you feel about yourself? Then keep your word with yourself and others for two days, a week, or longer.

Once this becomes a real practice for yourself, your word becomes law in your Universe. What you say, actually happens. There is hidden power in this exercise... the power of creation! When everything you say is true, then when you state an intention or affirm to the Universe something you want to create that is not yet formed, because your word has so much power and strength, by stating it, you believe it and make it so! You will begin to feel the energy and power that comes into your life by being in integrity and you will begin to manifest miracles!

Release and Forgive

For past experiences in which there is no action you can take to change what has been done, release and forgive yourself to move forward. Put a check mark next to any of the items that there is nothing you can or are willing to do, but you feel are still keeping you from feeling in integrity with yourself. For these items, ask yourself, 'Is there anything I can do to take it off my list?"

To release this item from your consciousness, close your eyes and take a few deep breaths. Bring the issue to your mind and say to yourself, "That was in the past. I am complete. I am now in the present moment." I suggest that for more in depth clearing for any of these items that keep you from your integrity, return to the Releasing and Forgiving chapter in Clearing.

Best Friend Exercise

This exercise is easy for most women because they can relate to this question, "How would you treat yourself if YOU were your own best friend?" I know for myself that I treat my best friend with great love, patience, acceptance and nurturing. I enjoy picking out cards and gifts for her. I enjoy treating her for a great meal, having fun nights out, listening to her. We make our "girls night out" a special occasion, eating well, lighting candles, enjoying the moments we have together. Women especially tend to nurture their female relationships in very sweet and loving ways. How do you treat your best friend? What if you could treat yourself that way? I ask my coaching clients to do something loving for themselves as if for their best friend. It could be anything from buying a rose, taking a bubble bath, getting a massage - anything that speaks to them and that demonstrates the love they feel for themselves. My clients who get this exercise for homework, at first, have great difficulty doing this, showing me how far away they are from loving themselves.

This also spills over into allowing yourself to have things and giving yourself permission to do things. I know there are times that I am stingy with myself. At a restaurant I may not choose what I really want to eat because it might be too expensive. Or I will put off going to a spa or getting my hair done, it manifests itself in a different way for each of us. Even on a budget, we can do things for ourselves that make us feel pampered and special. In looking at the Daily Dose of Happy Exercise that follows, most of those items do not cost a dime. Just as children do not really want things, they want their parent's attention. You, as well, will thrive in the act of treating yourself as your own best friend. By giving yourself this special treatment, you can cause more abundance to flow into your life. This is how energy flows. Watch the difference it makes when you are your own best friend!

I never loved another person the way I loved myself. ~ Mae West

A Daily Dose of Happy Exercise

 Sometimes it feels as if we are just focused on the daily grind of life – the job, the bills, or the crisis at hand. We forget that we are here on this planet to create, enjoy, and celebrate! When you find yourself in the doldrums I prescribe a daily dose of happy! Start adding to your day a practice of doing whatever makes you happy. Doing what makes you happy helps you get connected and helps you to attract what you are seeking. Here are some of the things that are on my list and may be on your list also:

- Petting and playing with animals
- Music
- Cooking
- Talking or going out with my girlfriends
- Seeing an uplifting movie
- Reading something inspiring
- Working in the garden
- Dancing with abandon
- Eating a great meal
- Singing

- Exercising
- Taking a nice walk or bike ride
- Seeing a sunset
- Being in nature
- Taking a bubble bath with candles
- Making love
- Acting like a kid, eating ice cream
- Intimate connections
- Playing with children
- Connecting with an old friend
- Learning something new
- Playing an instrument
- Going to a concert or museum
- Flying a kite
- Going to a beach

You will notice that a lot of these same items were on our list of Acts of Self-Love (page 34). There is a close connection between being Self-Loving to yourself and connecting with your Self! When you are making your own list, look at what feels really good to you when you do it - it nurtures you and brings you joy. This will be a list that makes you happy and it is also very self-loving. Put your list in a prominent place and begin adding these practices to your regular routine. The more of these things you can do regularly, the more you connect with yourself and raise your vibration.

Instead of taking a sick day, take a well-being day. I often suggest the practice of turning off the ringer, the computer, put on nice music, take a bath, take a walk. It shocks me at how hard it is for people to do this! On Sundays instead of chilling out and taking the sacred day of rest, people are running around, doing errands. We need to take time to rest and self-nurture. All of these things are really important to counteract the level of stress we are under. The bottom line is balance. Yes, we have to take care of our responsibilities and be in the world, but there is a way to approach this differently that is much more self-loving.

Don't forget to love yourself. ~ Soren Kierkegaard

Building Your Altar

An outward sign of your connection with your self can be an altar. Altars can be built for many different purposes. It is a place in your home where you can gather up your spiritual focus, where you can be inspired and perform rituals. It can help you connect with your creativity, vision, energy, and alignment. Altars are the place designated in your home where you get centered and connect with Self and Spirit. They can be placed any where you like as long as you are comfortable, with a place to sit and be undisturbed. Depending on the space you have you can place the altar on a desk, on a window sill, or in a corner. After you have found the space for your altar, look for objects that have some special meaning for you. These are the touchstones of your life: incense, pictures, crystals, a wand, statues, feathers, sea shells, anything that holds an uplifting energy for you and connects you with the Divine. Use your own creativity and imagination to customize your altar for yourself. This is the place where you can do your morning rituals, manifestation rituals, release, or uplift your spirit on a difficult day. Working with your altar regularly can change your being on the inside which will manifest as a life change on the outside. We always carry the most powerful altar, our spiritual essence, in our own being.

Getting Back in Connection with Our Physical Self

We have gone through some techniques to connect with Self, but what do we do when we find that connection and then lose it again? How do we get back into a place of connectedness? The physical aspect of our Self is a good place to start because generally it is the first place in our lives to go down the tubes when in stress or crisis. Most people will do something unhealthy when they do not feel connected to their Source. For example, some folks will go out for too many drinks, they will eat worse foods; they may not connect with the people that support and inspire them; they will exercise less; they will stop doing their spiritual practices; and they will watch more junk TV. So for example, if you have been waking up and grabbing a sugar filled muffin, drinking three cups of coffee and turning on the TV, the first step is to acknowledge these choices/behaviors. See if you can pinpoint when these unhealthy behaviors began and why.

- ❖ **Journal about where you are at, why or how have you gotten disconnected from yourself or out of alignment? What is out of balance? Write daily for a week. What really stands out? Are you overindulging in food or drink? Are you doing too much? Are you not doing your daily practices that keep you connected? As it becomes obvious, decide for yourself what you can do to return to balance. What is stopping you from being connected with Self?**

Food Choices Exercise

Do not be sabotaged by food. Our food intake is one of the first things to throw us off and is one of the easiest to change. You can begin to make some different choices and make a commitment to eat differently. If you know that sugar is throwing your system and your emotions off, try to cut it back. For some of us the foods we eat can literally alter our behavior. Look at what is off and make a commitment to change.

Share With A Friend Exercise

Get a buddy to do this with and support each other. There truly is power in numbers, when you share your practices with a friend, you hold yourself accountable. Begin by telling your friend that you are committing to one or more of these connecting practices a day. See if they want to make their own list and do it with you. Then, touch base either via phone or email and discuss what you have accomplished every day.

Start to notice how you are feeling. Are you feeling more at peace, more aliveness, more connected? After some time goes by, you may begin to feel some resistance. Clear any feelings of resistance through speaking to your friend or writing in your journal. See if you can express exactly what is going on in your psyche and put words around it. This will help you to get to the bottom of your resistance and help you to see why it is occurring.

Reward and acknowledge your efforts. It might sound juvenile, but our "little kid within" still responds to stickers. Place a star on the calendar every time you do a self- loving act. Keep a record of your accomplishments – "Today I ate an orange and an apple, instead of the donut I wanted, and I did a little exercise." BRAVO! For more ideas of how to jump start your connecting, see the Approaching the Day chapter.

Connecting with Self Emotionally

The key to connecting with Self emotionally is to *feel what you are feeling*. Alignment is being present. You can also be in alignment and be sad, you do not have to be happy and joyful all the time. But your alignment is about being present with the emotions that you are having in the moment. If possible, fully experience and express your emotions. Do not judge your feelings. If you are sad, be sad. Know that when you fully express and "complete" the piece of sadness, you will feel better. The lighter more joyous feelings that are always there will resurface. After all, the sun is always shining behind the rain clouds. This process of naming your feelings and not judging them is another way to get back to connection. Using the Weather Analogy, by giving your feelings particular characteristics, like stormy, or calling your mood, "thunderous," you allow yourself to feel your feelings. When you are sad and try to put on a happy face, you create more resistance. Let yourself be fully sad for an hour in the day. If you need to watch a sad movie, or look at pictures from a passed loved one, do it. Immerse yourself in that sadness for an hour or so and evoke the tears. Expression of a feeling, *moves* the energy of the feeling; moving that energy, (e-motion, energy in motion) allows it to dissipate. When you are present with your emotions, you are moving towards alignment.

Connecting with Self in Crisis

As mentioned, it is easy to get out of alignment and any crisis can knock us out of alignment. Looking at crisis as a temporary situation is a good way to connect with yourself in the present. When we are faced with a challenge that has lasted for a while, it is easy to get discouraged. Ask yourself, "has it always been this way? How long has this been going on? How long was this not going on prior to the most recent events?" Many times we look at our lives as if our financial, health or relationship challenge has always been this way. If you have been going through a rough financial time it may feel like it has been like this *forever*, but has it? Look at the reality of the situation. You might find that you had 10 years of financial stability, so the current situation is not forever. If you are undergoing a health challenge, it could be draining, even debilitating. But there was a time in your life where you were vibrant, healthy and felt great! Focus on that part of your history. Get a picture of yourself from a time when you looked and felt vibrant and healthy. Say the mantra, "This too shall pass. Things are getting better and better." Begin to create that connection of a more positive time in your life on a daily basis. By doing this and bringing in some of the other connecting exercises you will move more easily back into alignment and get through whatever challenge you are facing with more power, self confidence, and a better attitude. There is a whole chapter devoted to help you face crisis in a connected way.

Building Character

Crisis is character building. Your character is your temperament, your moral fiber, your Spirit, and your disposition. Facing any kind of challenge forces you to go deeper and get stronger.

Your most profound spiritual experiences can be your darkest days.

When you are in times of trouble, when your outlook is bleak and you do not see a happy ending to the story, even though it is difficult, realize in those darkest days that all is for good. All is in perfect, Divine Order. There will be another side to this pain. There will be an ending. And the person that emerges at the end of the story will be stronger, clearer, tougher, wiser, and connected. That person will know who her friends are and who she feels comfortable talking with about her deepest fears. She will know herself, her thoughts, desires and dreams. She will know what grace is and have a story of how it showed up in her life. Character building is a slow process. Real and lasting changes in our character often appear as a bulldozer rather than a pillow. Most times the epilogues to these scary, fearsome stories are a reflection back on the lessons that this painful experience resulted in. Eventually you will feel gratefulness for the character attributes that were won in those darkest days. You will be thankful for the woman that emerged at the end and you will truly know yourself better than you ever have.

Selfless Versus Selfish

What do we do when the crisis is not with us, but with someone close to us? We get a lot of messages from our parents, movies, books, culture and society in general that if someone is in need, you should drop everything and take care of them. If you do not give 100% you may be viewed as selfish. Maybe you have just started a new enterprise for yourself and life interferes, your husband gets laid off, or your parent needs an operation. When something like that happens, most women, who are notorious caretakers, put their own interests and creations aside. I am not saying that you should not help in whatever way you can, but there is a view in our culture that if you are not being selfless you are being selfish. The quality of being selfless is honored and admired. It is a character trait that is considered altruistic, giving without regard for self. But being selfless can also precipitate a loss of Self. What happens with people is that they can only be selfless for so long and then a meltdown is certain to occur. This happens mostly because one's life is way out of balance. You are not doing any of your personal practices that keep you connected, those go out the window. Maybe, there is a middle way as the Buddha would say. Especially in times of crisis, you must be willing to be *selfish* enough to create balance.

How can you care for another and still care for yourself? From my perspective one can at least strive to do both. Look at the situation that you find yourself and see if there are others that can participate in caring for the loved one or handling the details of the situation that you are presented with. Many times, because we are trying to prove that we are not selfish, or because we feel that we are the only ones that can do the job, or because of pressure from others, we find that we lose ourselves completely in the process. When you are coming from this place of disconnect and obligation, you are out of balance, not seeing the situation clearly. When you put your Self, your life and your dreams on the back burner long enough, this will lead to anger and resentment. Now you are the victim. Maybe you begin to blame the person for whom you are caring. The truth of the matter is that you are angry at yourself, because there is no connection with the part of our selves that makes conscious healthy decisions.

Self-less Versus Selfish Exercise

Here, again, we return to integrity. You have crossed over your own boundaries... yes, you chose to care-take for a good reason, but now what? The formula is the same for whatever judgments of yourself you are holding onto:

- Take responsibility, you chose to be the caretaker.
- Enlist the support of others.
- Forgive others and yourself.
- Go back to your daily practices that keep you connected to a strong sense of Self.
- Do self-loving techniques to nurture and empower yourself.
- Return or revisit your own vision and goals.
- What did you set aside when all this occurred?

These are the steps, in any situation like this, where you have left yourself, whether you are in crisis, or overextending to another. Following these techniques will be the path that will return you to your connection with Self.

CHAPTER 16
....

Connecting with Nature

I know nature speaks to us if we listen. Every animal has a story to tell. Every flower blossoms with reminders to be creative, and every tree whispers with its rustling leaves the secrets of life. – Ted Andrews, Animal-Speak

How can you connect with your Self and your Spirit through nature? Being in a time on the planet where we mostly walk on concrete rather than through meadows, looking at buildings rather than forests, illuminated by florescent lights, rather than stars, we have really come a long way from our ancestors who walked this earth without shoes, touching Mother Earth and experiencing the natural connection to Her. There is a rhythm to this planet, the seasons and the stars, the phases of the moon and the tides. There was a time when we were aligned with that which was created for our support, sustenance and healing. I believe the Universes' natural design infuses matter with presence and nourishment to allow us to connect with the One, our Selves, and our Spirit. This connection allows us to function optimally, and to balance the distractions in life with that which is peace. When I am distracted, worried, fearful, ill, hurt or angry, I am out of alignment; I am not in the moment. I do not feel that connection when I am not rooted in my heart center. Go outside and look around you... or imagine an abundance of trees, flowers, colors, smells, a cornucopia of abundance. Being in love in nature, with Self, with Spirit; that is your calling. It is a blessing, claim it. It continues to expand.

Nature is there for you always, supporting and nurturing
you, especially when you are out of connectedness.

Even when I look out the window at a beautiful tree, or take a walk where I can put my feet on natural earth, I feel a pulse. A vibration runs through me, and I know that this is real and alive and happening now. As I have explored this phenomenon by trying many different techniques, I have found a deep, sacred connection with nature that enhances my ability to *Clear, Connect and Create* my life. When I immerse myself in nature's beauty, I am clear, grounded, and connected. The following are ways that deepen this awareness.

The Web of Life

The Native Americans and many indigenous tribes around the world and throughout history have had an innate awareness of their connection with Earth, calling it The Mother. Their connection with Earth and all other living things was their connection with Spirit. The Web of Life has also been called the Mind of Nature. The idea is that all living things are connected by the life force through everything in existence. Man and woman, being human, are naturally part of this web. Today, it is harder to place ourselves in the Web of Life, yet it still exists around us every day. Remember fourth grade science for a moment, at the most basic level, the air we breathe exists because of the emission of oxygen from plants. Plants provide food for the animals we eat. We no longer kill our own food, our food comes from the grocery store, so we have lost the beauty of blessing the animals and plants we imbibe, as well as utilizing every last ounce so as not to waste and dishonor the spirit of the plant and animal. We have lost our feelings of being part of this community of life, and therefore we have lost a piece of ourselves. In this technological age, there is an apparent disconnection from our physical bodies and the earth, the plants, and animals. When was the last time you kicked off your shoes and walked in the grass? Feeling you are a part of the grand design of nature, the earth, the animals and plants, gives you a groundedness, a sense of the Sacred, while awakening your Spirit. It is a very self-loving act to give yourself permission to spend as much time as possible in and around nature.

Nature Exercises

- *Spend time in nature.*
- *Contemplate your place in the Web of Life.*
- *Imagine ways to honor plants and animals and feel yourself a part of the interconnectedness.*
- *Take some action steps after contemplating nature in your daily life, like journaling or drawing images from your experiences.*

Centering – Being Present, Open and Connected

When I began taking women on retreat in Sedona, I was given this tool by a company called Sportsmind that I used in hiking the high, challenging rocks. Many of the women I was working with were hiking for the first time, some of them were out of shape, or afraid of heights (including me), and some were just more used to being in their mind rather than present in their bodies. It was a learning experience for them to become aware of their bodies, connecting to the Earth (some for the first time) and to become very present. Several had a "breakthrough experience" realizing that this tool could be used anytime that they found themselves in a situation where they were afraid or on "unsteady ground." This is an excellent tool that leaves you feeling grounded, connected and centered to yourself. It allows you to break through perceived restrictions and fears and come into your power. Centering makes you more aware, and wakes you up by creating the connection between mind and body. Being centered is our natural state, so it should be "allowed" rather than forced. Centering will allow you to relax and regain your physical (and emotional) balance quickly. The three principles of centering are being Present, Open, and Connected. As you read through the following exercise (or listen to the sound of your voice if you can read it into a recording device) allow yourself to be and feel centered.

Being Present, Open and Connected Exercise

 Sit in a place (preferably outside) where you will not be disturbed with you feet firmly planted on the ground.

Being Present is being right here, right now, in the moment. This is the opening state to any form of meditation. As you listen to the meditation, (or read these words) your body is here with your mind and emotions. Give your attention to your body. You are fully present with the words. What is your physical reality? Notice your breath, muscles, nerves, heartbeat. You are fully present.

Being Open is to be relaxed and yet alert; aware of everything around you, not judging; letting everything in with focus. Tune into receiving external stimuli, with no judgment. Pay attention to the sound of your voice and all the details of the moment to moment reality. Feel your feet on solid ground, the air on your face, the feel of your skin, the warmth of the sun on your face. Accept and allow the sound of your breath, and notice the sounds around you. If any random thoughts try to interfere, just let them go. Imagine your heart center opening and expanding, with each inhale, open it wider.

Connecting is the process of getting in touch with the fundamentals you constantly experience, like breathing and gravity. Even though you are now completely relaxed, present and open, you can still concentrate on the tasks at hand. Accept what is going on around you and lightly focus on it. Feel the sensation of your feet rooted to the ground and feel the pull of gravity through the soles of your feet to the center of the earth. You are literally in touch with the Earth. Sense being a part of, rather than separate from things. Feel the air on your skin. What do you see? What do you smell? Extend your sense of connection out further, wider, higher, deeper. Now with your new sense of being grounded, begin to take a walk. Walk in silence, feeling Present, Open and Connected to all that surrounds you.

The process of being present, open and connected helps reduce stress in the moment. In a larger sense, it is a metaphor to empower you in difficult situations. Think of a negative situation in your life. Maybe you are arguing with a friend, having trouble at work, or need to confront a physical or emotional challenge. There are many times when you feel the future is uncertain, as if you are feeling you are on shaky ground. Create a vivid picture of the problem at hand in your awareness. Notice the feelings that are coming up as you imagine yourself in this experience. Are you willing to let go of these feelings? Begin doing part one of the exercise. Be conscious of your willingness and commitment to release this situation. As you feel your feet on solid ground imagine your feet connected to the earth. Release the situation to the Earth and imagine the earth taking this situation, transmuting its energy to love and power and feel it flow back up into the soles of your feet. As you shift your perception, feel your power, and know that you are grounded, present open and able to handle this situation to the best result for all involved.

Walking Meditations

 Here is what I wrote after my walk in the woods in Harbert, MI. This might help you understand my profound reverence for nature, as well as inspire you.

As I begin my walk with Muffin (my sister's dog), I start to relax and let all the stresses of the city go. I feel the earth under my feet as I walk and watch the light streaming through the trees. I see the light reflecting off the ponds as the birds whistle, communicating with each other. I notice a deer noticing me. I freeze and hold my breath, taking in her serene beauty, her sorrowful dark eyes, her magical presence literally changing the feeling in the air. And then she takes off running through the woods. Just being here with the cool air on my skin, the wind blowing through my hair, watching the light as it plays on the ground. The leaves are starting to turn. I feel all my senses come alive. I hear the sound of leaves crunching under my feet, the symphony of crickets and birds. I feel the wind blowing and see the trees swaying. I smell Fall. I feel the sun warming me on this cold day and I feel connected with the Earth. Nature is where I experience God. This is so magnificent - the perfect cycle of life as the seasons change. Only one hour away from the city and I feel all the

stresses and strains draining out through my feet, Mother Earth connecting me
with the solidness of earth and the Spirit that is mine.

Approach a walking meditation with an intention to be present, open and connected. Your intention, focus, and your silence make it a meditation. This process takes you out of your everyday thoughts into a directed and specific intention that you can set prior to doing your walk. You can select peace or clarity, healing, or just being present. You can set an intention to let go of something, an argument, a situation or person that continues to rattle around in your mind, and you can release it into the Earth. As you are walking on Mother Earth, to really feel your connection, ask yourself, "What are you ready to let go of?" Take that energy that is dark within you and literally send it down from your head, going down your body, to your legs, to your feet, from the soles of your feet into the earth. Know that She can transmute this energy, this vibration, this darkness into light and love. With each step, ask Her to send that light and love from the earth into your feet with your being ultimately cleansed, your head clear of the thoughts that you had, and the inspiration to see this situation in a new light.

You can also walk with an intention to get clear about something you want to create. With each step, ask for clarity about a project or goal. Ask for new ideas. Ask for energy to complete it. Say out loud as you are walking, "I am opening to nature to fill me with whatever I need to assist me to manifest my desire. And so it is!" If you do not get the inspiration that you are asking for in the moment, continue to stay open, allow it to come in its own timing.

Hug a Tree Exercise

Another technique you can use in the woods is to hug a tree. Put your whole
body on the tree, connect with it, and feel all the tree's energy. You can sit
up against it with your spine erect, and imagine that the roots of the tree
are climbing up into your spine. Imagine your grounding cord as wide as your
hips, going from the base of your spine, down, down, down, to the center of
the earth. Imagine it connected to the center of the Earth with some sort of
anchor. Imagine the roots of the tree, intermingled with your grounding cord.

You and the tree are one, draw your energy and sustenance from the earth. Picture any dark energies, fears, concerns, or negativity in your being that need to be cleansed or released going down this cord into the earth. I gather it up like garbage and send it down the chute deep into the earth. The earth then transforms it into light. Feel the base of your spine, your buttocks and your legs deeply connected with Mother Earth. Send a prayer out that Mother Earth will nurture and support and protect you and fill you with her being. Feel the love and support and strength that is constantly available to you by walking this Earth. And when you feel ready, open your eyes. You are more connected, grounded, clearer and centered by the Earth energy.

Touchstones

A touchstone is exactly what the name implies. It is a physical object that you can infuse with spiritual feeling. Like a souvenir will evoke happy memories from a vacation, a touchstone is an object infused with a feeling you want to remember. This object has the power to transport you back to those feelings you were having when you picked it up. Bringing in touchstones from nature can bring back those peaceful and connected feelings nature evokes. Arranging flowers that you picked while on a walk is a touchstone – a tangible memory of that walk and the feelings you felt. Every time you see those flowers, you are transported back to nature. Gather rocks, shells, leaves or crystals, anything you find that speaks to you of the beauty of nature. Keep it where you can see it and appreciate it. Create an altar to nature. Spend some time at this altar on days when you cannot get outside to enjoy it firsthand.

Color Connection

Another way of using nature is to get in touch with colors we find in nature and understand what they signify. In my studies, I have learned that the color blue, is connected with the throat chakra. It also signifies peace. It is so interesting to me that the sky is painted blue, it could be any color, but here we are literally surrounded by peace every day. Green is everywhere, from the grass to the trees. Green is the color of the heart chakra, the color of love, abundance and healing. Yellow gold is connected with the solar plexus and is signified by the sun. In many cultures, the solar plexus is the seat of your identity and power center. Feeling the rays and warmth of the sun, taking in the beauty of the golden light, you can consciously fill your solar plexus and strengthen that sense of self.

Color Guided Visualization

Settle yourself comfortably either inside or outside. If you are outside, it is easier to open your eyes and look at the colors that are surrounding you. If you are inside, you will have to rely on your imagination. Take a couple of deep breaths and imagine or focus on the color blue. Be aware of your throat as it is in this moment now. Remember that this is a place of power for you. "First there was the word..." from which we create our world, so clearing this chakra is of the utmost importance. Imagine this brilliant color blue enveloping you, filling, purifying and empowering you. Feel the blue of the sky; ingest it, filling yourself with the peace. See it surrounding your throat, front, sides and back. Imagine that each of your cells are filled to the brim with this beautiful blue light, vibrating with power. This light is pulling from your throat anything that needs to be cleansed. It imbues your throat center with the power of your word. Allow it to permeate and strengthen that part of your being. As this blue light fills your throat, feel the peaceful vibration of which it is made, deepening within your being. Take a breath to anchor the peace now! There is great power in your words to manifest and create your Universe. You now speak more powerfully in the Universe.

Move your attention down your body to the heart chakra. At this point, whether inside or out, whether seeing the green or imagining it, look around and notice the green of the grass, the trees and all the places where green exists in nature. Green is the color that speaks to the heart and signifies abundance and love. Take in that color and feel the energy that comes through to you. See this beautiful green light bathing your heart and chest area Allow every strand of DNA to pulsate with the vibration of abundance and love. Begin to allow the light to dissipate any wounds or blocks that have kept you from your heart's desire. Open up, allow this green to flow and to release the obstacles to your good. Take some deep breaths. Pause for a moment, and feel the void you have created. Open your eyes again and as you look at the grass, trees and bushes, consciously take in the energy of the color green again. Fill your whole being, from your head to your toes, focusing on the space created in your heart region with the brilliance of the green light. Use this empowerment to define your desires and manifest them in your world. Know that you now have this healing energy to more easily magnetize your abundance.

Gold is the color of the sun and is connected with the solar plexus. The chakra at the solar plexus is connected with the part of your being which is called the seat of your identity, of your well-being. It is the connector between the higher chakras and the lower chakras. It is the connection you feel for yourself and how you see yourself walking in the world. Picture or feel this golden sun right below the heart and above the belly button, the rays are spreading all over the whole region, fill up your being, heal all aspects of your being; healing anything that is in the way of your true identity. Release old, false and ego beliefs about yourself into the golden light. Let it bathe, heal, and connect you with your true essence. You have a bright, burning sun of golden light shining from your solar plexus. Take several more deep breaths. Imagine all three areas of your body; your throat is shining with the color blue; your heart is shining with the color green; and your solar plexus is shining with the color gold. Enjoy the sensation of your chakras being bathed in these healing lights. When you are ready, take a deep breath and open your eyes.

Change of Seasons

If you live where you get a change of seasons, enjoy it! Take some time to honor the change of temperature and the explosion of color. Take a walk contemplating the exhibition of life, death, and renewal taking place before you.

Sending Intentions Over Water

Water is the Divine energy receptor. There are several practices you can do using water to connect with nature and create and manifest. An exercise that I do regularly is to send my intentions out over water. This can be done over a real body of water like a pond, lake or ocean, or it can be done in your mind as a visualization. On my way to the water, I think about the things I want to let go of and things I want to create. First notice the vastness of the water. I used to live near Lake Michigan and the lake appears to be endless. I breathe in the smells and notice the change of moisture in the air. I take in the water and recognize it as a creation of God. Water is an expression of the feminine aspect of God because of its receptive qualities, balance, and traditional association with the emotions. I look at it and use it as a way to enlarge my perceptions. I think of it in terms of expansiveness and abundance. Many times, our ideas of our own abundance and what we are asking for from the universe can be compared to holding out a small cup. We can be small in our thinking and our creating. We may only be trying to fill our cup rather than overflowing the cup. Take in and accept the vastness of the lake, and the endless possibilities for water's flow (and in life!) Nature is so beautiful, large and expansive that it helps me to imagine what I want to create in a much larger way.

Releasing to Water

- *Pick up stones, and think about what you want to let go of.*
- *If you are upset or grieving about a situation, pull up the emotions happening within you and as you hold the rock infuse it with those feelings.*
- *Stand in front of the water, that vast and accepting water, and see if you are really ready to let it go.*
- *Throw the rock in the water with the intention of releasing.*

For cleansing and renewal, use the calm energy of the water. Swim, bathe, or immerse yourself in the water with the intention of letting the water cleanse your chakras, aura, and spirit. Imagine the refreshing energy of the water going to any dark spots in your energy to bring light and healing. You are now clear and cleansed and connected with nature!.

While in the sacred space that you have created in or near water, you are now ready to fill the void that you created from your releasing. What do you want to create in its place? For myself, when I want new clients to come in, I imagine that I am creating this great softball-sized ball of energy with my intention inside of it. I imagine sending that ball out into the water. I feel as if the receptive water is receiving my intention and sending it to the Divine.

For expansiveness and creativity, I stand in front of the water with my arms open wide sending out prayers to expand my ability to receive and be grateful for my openness to this beautiful abundant universe. This practice opens me up and stretches my capacity to dream and create.

Bird Meditation

Go outside and find a place to lay on the earth, in the grass, or on the beach (if that is not possible, find a spot you will not be disturbed in your home). Close your eyes and begin to relax. Let anything that is bouncing around in your mind melt into the earth. With your eyes closed, take a few slow deep breaths. Breathing in the smells of the earth and breathing out any tension. Breathing in that grounding energy of the earth and letting go of everything else on the exhalation. This is your special sacred time to connect with nature. Feel the energy of the Mother Earth supporting your back, almost like being cushioned with the feminine embrace. Begin to notice the sounds around you. Tune into the conversation of the birds as they sing their song. They create a beautiful, uplifting symphony, with a high spiritual vibration. Let go of any thoughts and focus on the birds' songs. Notice the different types of birds communicating with each other. Can you hear their call and response? Sometimes, I make a sound mimicking the birds, and I like to think we are communicating back and forth. Allow this beautiful chorus to bring you peace and healing. You may not consciously know what the birds are saying to you, but I feel they have a message for us that we can understand on some level.

As the cares of the daily grind melt away, you are transported. Read these words to yourself to fully connect with this energy.

Blessed Being of Light, listen to the birds' symphony. The birds' song, carries a very high vibration. Close your eyes and really tune in, you will be uplifted to the heavenly realms. Fill yourself, my beloved, fall in love with nature, Self, and Spirit. You will find that it loves and nurtures you back. Lay in the grass and be serenaded. There is nothing to do. Just be, be, be.

When you feel ready, take a breath and begin to bring yourself back into the physical. Wiggle your fingers and toes to begin to get that energy moving. When you feel ready, slowly and gently open your eyes, sit up and look around you, notice how you are feeling; you are calmer and more connected to Self, Earth and Spirit..

Animals Totems

Perhaps there has been an animal in your life to which you felt a close association. It does not necessarily have to be a pet. It can be any animal, bird, insect, fish, etc. to which you feel a connection or an expression of energy that you liken to your own. It can be an archetypal force or an actual spirit represented by this being of nature that you hope to awaken within yourself. You can use this picture or touchstone (such as a feather) of that animal as a totem – a tool to facilitate a shift within you. Legends, folklore, and mythology are filled with the metaphysical qualities of animals and what they represent. For example,

- Otter is playful and fun loving
- Butterfly is transformation
- Lion is strength and courage
- Rabbit is fertility and new life

Spend time with your animal totem, consciously bringing forth the qualities you wish to nurture within yourself.

Every existing creature manifests some aspect of the
intelligence or power of the eternal One... - Manly P. Hall

Journal excerpt from Margaret Brown: When my son Elliott was seven he decided one sunny afternoon that he wanted a dragonfly to land on him (there were many buzzing around our yard at the time). I told him to be very still and invoke the spirit of a dragonfly. He was standing still but, inevitably, while the dragonfly was making his circles of flight, my son would flinch and the dragonfly would land farther away. After about 20 minutes or so Elliott proclaimed, "Well the dragonfly didn't land on me." I said, "Nope, not this time." He said, "I think I get it though, Mom. In order to be one with the dragonfly, I have to be one with myself." Out of the mouths of babes! Children have an innate ability to fully accept and understand nature.

I hope this chapter has inspired you to reawaken your connection with nature, to enhance and evolve your Self and Spirit. This grounding in nature is integral to our commitment to Self-Love and bringing forth your manifestation in later chapters.

CHAPTER 17

Connecting with Spirit

n this chapter, we consider the Universe's unseen forces. If energy exists everywhere, and everyone seems to agree on that, then that force, universe and Spirit is within you also. When we connect with our Self, connect with nature, approach the day with intention, we are in the wholeness of who we really are. We are utilizing the tools to access our own Spirit, the unseen part of our self. By doing this work, your Spirit, your soul becomes activated, leading you to full actualization – leading you to experience yourself as your own true essence in physical form. This physical form is the container that holds the Divine. When we connect with Spirit, we connect with the most real part of our being. These unseen forces that we are referring to in this chapter may seem outside of yourself, but when you connect with Self, Earth and Spirit, you are empowered from within!

Who You Really Are

When we connect with Spirit, we reach for that higher part of ourselves that does not judge and evaluate. It is the empowered, nurturing, larger aspect of Self. This part of your Self, God-Self is composed of all the Divine Love, total abundance on every level, all wisdom, all peace. It is called many things: higher self, soul, authentic Self, immortal divine essence. Some of us may be more aware of the higher part of ourselves than others. This higher part of our selves awakens when we acknowledge that it exists. It is experienced as real when we practice empowering techniques to connect to it. Connecting with this part of your Self and these attributes will allow you to more easily manifest them in your life. The more we are aware of the Divine Design, that we are spiritual beings having a human experience, the more real this becomes. The Divine Design is to first remember who we truly are, Spirit and form, aligned, awakened and connected. By perfecting ourselves through the Clearing and Connecting practices, we can begin to merge fully with Spirit. Now, from this place of connection you can move into creation.

We call upon the Universe with a request to create something from nothing. Connecting and creating with Spirit is the sacred act that we were put on this planet to do. This act of merging the physical with the spiritual, the act of creating, fully expresses the powerful beings that we are! When you connect with Spirit for the manifestation of your creation, Spirit is awakened by your beckon.

Lotus sits on top of the water, many times the water is dirty or muddy, but it remains untouched. Lotus is like the Spirit part within our own being; surrounded by, at times, the darkness, the shadow part of our lives, the drama. That Spirit, within us, like the lotus remains untouched. The power is in connecting with the lotus part of ourselves, merging with that part so that we come from that place into our lives.

The opposite is true as well. When we disconnect, do not honor, acknowledge, or connect to our higher self, our small mind (ego) will take charge. In my observation, the masses mostly live their lives focused on the outer. When not aligned, we give the mind the power. The mind judges, compares, and evaluates. It is not in the present moment. Have you ever noticed you were in your head? The small mind worries, gossips and manages our fear-based thoughts; all of this blocks support from the Universe. This is a deadening existence and it is almost impossible to create from this place. When you take a moment, breathe, get quiet and go within, there is an opening to awaken. If you start to connect on a daily basis with your Self, for example through the morning ritual, regular meditation, and appreciating nature, this connection inspires and uplifts you.

I have found through my studies, and in working with my clients, that how you treat yourself is how you will be treated. It is reflected by others and by what you attract. For example, when you love yourself, give yourself kind words, praise, respect and so forth, the Universe reflects that. Your life becomes more peaceful, joyful, and there is an ease, a flow and a vitality beyond your wildest dreams. Love of Self, connection with Spirit, and experiencing the oneness, allows you to not only to feel the joy, but to move forward in manifesting your purpose and your heart's desire.

The Energetic Container

Once you have achieved alignment, it is beneficial to have a context to maintain this state of connectedness. I would like to introduce the concept of the Energetic Container. An energetic container is similar to the aura, and it has also been called the Etheric Web in several cultures. St. Germaine talks about it as a tube of light surrounding you. For me, the words *Energetic Container* is a visual representation of the energetic field around myself. I can see mine in my mind's eye and, at times, I can even feel it.

The purpose of the Energetic Container is two-fold. Its first job is protection, it feeds you personally, and it strengthens your intuition. Because you are a vessel of the Divine, your Energetic Container is your connection with Spirit, purity, and light. As we feed it love and light, it gets stronger and stronger. You support it by being the best you can be, and it supports you and nurtures you. You are a co-creator in constructing and maintaining your own Energetic Container, and it is your job to keep your vessel stable and strong. We strengthen our containers by following a discipline of positive behaviors and acts of Self-Love: have a conscious intention of good thoughts; do meditation, prayer and commit acts of kindness; love and support the people close to us; do our clearing work regularly. All of the ideas in the Connect chapters contribute to, and build this force field. The second job of the Energetic Container is to magnetize the pure intention of what we desire. We shore up this aspect of your Container by taking clear and decisive action steps towards our creation on a daily basis; by keeping positive thoughts, words and deeds around our creation; by being crystal clear about what it is we want to create; by reciting and repeating our visions daily; by keeping our body and mind healthy and strong. A strong Energetic Container will radiate like the sun, beaming to all those who are ready to receive our light, attracting to us all that we desire, easily and effortlessly!

If you wonder why things are not coming to you, sometimes the Energetic Container, is weakened, as if it has holes in it. These "holes" are created by less-than-whole thoughts and behaviors, such as: excessive fear, drugs, alcohol, negativity, stress, trauma, and poor choices or behaviors that are not in alignment with what we want to create. Our Container's strength varies based on our discipline. If, for instance, you want your soul mate to come into your life, but you keep sleeping with the wrong guys or harboring beliefs that he may not come, this weakens your Container. It is your responsibility to maintain and strengthen your personal Energetic Container. No one can do that for you. It comes down to the moment-by-moment decisions and choices, thoughts and feelings, that are either Self-Loving and healthy for you, or not. Your Energetic Container is literally built on these *choice points*. If you are not clear and not caring for your personal vessel it is harder to send out signals of pure intention. The signal becomes distorted and loses its power, attracting nothing or a less desirable version.

As you grow spiritually, you will have more awareness of this Energetic Container in which your being resides. The following exercise assists you in seeing and feeling your Energetic Container. You can begin to interact with your Container to learn what it needs from you to become stronger.

Guided Visualization of the Energetic Container

 Find a time where you can be undisturbed and alone. Sit down, close your eyes and take three deep breaths. First, create your grounding cord as we have done earlier in this book. Imagine at the width your hips a cord that goes vertically down through the floor, deep down into the earth. Take an anchor or a rope and tie it to the center of the earth. Be sure it is strong and sturdy. Take a moment and think of anything going on in your life or any energy that is not of love and light,

that you are ready to release. Imagine putting it into a box and imagine you are sending it down the chute and it is going all the way down to your anchor in the center of the earth where it will be transmuted into love and light. Let that light travel up your grounding cord through the layers of earth and up into your being to fill and bless each of your chakras from your root to the crown (more information about the Chakras comes later in this chapter). Clearing and purifying chakra by chakra as it fills your being with light.

Imagine yourself surrounded by a tube of light. Ask your guides to enfold you now in the mighty magic energetic tube of light substance! See it around you as bright as possible. Some people see a color in the light. This is a great practice to do on a regular basis because you are strengthening your own force field. See if you can see it and or feel that beautiful tube of light around you. Notice if there are any dark spots or holes and send your Energetic Container love and healing energy to those places. Ask your guides to fill these holes with light. Let your container know you are now consciously aware of it and you are ready to be responsible for its strength and caretaking. Ask the Energetic Container or tube of light to tell you what behaviors or thoughts need to change in order to strengthen its power. Be silent and wait to hear the answer. Feel the energy of this beautiful light. Take a breath to anchor this Divine protection. Slowly and gently open your eyes.

Energy Shields

Energy Shields can be a part of one's morning ritual. Many of us are very sensitive to energy from other people. The more you work with your own personal container and grow spiritually, the more sensitive you will become towards other people's energy. You may find yourself entering someone's house for the first time and feel negativity, or you meet someone new and feel sad. It is not healthy or beneficial for you to pick up and carry someone else's feelings, or the residual energy left behind. By putting up an energy shield, you can protect yourself, and in some cases allow yourself to be with a person or situation that would have been difficult for you otherwise. In my work, I coach and consult with many caregivers, who classically have difficulty separating their feelings from their clients. Energy shields allow you to be with people without picking up their energy. I disagree. By using a shield, we can be present and more connected with the other without fearing their emotions or the drains that can ensue.

Putting Up an Energy Shield

How do you put up a shield? There are many types of shields from simple to complex. The simplest way to practice doing energy shields is to close your eyes and picture yourself in a bubble of light. As I see myself in this bubble of light, I affirm that I am holding in my good energy and any outside negativity or energies that I do not want to absorb are bouncing off my bubble. An easy way to reinforce the bubble is to visualize mirrors outside the bubble. These mirrors reflect whatever is being projected onto you back to the sender, or out to the universe. If you are very sensitive or feel like you are being drained in your life, create this bubble as part of your morning ritual. Do it daily, as regularly as you brush your teeth. Picture the mirrors on the outside of your bubble and affirm that you are protected. This allows you to walk through your life with confidence, strength, and knowing you are able to be with whatever situation comes up.

Chakras

The Chakra is a concept originating from Hindu texts and practices. Its name comes from the Sanskrit word for "wheel" or "turning" referring to wheel-like vortices which are said to be "force centers" or whirls of energy within our bodies. Like we referenced in Clearing, when our emotions get blocked, the corresponding chakra can be affected.

1st Chakra – The Root Chakra and the color is red. Located at the base at the lowest point on the trunk of your body, this chakra is the home of our basic instincts and survival. This is the one that is truly about a person's need for security and stability. The Root chakra is our connection with Earth. It can get imbalanced by our reaction to emotionally unstable parents or being around or part of addiction to drugs or alcohol. It can manifest in problems around money or a general inability to create stability and happiness. Healing this chakra is about working on the emotions, healing basic stability and survival issues.

2nd Chakra – The Sacral Chakra. This is the chakra related to sexual and creative energy, relationship and emotional desires. Orange is the color associated with this chakra. It specifically is located behind the sexual organs. Blocks in this area can affect your sexuality and your creativity and sometimes will manifest as boundary issues. Balancing this chakra allows you to create intimacy and be creatively self-expressive and more self-confident.

3rd Chakra – The Solar Plexus. The color is yellow. It is just behind the belly button along the spine. It is related to power and control. It is the intersection of your self and your identity. This chakra pertains to your personality, your confidence, your knowing of yourself, and who you are. The ego makes its home here. When we feel good about ourselves this chakra is open and clear. When it is out of balance, you may find yourself being overly controlling, feel excessive anxiety and stress. Your reaction to over-controlling parents or an abusive home can shut this chakra down in childhood and create an adult that is controlling and fearful. Healthy human relationships, relaxation, meditation and therapy helps.

4th Chakra – The Heart chakra is located in the chest. The color is emerald green. This is the chakra that relates to compassion and love, and overall balance of the three higher and three lower chakras. A path to opening the heart chakra is learning to love ourselves. With Self-Love, we can then love and have compassion for others. When the heart chakra is blocked, it can manifest in an imbalance, needing to please others. We may not be comfortable taking responsibility for our emotions and actions. We can be overly critical of ourselves and others. It can be damaged from abandonment, loss, and can manifest as jealousy and mistrust. In order to heal your Heart chakra, we must learn to self-love and accept others.

5th Chakra - The Throat chakra's color is blue. This chakra invites communication and freedom of expression. This is where you speak from and from where your voice is created. The throat chakra, in particular can get blocked if people have not been raised to speak up or tell the truth or speak their own truth. It is a place of power because we create from our word and our thought. If this chakra is blocked, it can seriously get in the way of manifesting. Many people get shut down in their ability to speak up for themselves. Because of this, it is related to your own independence. In addition, sometimes an inability to listen is a problem among those with an inefficient throat center. Too much energy here causes people to be overbearing.

6th Chakra The Third eye is located right between your eyebrows, above the bridge of the nose. The color is indigo. This is the place from where you create your visualization and where you send out your vision to the universe. It relates to your inner sight, spiritual communication, and receiving guidance from other levels.

7th Chakra - The Crown chakra is located at the top of your head. The color associated with the 7th chakra is violet. The 7th chakra on babies is known as their soft spot. It is the channel that connects you with the Divine. It is an important chakra to keep cleared so you receive inspiration, intuition, and guidance. It deals with pure consciousness and oneness with the world. If you are blocked spiritually, this is where a conflict with God would manifest, spiritually, emotionally, and physically. If you consciously work on clearing the 7th chakra and opening the 7th chakra, you will have more ability to channel and receive information.

Chakra Meditation

There are many different techniques to heal and balance one's chakras, including: chanting, breathing, and meditation. We will be doing both a visualization and an affirmation with this meditation. We will be looking at each chakra, getting a sense of your feelings when you go there and making sure the color is clear and bright, with no holes, darks spots or muddiness. We will also be looking at it from a perspective of its motion. Is it stagnant or spinning, clockwise or counter clockwise? At each chakra, we will be saying the words "bless and dissipate." We will bless each energy center of our body, and dissipate and clear any energy, feelings, or attachments that do not serve.

When you are working with the chakras, make sure that you start at the root chakra and work up. Sit in a quiet place, making sure your back is straight. Begin by doing a grounding cord technique. Imagine a tube as wide as your hips going deep, deep down into the center of the earth, as far as you can imagine. In the center of the earth, anchor it in (tie it or anchor it). In your imagination, go back up and strengthen the cord as you go up so you have a firm solid tube from your hips leading down to the center of the earth.

Beginning with the root chakra, concentrate on the area behind the sex organs towards your back and buttocks. What are you feeling? Do any images, colors, or words come to mind? Can you begin to sense and feel your chakra? Imagine it as a red globe or spinning ball. When the chakra is open and working properly it is spinning clockwise. Imagine this chakra, red, bright and full, spinning clockwise and say the words, "Bless and dissipate."

Move up to the second chakra, the sacral chakra which is located in the groin area, again near the sex organs but a little higher and closer to the front of the body. Repeat the same process of first locating that area and seeing what you sense and feel. Since the sacral chakra is related to sexual energy, if there has been any sexual issues in your life, this may be the seat of an emotional wound for you. Just sit with your feelings and notice any images, words, colors or discomfort that you might experience. What do you see? Begin to imagine a bright orange ball there, spinning clockwise and again say the words, "Bless and dissipate." Take as long as you need to see your chakra spinning properly, glowing bright.

Then move up to the third chakra, this is the Solar Plexus, located just below the chest and above the belly button. This is the seat of your power and ego. How do you feel when you concentrate on this chakra? Imagine a glowing, golden ball of light shining and spinning in a clockwise direction. To yourself, say the words, "Bless and dissipate."

As we move up to the higher chakras, these are mainly associated with what we manifest in the world, as well as our connection to Spirit and the Divine, so it is extremely important that these be clear and spinning appropriately. We are now at the 4th chakra, the heart. Sit with your heart chakra for a moment and see what you feel. Do you feel sadness or longing, are any emotions or images coming up for you? Feel what you feel and begin to bathe the chakra in loving, healing emerald green light, seeing it spin in a clockwise direction and saying the words, "Bless and dissipate."

The 5th Chakra is at the throat and the color is blue. This chakra is related to your speaking and communication. How do you feel as you focus on this area? Does it feel closed or sluggish? Do you have any issues around communicating or speaking up for yourself? Imagine this chakra spinning clockwise and glowing brighter and brighter blue, all the time blessing and dissipating any stagnant energy here until the chakra is spinning and glowing on its own.

We now move to the third eye and 6th chakra. As you concentrate on this area between your eyes think about your own intuition. Do you feel you receive guidance from your highest self at times? As you spend time in this chakra picturing it spinning clockwise, bathe it in the color indigo (indigo is a cross between a blue and violet color). Continue to bless and dissipate the energy of this chakra until it is glowing bright.

We are now at the 7th Chakra at the top of your head. This is your channel to the Divine. Begin to imagine a bright violet ball there, spinning clockwise and again say the words, "Bless and dissipate." Take as long as you need to see your chakra spinning properly, glowing bright.

Calling on the Archangels

Another way to put protection around yourself is to use the Archangels. This allows us to feel connected and calm. It allows me to walk in the world confidently and not from a place of fear. By calling on the Archangels, I affirm my protection, strength and trust in my Source. I work with the Archangels as part of feeling supported in the world, and I call upon them when I need powerful and immediate assistance for small or large undertakings. Each Archangel has a different role.

Michael – Michael is called upon for protection and clearing negative energy in your home or work place. His is the role of "cutting of bonds," with his mighty sword. If you find yourself any place where you feel unsafe you can call upon Archangel Michael to guide and protect you. If you find yourself in an argument with someone, silently call upon Michael to intervene. He helps to clear worries and fears.

Gabriel – Gabriel is God's messenger. If you are wanting to conceive a child, or start a new business or get a new home, for example, call upon Gabriel to assist you. He is in charge of dreams and visions. You can, at the beginning of saying your vision out loud, ask Gabriel to carry a message to God. If there is an area of your life that feels stagnant, ask Gabriel to blow his mighty horn and shake things up!

Uriel – Uriel's name means "light of God." He is the archangel of clearing and creating. He will help us to heal and release the past and transform situations so we can see the good in people and ourselves. Call upon Uriel when you are having a difficult time letting go of your story, forgiving a trespass, or forgiving yourself. He helps you to find peace of mind. Uriel helps us fulfill our intentions and brings our ideas to fruition. He keeps us on track and inspired with our projects. Be open to Uriel's support when working on creative new ideas.

Raphael – Raphael is an archangel of healing, helping with challenges related to the physical realm. He intervenes when you have any healing crisis or ongoing health issues. Raphael can be called on for yourself and your loved ones. Raphael even works with your thoughts that might be causing the manifestation of disease. His is the emerald green, loving heart chakra energy. Call upon Raphael to bathe your cells with this healing energy.

Archangel Visualization

When I feel the need for protection, I see the Archangels around me forming a circle. They are in front of me, on my sides, and in back of me. Anyone that would want to do me harm would feel that energy of protection. I suggest that you visualize them around your bed when you sleep and around your house in the North, South, East and West. As you become more sensitive and tuned in, having the protection of the Archangels supports you on your journey.

Your Celestial Team

Who makes up your Celestial Team? Angels, guides, masters, teachers and loved ones; these can all be members of your Celestial Team. The Masters are the Avatars and the highest, most evolved teachers like Christ, Buddha, Moses, Abraham, St. Germaine and Mohammed. There are the archangels who are in charge of all the angels, previously discussed. Then there are those loved ones who have passed on who are assigned to your keeping, watching over you. Native American people have strong connections with their ancestors. Everyone has a team of guides. Often when I do an Akashic Reading, I see their team circled around whoever I am reading for. In my experience, the more you call upon them, the more you will sense their presence. Some people believe the whole hierarchy of the beings including your own personal higher self is God. My belief is that there is an unseen force in the universe, that when called upon, is behind our intentions. Your team is there for your support, protection and upliftment. They are there to guide you and teach you, especially in times of despair or crisis. I suggest that you call upon them to support you in all your endeavors, large or small.

Prayer

Some people pray to God using formalized, ritualistic prayers based on their religion; others keep up a dialogue with God, their Higher Self or their Celestial Team. There is no right or wrong way to pray. The key is to speak from your heart. Feel free to ask for what you want and need. Your belief in the outcome should be positive and unwavering. Ask with respect knowing that if it is God's will, (and remember God's will is *your highest good*) then it will be done. You can also just ask for the highest and best good to be done for all. And so it is!

Gratitude

Give thanks and rejoice in all things. – Bible

Gratitude works the same way as prayer. When we pray we are sending out a request for help, when we have gratitude for something we send out the energetic vibration of "I appreciate this thing." The Universe automatically responds by giving you more of all that you are grateful for. When you think of Spirit, it is overflowing abundance. It is a constant giving forth – a cornucopia of more, more, more. When you give gratitude, it aligns you with Spirit and opens you up for more. The power of being in gratitude comes from being thankful for what you do have, instead of focusing on what you do not have or want to have. Focusing on gratitude quiets the critical and judgmental mind opening you to create more peace, joy and abundance. Make a list of what you have in your life that you appreciate. Write it down, read it regularly and add to your list as more things come to mind. If you are working through this book with a partner, speak your list out loud, or into a recorder. Being in a place of gratitude connects you and your vibration with all that is good in your life and with the abundant Spirit of the Universe.

The Four Directions

The Four Directions ritual has many uses. You can do this ritual to ask for the Universe's support for your intentions. You can use it to clear and heal an issue, or connect with the Divine for any spiritual practice. I also use it to start my workshops or retreats to empower myself and others. It is a spiritual practice of creating sacred space and it helps to gather up the energy, so that my guides and my celestial team are behind me in all my endeavors. In my studies of Peruvian Shamanism, I was taught this particular method. I have also encountered other methods from Native Americans. If you are someone who has learned a different method, see if you are willing to try this one and see if it resonates with you. We will start by describing the animal symbols for each of the four directions with a short description on how it can apply to your life. In this method of working with the four directions, we begin in the South.

South - The animal that represents the south is the serpent known in many cultures for its transformational nature. Here we focus on the fact that a snake will periodically shed its skin. It does this very quickly and the skin is always left in one piece. This represents the awareness that we, like the serpent can shed that which no longer serves us. I liken this to someone who believes they have to sit on a therapist's couch for twenty years to let go of their childhood trauma. With the serpent's help, I believe, we can let go of both small and large issues, when our intention is clear and we are fully committed, in a moment of transformation, in an instant! Just as the serpent sheds its skin with ease, we too can let go of that which we no longer need.

West - The animal that represents the West is the jaguar. The jaguar represents courage; courage to move forward and the courage to let go. The jaguar is known to stalk its prey. We ask the jaguar's Spirit to help us to stalk those things in our life that are stalking us, and give us the courage to release them. For example, if you are having a problem with an addiction, a recurring, fear-based thought pattern, or trying to shed an issue that feels like it just never goes away, ask the jaguar to give you the courage to confront the situation and release it.

North - Then we move to the North and meet the hummingbird. The hummingbird is this very small creature that performs amazing feats. It can beat its wings up to 90 times a second and fly forward, backward, up and down, in that tiny little body. The hummingbird, not knowing it is doing something amazing, just goes on living his little hummingbird life. We are like the hummingbird. Stop and imagine the amazing feats we accomplish every day. We are these spiritual beings in human form, accomplishing these feats of perseverance and strength, and yet we just go on, having what we think is just an everyday human experience. The hummingbird is a reminder that we are so much more than we perceive and appear to be. We are spiritual beings having a physical experience!

East - The East is represented by the eagle, or the condor in Peru. The eagle is known for its keen sense of sight. It flies very high in the sky and see from that vantage point a larger perspective. The eagle to us represents vision. The vision is for all we create and all that is held for us that we are invited to step into. We ask the eagle to help us to see our life or our situation from a larger perspective. We ask eagle to remind us of our vision, purpose, and to be empowered to fulfill these.

Below - Then we lean over and touch the earth where Mother Earth (as named by our culture, or Pachamama, as named by the Peruvian culture) resides. She is the feminine Earth goddess, she is Gaia, the spirit of the Earth. She is the energy of maternal reproduction, the cycles of life. We ask her to nurture us and ignite the feminine principle within us, so we might remember our ability to create, to nurture, and to express love.

Above - We rise up and put an arm up to the sky and call in the Great Spirit, God, the Force, whatever your name for this power. The Great Spirit is the masculine, father energy of the Earth. He reminds us that this life is meant for celebration. We ask the Great Spirit to be with us on our journey, to help us remember who we truly are and we ask him to help us fulfill our purpose on this Earth. One last word, "Ho," is used by the Native Americans as an ending to a prayer. "Ho" is said at the end of calling in each direction. It can be likened to *Amen* in Christianity, or *And So It Is*. It is a powerful way of both accentuating your statement like an exclamation point, and professing your agreement.

Creating Sacred Space

 To create sacred space, get a sage stick and use it to clean your aura and your energy field. Start by waving the smoke over your head and slowly and deliberately running it in front of and around each chakra, saying out loud, "I bless and dissipate." Take the smoke all the way down to your feet and then pass it over your body from front to back. Be clear and focused. As you are turning towards each direction, raise your hands up, and use your intention to literally "call in" the winds and the totems in all six directions. Say the following, and add your own feelings and intentions. The more personal you make this ritual, the

better. Before starting your ritual make sure you will not be disturbed, you will want to be able to do this process from beginning to end without interruption.

Turn to the South and begin.

South – I call on the winds of the South, the serpent, to let go of that which no longer serves me. As the snake effortlessly sheds the old skin to make way for the new, with great ease I learn this through my own intention, I, too, can make the changes necessary for my life. Let me remember that I, like the serpent, let go. I am ready to release. Allow me now to let go of this burden. Thank you Great Spirit of the South, Ho!

Turn your body to the West and raise your hand.

West – I call on the winds of the West. The jaguar, imbues me with courage. Help me to stalk that which is stalking me now. As you stalk your prey and stalk that which is stalking you, teach me, jaguar, to turn and face that which I do not want to look at, but which I must see for full consciousness and awareness. I ask that I may look fear in the face with courage. Thank you Spirit of the West, Ho!

Turn your body to the North and raise your hand.

North – I call on the winds of the North. The hummingbird reminds me of who I really am. Just like you, hummingbird who performs amazing feats as a tiny bird, I, too, am a great Spirit who asks to remember and to know what and who I am. You fly forwards, backwards, and up and down, flapping your wings many times a minute. Remind me that I am much more than what I believe I am, a truly remarkable spiritual being, having a human experience. Remind me, hummingbird, that I am amazing! Thank you Spirit of the North, Ho!

Turn your body to the East and raise your hand.

East – I call on the winds of the East. I call on the eagle who holds the vision for my path, who flies above the earth and sees the bigger picture. I ask that I am able to step into my vision and that it manifests for me now. As you, eagle, fly high above this earth, help me to see the bigger picture of my life. Empower me to walk forward on my journey and fulfill that which I am here for. Thank you Spirit of the East, Ho!

Bend down and touch the ground.

Pachamama – I call on Mother Earth, the feminine, and ask for nurturing grounding support. Fill me now with your loving presence. Ignite the feminine principle within and remind me that I am co-creating this beautiful experience. Thank you Pachamama, Ho!

Raise your hands to the sky.

I call on the Great Spirit, Father Sky, and the remembrance that life is for celebration. Be with me now, and remind me that this life is for joy and celebration. Strengthen me, empower me. Align with me now so that I may walk forward on my path knowing that you are with me. Thank you Great Spirit, Ho!

You are now present with the energy of the four directions and the power of the totems you have called in. In this sacred space you can pursue any further clearing, connecting or creating rituals, visualizations or meditations, or just bask in this sacred space and the power and peace. When your connecting session is completed, take a few deep breaths, thank the forces of the universe who aligned with you and release them.

Column of Light Visualization

Something that I learned while studying the Akashic Records with Linda Howe is the Column of Light which I use as a shield of protection for myself and my house. I use it when I am doing spiritual work.

Sit, close your eyes, and breathe. Get relaxed. Call upon Mother Earth, the feminine earth energy. We are calling upon her to send a ball of healing energy up through the layers of earth into the soles of your feet. Slowly visualize that energy travelling up your legs and into the trunk of your body expanding out through the trunk up through your stomach, solar plexus, your heart center, and your throat. Let go of any thoughts. Bring the energy up into your head and fill your entire head with this nurturing feminine energy and send it out the top of your head and let it go. Imagine a ball of white light a foot above your head and see a shower pouring forth on the front, sides and back, of you, clearing away any energy in your aura that needs to be released. This light is bringing to you what you need at this time. Create an opening in the top of your head allowing the shower to pour forth into your head filling your head, eyes, nose, jaw, down your throat, into your neck, shoulders, arms, fingers; bringing it down to the heart center, the solar plexus, stomach and down the legs into the feet and out the toes. Fill every cell and strand of dna with light until it feels as if your body is bursting with light. Bring your awareness to your heart chakra and send a stream of white light out creating a column of light before you. The column of light goes down through the floor, deep deep, deep down to the center or core of the earth. Imagine tying a rope or an anchor to the center of the earth. When that is done visualize that a column of light is travelling now up through the layers of earth, through the room your seated in, going up through the roof, and into the sky. Expand it in your mind as far and as wide as you can imagine and then let it go out into the sky. Take the column that is in front of you, and in your mind's eye imagine that it is now around you where you are seated. Lastly, visualize the column expanding out to the walls, the floor, the ceiling and windows so you are then within a container of divine light. Now that you have established this column of light, you can use it as a shield of protection, or you can go into a meditation or another visualization. You are much more connected with spirit and relaxed!

CHAPTER 18

Connecting in Crisis

hat would be more valuable for us to do in times of crisis than to call upon and connect with Spirit for support, healing, and nurturing? And yet, if you think about the times when you have been in the most dire straits, most of us panic and go into fear mode. During a crisis, we move as far away from our connection with Source as possible. Some people pray, or ask God for help, but as far as a regular daily connecting practice within – this rarely happens. Connecting with Spirit is a powerful way out of crisis!

This chapter is a step-by-step method to remind ourselves that when we find ourselves in crisis, we need to remember to connect. Connecting with Spirit allows us to draw the strength needed to handle the crisis from a different perspective. When we are in connection with Spirit, there is less fear, panic, anxiety, and illusion. Spirit is a place of peace, joy, abundance, and truth. Are you going to choose fear or love? Choose the path of Self-love. Love is the true essence of who you are. When we are fully aligned and connected; Spirit and Self-Love dispel the darkness. It is ideal to have the strength and fortitude built up from a solid, consistent connection with our Spirit. When crisis strikes, we then have the ability to deal with it from a higher perspective. We see the truth more clearly, rather than the illusion, fear and drama that swirls around. When we come from this centered place, it is like watching a play. We are connected with something that is immortal and Divine, and our awareness of this, allows us to be more detached. This awakened perspective makes you the director and not the actor in the play. This change in perspective shifts our ability to stay centered and clear during the challenge, and it may shift the outcome of the situation as well.

Yes, there are things here in this chapter to do in crisis that can support you, but the real message here, is to be willing to do a daily practice which is the key to having constant and continued alignment with your true essence. Doing these exercises during a challenge will prepare you so that you can face it empowered!

Just Breathe

The first thing you can do in crisis is remember to breathe. As soon as something rocks our world, and we are off-center, we start to breathe from up high in our lungs. Many of us take shallow breaths, hunch our shoulders, and our voice may be strained from the lack of breath. Taking deep slow breaths is one of the most powerful methods to slow down our nervous system, calm our self, and bring us back to the present moment with more clarity and connection to Self and Spirit. Breath is the simplest way to connect.

You may have to remind yourself to breathe deep, expanding your diaphragm. Put signs up, at work, on your computer. Write it in your day planner. While taking a walk, take conscious breaths with each step. Aromatherapy, specifically lavender, is a good scent to apply in crisis because it lingers and is calming. Throughout the day, every time you smell the scent on yourself, take in a deep breath. You can wear a rubber band around your wrist, or a string around your finger to remind yourself to breathe deeply. Carry a crystal or a stone in your pocket, so that when you touch it, it wakes you up and reminds you to breathe slowly and deeply.

Re-Creation

Another way to connect in crisis is to express what you are thinking and feeling through Re-Creation. It is important that you select the right person to speak with who will be able to hear you without judgment and without trying to fix the situation for you. If you have chosen someone who has not done a Re-Creation with you before, or does not know how to do the technique, the process may "add mass" or energetic weight to your already burdened shoulders. On the other hand, when you speak "into the listening" of someone that is clear and holding space for you and your communication, then the weight of your feeling disappears, or at the very least, lighten. Refer to page 23 for the Re-Creation Exercise. Fully express every thought and feeling until you feel empty, and you have nothing more to say. The word here is "dumping!"

Absolute Needs

When we are in crisis sometimes our minds get so overloaded with worry that conscious thoughts go out the window. Stop and create a plan to meet your absolute needs. Look and see what you absolutely, immediately need to handle. Is food and shelter for yourself and family at risk? If the crisis is financial, is there someone you can call regarding postponing a payment, or speak to someone who can advise you? Use discernment and look at all of your options. Answer the following questions: "If I do nothing, will it get worse?" "Is there anything to do?" Is the crisis at hand even in the realm of your control, or is your state of fear and worry, just a state you have gotten yourself into? The mind is powerful. People handle stress and crisis in different ways. Some will shut down while others will move into overdrive and try to control every aspect of a situation. For the "doers" out there, when you are able to let go and not count on yourself to make everything happen, things may go much better than you think. Many of us are afraid to let go of the details, fearing things will get worse. Is there anyone else to help? Are you hanging on to control for the sake of your ego or power? This is our attachment to the worry and need to control. I encourage you to let go of some of the details.

Self-Care

Self-Care equals Self-Love. Yet in times of crisis, the last thing we do is care for ourselves. You absolutely need to take good care of yourself during times of crisis.

Surrender and Release

We will be discussing more about surrender in the Create section, but that is more geared towards surrendering the outcome of your creation. Talking about surrender during a time of crisis is a different type of surrender. There are times to take action. There are also times to surrender. Surrender is a scary concept for most people. Does it mean I give up and let go of my will? If I do nothing, will my needs be taken care of? Surrender is a decision to choose faith over fear. Fear is the unknown and all of the "what-ifs." Faith is to know and trust that you are taken care of. Your life is changing. You may be losing your home, your job, and/or your way of life as you know it. You may want to hang onto that past identity and you may fear that you will be lost if that way of being ends now. Ultimately, there is a bigger picture, a greater plan for you. The growth is in the journey. When you are at your lowest, the real YOU is not far behind. You have dealt with the mind, spoke to friends who could listen and not fix, and there are no outer actions to do. Now it is time to pray, hand it over to the Universe, and give it to God. Surrender and release.

The Universe has a plan that will take you to all the places within yourself that you could not get to on your own.

When you feel the need to control a situation, you are discounting your intuition, your support from the Universe and your own inspiration. After all, if you trust you need to manage every detail, then you do not feel you have any support from others, from God, and your celestial team. If you believe you have to do it yourself, then you *do* have to do it yourself. When you surrender to a situation you must turn it over, releasing the control, letting go of focusing on the end result you can envision. To surrender is to be open to all the possibilities with an endless list of wonderful outcomes you have not even begun to imagine!

God has the ability to create miracles.

Ceremony to Surrender

Come up with a representation of what you are fixated on, a meaningful symbol to what you need to surrender. If someone is sick, bring out their picture, or something that reminds you only of that person. If you want to surrender a situation, like you just lost a job or a relationship, add something to your alter that reminds you of the situation. It should be an item that completely draws you into the feelings that are disturbing you. Burn some incense and create sacred space. Sit in front of your altar and pray with the intention of letting this issue go and allowing God to come in and remove or move this obstacle or challenge. When that feels complete, cover the altar with your items still on it with a colorful or soothing cloth. Something that makes you feel good when you look at it. Maybe add an affirmation or a flower or something that further makes you feel good when you look at your covered altar. When you look at the covered alter, say an affirmation to yourself (see below). Remind yourself that you have nothing more to do and it is now in God's hands. At some point, you will want to remove these items from your alter and maybe do a burning ritual to complete these feelings for yourself. Keep your altar covered until your feelings or the situation itself has shifted. Some possible surrendering affirmations include:

> *I let go and let God.*
> *I surrender, I let go.*
> *It is complete, now rest in peace.*
> *I am done, the angels come.*
> *I trust my Celestial Team is at work.*
> *I give it away, my worry is at bay. I play!*

Call on the Team

God, your angels and your Celestial Team are there, but they have to get called upon. Like we said earlier, if you believe you have to do it yourself, then you have to do it yourself. It is your belief that closes the door on that support that is there for you. It is like trying to climb a mountain without the proper gear. You fall down the mountain, you get back up. You do not have the training or the gear to do this by yourself and you were not even designed to do it yourself. You need the support and faith and trust and inspiration to make it to the top. Do you believe God wants you to be happy, healthy, and abundant? Can you imagine you are part of a bigger plan than the crisis before you?

When we surrender, we open the channels to the universe, and we trust the Universe to take what we want and give us that or something better. We are conditioned by our families and culture to make it on our own. That mindset can take us only so far. Who can you call on for help? God, your angels and Celestial Team are always available. Call. Ask for help now.

Asking for Divine Guidance

According to the angel experts, angels cannot enter our lives without our expressed permission. Giving up our problem to them is like mailing a letter. You have to release the letter from your hand before the post office can deliver it. By mailing the letter, we give it away; we take it back when we give into the worry and fear. Surrender and trust. We must not write a script on how to resolve the problem. The angels and God will have a much better plan for fixing the problem. God's will is that we be happy. If you totally trust, a solution will come.

Discipline

People who really want to make a change must do the Clearing and Connecting work regularly. Your level of commitment to what you want to create and manifest in your life will fuel how much work you do with yourself. With my clients, I see them come to me for a crisis, we work through it and sometimes they come back four months later with the same issue. Clearing and Connecting requires you to be vulnerable. You have made a commitment to yourself to go deep, do the inner and outer work, and invest in your Self and your creation.

Mastering the mind in the face of fear is a discipline. I am inspired by the athletes in the Olympics. They have set a vision of gold for themselves and they persevere with their goals through family drama, through injuries, and through days of despair and doubt. Sure some days they wake up and say, "I cannot do it today. I hurt. I am exhausted. I am not as good as the rest. I doubt I will win anyway." They, too, get discouraged and downhearted. But they do get up, and they do their workout routines. Here I am asking you, too, to treat your Connecting tools as a discipline and daily practice. Sometimes the only way to push through discouragement and despair of a crisis and achieve those results in life is to practice with an Olympian's discipline! Ask yourself about your resolve, your vision of what you want to create. Are you going after it as a gold medalist, or are you taking a few steps forward and a few steps back? If you really commit to the practices here in this book, you will make progress. You need to be aware and notice when the fear begins to take over and immediately take action.

When we are in crisis our mind tackles the situation like a puzzle, analyzing, picking it apart, trying to find a loophole, trying to discover some form of action we can take to resolve it. When there is no resolution, when the only solution is to wait and see, or accept our situation as it is, our mind drive us crazy seeking out something, anything to do, do, do. It creates scenarios, what ifs, scenes of cause and effect, "if this happens, then, this... and I'll be fine." At this moment, our mind is writing the script to resolve our problem or replaying an old script. When we are coming from a place of fear, we do not trust that this situation is for our highest good. We do not trust that the Universe has a solution for our situation. We do not believe that God's solution is better than our own.

Giving it to God Visualization

Close your eyes and take three deep breaths to center yourself. Imagine yourself sitting down at a desk, the desk can be as simple or ornate as you desire. You pause for a moment, pen in hand, to fully reflect on your problem, fully experiencing all the emotions, sorrow, fear and worry this problem is causing in your life. You look down at your paper (parchment, scroll, papyrus, again whatever you desire), and as you look down at your paper, it is as if your soul is writing the letter in a beautiful gold script. Your prayer to your Celestial Team fervently composes itself before your eyes. You state your problem. You ask for what you specifically need. This beautiful request of the Universe is the prayer written from your soul. When you feel complete, you thank the Team for their assistance. And you end the letter with the phrase, "This or something better is now manifesting for me in totally satisfying ways." You fold the letter and place it in an envelope and seal it. You walk out of your home and there is a mail box. It can be a traditional mailbox, or since this is a heavenly request, your imagination can create any kind of mailbox you desire. You drop your letter into the mailbox. As soon as the letter has left your hand you can rest assured in the knowledge that your Team has received your letter and has heard your prayer. You no longer need to worry over this problem. You have released it to the Universe. You are at peace. Feel the peace that the situation has been perfectly handled. When you feel ready, open your eyes.

Once you have completed this visualization, your job is to harness your worry. When you begin to worry about this problem again, you have, in effect told the Universe and your Celestial Team, "you are not handling this fast enough, and I think I can do a better job anyway, so I am taking my letter back." Follow any and all directions you receive after this exercise. Once you release it to the Universe you may receive directions from your heart, in the form of a voice, a dream, a vision, or a knowingness or intuitive feeling.

Surrender Again

Use the Surrender affirmations (page 229) whenever that niggling problem re-enters your mind and threatens to take over. Saying something to master your mind will bring you back to the peaceful place of trust and surrender.

CHAPTER 19

·······················

Approaching the Day

How we set the tone for the day has a significant impact on how our day turns out. Most people wake to an alarm or someone else waking them. Some people might jump right into responding to other people's demands, and become irritated or frustrated shortly after rising. For those who languish in bed for a few extra minutes, their mind may be prioritizing the list of chores and activities for the day. Changing how we enter waking consciousness from the dream state, has a dramatic effect on our mood, expectations, and how the day unfolds. I suggest that you connect with your Self before all of the distractions of the day pull you away from your center. Give yourself a few minutes to connect with yourself spiritually, emotionally and physically. Put your own Self first upon waking, and it could very well align you with the higher part of yourself and transform the circumstances that you create. Experience the beginning of the morning in a new way to change the way you experience your life.

When we first awaken, we are open, receptive, and energetically vulnerable from the dream state. We have spent the last eight or so hours, tripping around the astral plane playing with our subconscious. If the first thing we do upon waking is to turn on the news and hear about murder and mayhem, then that is what we ingest and bring into our space. Be sensitive to your energetic state upon rising. By consciously creating your morning, you allow your mind, body, and spirit to reunite. These morning routines help us connect with our spirit, control and tame the overactive mind, and be connected in our bodies.

The Approaching the Day Techniques are any and all experiences that put you into a place of connection with Source that is centering and grounding for you. By taking these actions, you honor and love yourself, and put yourself first before you extend and respond to others. It can be a very powerful declaration to your Self and the Universe of your commitment to your own well-being. It is a sacred practice to work on the connection to Self and Spirit. With this early morning connection, you strengthen your energy field, wholeness, awareness, intuition and appreciation for something greater than yourself. It has a cumulative effect. As you continue this practice, for a minimum of 30 days (again, it takes 30 days to change a habit), you will begin to *not* want to start your day in any other fashion. It will feel strange to *not* do these practices and to not give yourself this daily connection. After the first 30 days are over, begin to notice how you are responding to the circumstances, people and events in your life that may have been a trigger of stress or anxiety for you. It has been my experience that when I do this practice, I feel more patient with others. Throughout my day, I am able to pause and draw upon my deepened sense of peace within.

We are so distracted in our days with all of the outer activities and the busy-ness of our minds. By taking the time in the morning, honoring our Self and doing these practices, we build a foundation of strength. The deeper our foundation, the more we can expand our spiritual development. This also enhances our ability to be empowered in the world, and our ability to stay centered in the midst of any storm. Just like a house that has a strong, deep foundation, your morning practices reflect how you approach the day. You will feel more grounded. You will be in the world, but not of it. You will discover what it feels like to be a spiritual being having a human experience, remaining centered and clear.

Suggestions to Consciously Create Your Morning

Physical Connecting: It is a perfect way to transition from sleeping to waking. Walk, dance, stretch, do yoga, tai chi, or any form of exercise. Exercise is a perfect way to connect with the physical aspect of your body and momentarily quiet the mind during its performance.

Breathing, Mantras, Chanting: Simple breathing techniques – taking several deep, conscious breaths will go a long way to clear your mind and ground you in your body, in the now. Mantras are traditionally associated with Vedic, Hindu and Buddhism traditions. Mantras are energy-based sounds, syllables, words, or group of words that derive their power from the user's intention and the meaning they convey. They are considered capable of creating spiritual transformation. One will generally repeat a specific mantra related to what you are working on in your life. For instance, a one syllable mantra is Shrim (pronounced shreem) which is the sound for the energy of abundance in all forms. Repeating the Shrim mantra helps you to attract and maintain abundance. Chanting is another great way to greet the day. Even if you just chant Om three times, it is a practice to differentiate the dream state from the awake state; something to honor oneself, to honor God, to honor the day.

Meditation, Reading, Affirmations: At times, I meditate in bed right when I wake up to make sure I get it done. Listening to the birds, watching the sunrise, or gazing out at the sky or a tree can connect you to something bigger than yourself and bring peace and alignment. I have books by my bed to inspire me. Try closing your eyes, ask the book for a personal message for today, and open it to a random place. When I do this practice, nine times out of ten, the passage I read will "coincidentally" be meaningful to the course of the day. Read your affirmations. Throughout the course of this book we have crafted affirmations to reinforce our new thought forms, creations and behaviors. This is a perfect time of the day to, either lie in bed and read them out loud to yourself, or to say them while standing in front of the mirror.

Journaling: Upon waking, take out your journal and write at least three pages, uncensored, especially if you have had a vivid dream. Recall the people and places that appeared in the dream; what were you doing in the dream; and what feelings it evoked in you. These recollections can be instrumental to the Psyche Detective. If your feelings from the dream state are not acknowledged and cleared out, they can be carried like a cloud over your head throughout the day. Examine and express your feelings in your journal. Also, write free associations about random thoughts, to help you be more in touch with your Self and your Spirit.

Gratitude

In your journal, write, or say out loud, three or more things for which you are grateful. Make it part of your practice that upon waking, you think of a minimum of three things you are grateful for today. You can also create a gratitude journal. At times when I am feeling especially grateful, I sit and give thanks and create an entire gratitude list. Any time I feel a dip in my energy, I pull out my gratitude journal for inspiration. Acknowledge your gratefulness for ... this body, my health, this breath, this home, the loves in my life, my consciousness. Gratitude is a way to connect with your Self and your Highest Self. It is a way to say thank you to God for all the good in your life. Approaching the day from a place of gratitude is an important way to connect. Whatever you put your attention on expands. So if you emphasize the good in your life, it expands. When your mind focuses on what you do not have, or what is not working, it is a great idea to review your gratitude list of good. Read it periodically, add to it, change it, update it. Practicing gratitude is a simple way to expand your prosperity, open up your mind, acknowledge yourself, acknowledge God, know yourself, love yourself, and be open to even more abundance by focusing on the good. Another way I reinforce my gratitude is to speak my gratitude out loud while walking. "Thank you for the trees, birds. Thank you for my breath, my energy!"

Daily Visualization: This technique will be described in more depth in the Create section. It deserves to be here, as well, since it is such an important practice for a morning routine. Regularly, I imagine a vision for my day.

It can be as simple or detailed as you like, and when there are important events occurring, where I want to see a specific outcome, I will go so far as to write out my vision for the day. Basically, what you are doing here is placing your order with the Universe. You are putting your preferences out there, consciously co-creating with the Divine. Review in your mind all you really want to accomplish and decide in your mind the absolute "best case scenario" that you can envision for the circumstances. Write, speak or imagine your intention or vision for the day. For example, when I have an important business meeting, I will state my intention for that meeting. The statement is in present tense, as if this is already occurring. So my vision might look something like: "I have an extremely successful business meeting with Jim and the results far surpass my original expectation!" Then you would add details that you specifically would want to see happen. Or you might set the intention to stay peaceful and calm when you talk to your mother today. Instead of allowing the day to just unfold on its own, by putting forth your specific intention in a visualization, you connect with your Self and Spirit as a co-creative force.

Speak Your Vision: As we begin to re-design our lives and deal more with the Create portion of this book, you will craft a Vision for your life. Reading your vision first thing in the morning is a powerful way to begin every day. It will work like an affirmation, stated in the positive, and the present. To speak your vision is to inspire you to create the life you desire.

Praying at your Altar: Praying at your alter is another powerful way to begin your day. I sometimes sit in front of my altar and do breathing exercises, pray, meditate and ask for guidance. This is your sacred space that you have created to connect with Spirit. If you have very little time, just being in front of your altar and taking in this sacred energy can enhance your day, align you with your Self and deepen your connection.

Sunrise Meditation: Indigenous peoples and the Priestesses of the Goddess temples would arise at sunrise to do their rituals. This time was chosen because of the powerful energy available to them to enhance their ceremony. By rising early, you can use this power for yourself. Ideally, you choose a place outside to sit where you can see the rising sun. If that is not possible, face East. Take a few moments and center yourself. I create a grounding cord to connect to the earth. Do a short meditation or take some deep breaths. I lift my arms and envision that I am gathering in the energy of the sunrise. I close my eyes and visualize the colors of the sun unfolding before me. I am pulling in these colors and beauty into all the areas of my body, all my cells, especially the places in my body that need healing. This is a good time to call in the Four Directions tapping into the vibration and power animals as you move around in the circle. Honoring Mother Earth and Father Sky will align you with the power of these forces. I bless the planet and ask for protection and blessings for myself and my loved ones. Then I thank the Universe for the divine fulfillment now. It sets a wonderful energy for the blessed day.

Guided Visualizations and Music: Sometimes it is difficult to do your own guided visualizations. We have several visualizations on my website, www. cindypaine.com, so if you have a favorite, make it a part of your morning routine. Music is also a great tool to raise your vibration. Pick a piece of classical or new age music that inspires you and uplifts you as you do some of these techniques.

Grounding Technique: A grounding cord is a great way to anchor some of the energy that will be raised by these spiritual and emotional techniques. Using a grounding cord upon waking can also help you feel more in your body and connected to the earth.

Shielding Techniques: Shielding is as simple as putting a bubble of light around you. It is great to do after you meditate or after you have cleared your energy. It is a way of holding in the good energy and refracting or bouncing the negative energy or other people's energy off you that you don't want to absorb throughout the day.

Reflect and Create Your Own Morning Rituals: It really flavors the day when one experiences any or all of these techniques and takes the time for one Self. Go through the techniques listed and circle the things you would be willing to do. Try to do the practice of at least one per day and build up. Write down five things that bring you peace, centering and grounding, so that you can begin to interject your own ideas into your morning routine. Begin to wake up a little earlier so you are not rushed. Give yourself a minimum of 20 minutes to a half hour. Do not turn on the TV or radio. Write down your experiences both about how this has affected you and how your interactions with others have changed by starting your day in a different way.

CREATE

CHAPTER 20

Creating Is Sacred

The act of Creating is sacred. While on this path of Self-Love, we have learned that we are designed to be in harmony with our Divinity. We are awakening to who we really are, the vessel that holds the Divine – a physical being having a spiritual experience. We are sacred beings and deserve to be loved and honored and to awaken to our true essence and to our true potential. We are learning to love and appreciate that presence within. We have cleared and connected and anchored that connection, and now we are at the place on our journey where it is time to practice creating from a place of Self-Love. Congratulations! We are at the journey's core. We are in divine relationship with Self, and consciously playing in the creation field. We are here to create, we are creative beings. We are the creator in action, in physical form. You have been given free will to play in the physical universe and to create. As a manifestation and a reflection of God, the Creator, our job here and now on this planet is to create - our mandate from the Source is to co-create with the Divine and awaken to who we are.

To create is the impulse to cause something out of nothing. To create is the action of accessing the energy of Source, based upon our heart's desire. If it is in accordance with the highest good for us and others, it will form into matter. All of us are always creating all of the time - consciously or unconsciously. So, basically, we can receive what we desire, or we can get what we do not want. Creating consciously is a much more powerful experience than creating unconsciously, not to mention that the end result is better. Conscious creation allows our heart energy and desire to cause experiences or things to come into physical manifestation. Real creation is happening all of the time. We are creating with our speech, our thoughts, our attitudes, our feelings, and the way we walk in the world. You can look at your life and see what you have created. If you do not like what you see, you need to *cause* something different. Are you creating what you desire or are you creating out of fear? Are you creating consciously or unconsciously?

Most of us spend much of our time in survival, to maintain the status quo of our lives. We are playing a game here in this universe. Sometimes we forget it is a game and that it is supposed to be fun and easy. Some of us forget that we have the ability to co-create the outcome and we get too caught up in the drama, the suffering. The suffering comes when we forget it is a game. We sometimes get attached to our humanness and forget who we really are. We forget how powerful we are. Herein lies the lack of Self-Love. We will berate ourselves, when we do not create what we want, or we blame others, ourselves, and God... and we suffer.

As you nurture and treat yourself better, and as you clear your psyche and connect to the Source from where your essence comes, you have become aware of the truth – the truth of your power. Now, you are ready to create and do it from a lightness of being that is aware of the truth. Manifestation comes from this much higher place of connection, not from the survival mind, a place of fear or lack of trust.

What is True Abundance?

Abundance is not just physical things – money, houses, cars, and toys. All of these things may give you a certain amount of pleasure, however, this is not what the creation game is about. True abundance is our natural state of being. True abundance is a state of being along this path of self-awareness. When I experience true abundance, I am vibrating at my highest level of awareness and consciousness. I am connected to Source. I know in the deepest part of my being that I am co-creating my experience, that who and what I am is Source, God, whatever you want to call it. I am in a higher vibration and energy. I am at peace. I am in joy. I am trusting from my heart, and soul. I know that I can create whatever I desire for my highest good. That is true abundance. The physical manifestations are a reflection, a *result* of that state of being. They are the outcome, the effect of operating from that state of being; from that highest vibration. You will get the appearance of the physical manifestation when you are at that level of consciousness. When you are fully resonating with the Divine, that is true abundance and getting there is the Self-Love journey. From that place of being, your true heart's desire of a great relationship, optimal health, financial freedom and connection with the Divine will manifest with ease. All of it will be a natural outcome of your state of being. How do we get there? By doing exactly what we have been doing, clearing and connecting and taking the Self-Love path!

Deserving

The dictionary definition of deserving is, "to be worthy of," Ask yourself, "who decides what I am worthy of?" *You do!* What you feel you deserve is something most people never reflect upon, yet this decision we make about our lives is operating in the background, constantly, affecting what we attract and what we create. I have spent a lot of time looking at the so called "haves and have-nots." When you examine what people create and you look at their relationship to deserving, it tells a profound story. When people do not feel they deserve good, their lives and their outer manifestation reflects that.

Examining Our Deserving

Below are common messages from childhood related to deserving that still may be operating in your consciousness which illustrate the full deserving spectrum. See if any of these circumstances sound familiar to you. At one end of the spectrum, we have a person that has a severe issue around deserving and their life reflects that conflict within. They say they want a new house and a great relationship and good health, but their life and their choices, do not reflect that. This person might feel they need to be punished for something they did in their life, or they might have a negative belief about themselves. They may have a belief that they have to work really hard to make a living, or they may have come from a childhood where they rarely saw anyone succeed or prosper. In the middle of the deserving spectrum, we have the person who feels they deserve very little or just enough. This person might have issues around abundance being bad because of a religious belief (you are holier if you are poor), or because they feel they have been selfish and not deserving of good. This person may feel, for example, "if it was good enough for my dad to earn a meager income, it is good enough for me." With these unconscious messages operating in our psyche's background, it is difficult to break through and manifest beyond what we feel we deserve. On the opposite end of the spectrum, we see people, seemingly effortlessly, manifest the ideal job, high salary, perfect relationship and vital health. This person believes they *deserve* all of these things and their life reflects it. If you were to look more closely, they may have certain areas of their lives that are challenging and their deeper beliefs may not be *as deserving* in those areas. If you desire something in your life and you are having difficulty manifesting it, look at where you are in the spectrum around deserving that thing. We all have a full spectrum of feelings, thoughts and beliefs around deserving and worthiness which need to be examined before going into the manifestation process.

So the question becomes, if I do not have an ingrained, healthy sense of deserving, how do I get one? The next exercise will help you to examine and begin to clear your deserving spectrum.

Exercise to Increase Your Deserving

In the Clearing chapters, we removed the blocks that may have been in your way of manifesting that which you desire. Now, in the Create process, you may need to revisit the Clearing and Connecting chapters to see if you have issues around deserving. Like I offered you in the Clearing chapter, you can analyze this for yourself by writing down your history regarding deserving and the thoughts and beliefs you may have created as a result. Then write down the opposing belief or affirmation and say it out loud to yourself for thirty days. Do not place any negative judgments on yourself because you may have to go back Clearing for the area of deserving. This step, Clearing to Create, is the most important step to getting what you desire, and the step where most people get tripped up. My goal is for you to have an unfettered path for your intentions to manifest.

- **Read through the following examples of deserving statements. Take some time for yourself and develop your own statements of deserving in each of these areas. If you feel a "charge" on any of the statements below, practice some of the following exercises related to Deserving or go back to Clearing and begin to heal this area before moving forward in the Creation process.**

Statements of Deserving:

Relationship:
- I deserve to be treated really well in all my relationships.
- I deserve for my partner to be in integrity.
- I deserve great friends.
- I deserve family members that are loving and supportive.
- I deserve a great community.

Money/Career:
- I deserve financial abundance.
- I deserve financial independence.
- I deserve financial integrity.
- I deserve peace of mind around my finances.
- I deserve a job that is fulfilling.
- I deserve to have passion about my job daily.
- I deserve a workplace that is supportive and nurtures and stimulates me.
- I deserve opportunities that keep expanding.

Health/Wellness:

* I deserve to be healthy!
* I deserve to thrive (not just survive)!
* I deserve to feel sexy and attractive with a fit body.

Spirituality:

* I deserve peace!
* I deserve to grow spiritually and to be surrounded by other like-minded people.
* I deserve to be inspired daily through nature, reading, and music.
* I deserve joy and bliss and ever-expanding consciousness.

The Abundance Barometer

What you attract through the Law of Attraction is your deep, deep knowing of what is natural for you to attract. What you *think* you deserve, is what you get. What you *feel* you deserve, is what you get. I would like to introduce the concept of an esoteric tool that we will call an Abundance Barometer. The Abundance Barometer, if it existed, would show us what our level of "believed deserving" was in each of the areas. If you feel you do not really deserve much, there would be a direct equation from the Abundance Barometer to what you asked for in life. People that have issues around what they deserve also have the issue of not asking for enough. These people will just get enough to pay their bills, never even entertaining the idea of financial independence. If you grew up around poverty, where no one is succeeding, how do you stretch your Abundance Barometer?

Self-Love

Every time you are more loving to yourself, forgive yourself, and fall in love with yourself, you deepen your level of deserving. When we exhibit what I call a "stinginess of spirit" for our own Self, it causes our ability to attract to shrink. Repeat the Falling in Love with Yourself Exercise in Connecting (page 170). By revisiting all of your amazing attributes, gifts, and abilities, I hope you will realize you are worthy of so much more! When you are clear about what you deserve and you have connected with what you authentically feel you deserve, then the key going forward is not to compromise. When you lower your standards, you demonstrate to the universe, yourself, and others, that you deserve less. Do not lower your standards! If you have a conscious standard, a requirement, of reciprocal love, and that is what you feel you deserve and that is what you give, then that is what you require, and anything less than that is a "no."

Look in the areas where you are clear that you deserve the best. These will be the areas of your life where you effortlessly manifest all you desire and need. Maybe you have a really great supportive circle of friends and family and you have a beautiful home that nurtures you and keeps you safe and warm. Ask yourself, "why do I know that I deserve in this area?" Maybe you were brought up in a beautiful home with close family. These things came naturally for you. If the opposite is true, and your grew up in a broken home without a loving family, you may have been determined growing up that you wanted something different, so without even thinking about it, you knew you *deserved* better, and you created that for yourself!

When you notice an area in your life that is more difficult for you to manifest what you desire, creating in that area can bring you much closer to Source. It is never a loss. Whatever area you are having difficulty creating in, always will point to a possibility for healing in that area, that which needs clearing from the past or a belief or a decision that needs tweaking. Sometimes, we think there must be a problem with us because we are unable to create abundance in a certain area. In our humanness, we may tell ourselves, *I will never have enough*, or, *my life is a struggle.* Instead, there can be a powerful shift, if we hold it as, *I do have abundance in these areas, and I am open to learning and receiving in this other area.* Or, you may acknowledge, *I am challenged in this area and I ask for guidance and support.* Now you have an opportunity for healing.

In the next chapters, we will get very clear about what we desire to create. It is easy to say, "Yes, I deserve more," but is that really true for you?

Make sure that when you do your intention with all of these thoughts around deserving-ness that you do not just add ten or twenty percent to what you feel you deserve now. Our intentions are not based on what we currently think is possible. For example, our desires are not based upon what you are currently making or based on the economy. What I want you to do here is to *stretch beyond to the miraculous!* Expand the limits! The practice of resetting our Abundance Barometer is not something that happens overnight. Take the time to expand your deserving-ness in each area of your life.

When we are not sure what we deserve and we are not sure what we desire, we give ourselves and the Universe mixed messages, and our Abundance Barometer reflects that. When we expand our Abundance Barometer and know we are worthy of more and more, then better and better manifestations occur. When we allow ourselves to deserve more, we hold our relationship with Self as sacred. We are committing loving acts to our Self and the Divine. We continue to clear and connect, and the circle of manifestation becomes complete. All of these steps raise our vibration. That, coupled with our clarity of intent, and single minded focus, goes out into the universe and draws back to us what we desire. The clearer the path, originating in the place of Self-Love, honors one's sacredness. As we know all that we DESERVE, the universe brings forth your heart's desire in physical form.

CHAPTER 21

Expanding

Giving Exercise

This exercise will help you expand your Abundance Barometer. The actions to give and receive start the action of creating. You can do the following exercise anytime your manifestations are slow to come in, or at the beginning of the creation process. When we manifest more abundance we have more to give and to help others. Beginning the process by giving is a little like putting the cart before the horse, playing the game backwards. By giving first, we start the energetic flow of magnetizing our good. Plus, the act of giving makes us feel better, and puts us in the vibration of attraction.

Giving to someone else, even if you have nothing to give, begins the process. Go in your garden and give a flower to someone. If you do not have a garden, pick a bunch of dandelions and tie them with a piece of ribbon, or place them in a glass jar. Pay for the person behind you at the toll booth. Let someone go ahead of you in line at the grocery store or cafeteria. Practice little acts of kindness towards others for 30 days. Giving something of yourself everyday brings in the abundance and puts you in a high vibration of joy. Ask yourself, "What can I give today?"

Many people, when looking at creating abundance for themselves feel a moral aversion to having a lot of money or material wealth. I have heard people say, "movie stars and athletes should not make so much money when other people have so little." My response to that would be, if you are someone that really wants to make a difference in the world, wouldn't it be easier if you had a lot of abundance to share? Something to consider... Many people are pushing their abundance away because they hold negative beliefs around having much.

Giving to Expand the Abundance Barometer

Here are some lists you can make to begin to expand your Abundance Barometer.

- List what acts of kindness and service you could do to help others.
- List what you could and would do if you had as much money as you can imagine.
- What can you give to yourself today?
- What can you do for your friends and family today?
- What can you do for your co-workers and the people you meet today?

Receiving

Many people know how to give, and they are blocked in the area of receiving. When you have a block to receive, very little can come in. To the degree you are open to receive is the degree to which love and material items can come to you. We are trained by religious and societal beliefs, such as, "it is right and good to be a giving person." Notice there is no emphasis on receiving. I see it as a circle. You have energy coming out from you as the giver. Imagine it like an arrow going from you out and forming a semi-circle. When you are only a giver, half the circle is missing. There is no energy coming back to you in the form of receiving. Many of us have over-emphasized the giving part and we do not get the receiving part. Thus, we do not get what we want. We are not open to receive. Giving and receiving forms a full circle. You can visualize all day long; however, until you are open to receive, it will not come to you. It is difficult to be an open, expanded visionary being, if you have limiting beliefs from your past.

◆   **Ask yourself these questions to make sure you are clear to receive: Do you need to clear anything from your past around an incident of receiving? Were you ever in a situation where you did not receive what you deserved? Did you ever settle for less than you deserved?**

This experience can create a block to your flow of abundance. We need to learn how to expand our ability to receive our good. The following exercise expands your Abundance Barometer, and opens you to receive, so you can manifest in larger ways.

Giving and Receiving Exercise

 This exercise requires a partner or you can speak it into a tape recorder for yourself (when doing this alone, you would play the role of the "giver" and when you play it back, you would be the role of "receiver"). When you work in pairs, one of you will be giving and the other will be receiving. Sit across from each other. In doing the exercise you will both have your awareness on your chest area or heart region. Begin by breathing into that area and consciously envisioning expanding that part of your physical body. Close your eyes and take a couple of deep breaths. Breathe slowly and deeply and make a sound of exhalation. Do this 3 times. Get centered. Find that quiet place within yourself. Get grounded and connected, bringing your Self back into this moment now – a clear space in which to express and to listen. Get quiet and connect with your Higher Self with an intention to expand your ability to give and receive.

When you are ready, open your eyes and pick an A (giver) and B (receiver).

A's job is to give the gifts to B. B's job is to be the receiver of the gifts and to listen. As the giver, you will be offering gifts to your partner that come from your own inspiration, allowing the universe to inspire you to speak these gifts to your partner. Say the first thing that comes to your mind, be expansive, do not limit yourself to what is possible, or what you think the other person would like. For the giver it expands their ability to be generous and to be inspired to give. Oftentimes the receiver will be amazed at how attuned the giver is in his gifts, how perfect the gifts are. When you truly are open to messages from the Universe without censoring those messages, you are allowing that divinely inspired intuition to come forth. Allow your crown chakra at the top of your head to open up and receive the inspiration of what B needs and would love. The inspiration comes down through the head and out through the throat. It can be material things, emotional, and spiritual attributes. The giver should also keep coaching the receiver to keep opening up, keep breathing and keep expanding his/her heart center. This exercise can be very powerful for both the giver and the receiver.

As the receiver your job is to open to receive the gifts that you are given. The giver has his/her conscious attention on the crown chakra, and you have your attention on the heart and chest area. As the giver is lavishing you with amazing gifts of abundance from the universe, your job is to accept them, to take them all in, and to vision yourself from your heart area, being, doing and having all of these gifts, qualities, and attributes. Your job is to remain present while the gifts are being lavished upon you. As you are doing this exercise, you may feel a tightening in your chest. Do you feel like hunching over? Do you have thoughts like "I don't deserve this" or I am not good enough" or "This is too much... too good for me... too big." If you feel like shutting down or wanting to resist, this is normal. Ask the giver to pause a moment, notice for yourself what was said that caused your heart to constrict, and where you still have blocks to receiving your good, and make a mental note to have your Psyche Detective investigate this area at a later time. Keep expanding. Keep breathing into your heart. Keep opening up to receive the gifts. Open your eyes and share your experience. Now switch and do the process over again. At the end of this process, share again.

If you are doing this for yourself into a tape recorder, make a list of all the things you desire to create in your life. Think outside the box, really let your imagination go! Say, "I am giving you the gift of _____(ex. unlimited wealth, peace, love, quiet, travel...)" Pause after each one, keep going until you feel complete. When finished, close your eyes and feel what it is like to give that much to another, feel the energy in your body as being the giver. Play back yourself giving the gifts and feel what it is like to be the receiver. Journal your experience.

This is a really good exercise to start the process of manifestation. You will feel empowered as you have stretched that deserving, receiving and giving muscle that has been contracted. This process will expand your ability to receive your good. The Universe is a naturally abundant place. We just have blocks to receive it. When you stretch and expand to know that you deserve abundance, you will come into the realization that this is an abundant universe and be much more open to receive your good.

The Emerald Temple – Treasure Room

We are generally stingy with ourselves with what we expect and feel we deserve, not only in terms of money, material items, and from true abundance like love and joy. This meditation will allow you to keep expanding your ability to have and receive large amounts of abundance in every area of your life, continuing to stretch that Abundance Barometer. Emerald green is associated with the heart chakra and healing. It is also the color of money and its meaning relates to abundance of all kinds. It is fascinating that true abundance is directly related to our heart's desire. This is significant because as you are in the creation process, always "think" or center yourself in your heart and not your head. We will be working with this color to fill our being. Record this meditation for yourself and play it back.

Sit down, close your eyes and take a few breaths to get into a relaxed state. Let go of your day and get into this moment now! Glance up with your eyes closed and imagine a ball of emerald green shimmering light above your head, focusing on that color and light. Imagine from that ball comes a shaft of emerald green light from the ball to your crown chakra. See it filling your eyes, nose, and cheeks as your entire head is filled with the emerald green light. Bring that light down into your throat, the front, sides, and back of your throat are filled with green energy. Bring it down into your heart, and allow your heart to be bathed in this healing vibration, clearing away any blocks that are ready to go. Bring it down into the solar plexus, into the stomach and organs, pelvis, hips and flowing down both legs into the knees, and ankles, filling the feet and send that emerald green light out your toes. Imagine that every inch of your being is filled to the brim with the emerald green energy. Bring it up the back of the legs, thighs, buttocks area and bring it up the back of the spine, one vertebra at a time, covering your back like a beautiful green blanket. Allow it to go up the back of your neck, head, and out the top of your head. Imagine a bubble of light around your body and the bubble is emerald green. Take a breath and presence yourself in the emerald green energy.

Imagine your special elevator appears before you. It is iridescent in the colors of the rainbow. Step inside it and notice the numbers from one to twelve. Press twelve and watch the numbers light up as you are lifted off the ground into the clouds. One, two, three... you are above the trees and into the sky. Four, five, six, you are above the clouds. Seven, eight, nine, you are into the stars. Ten, eleven and twelve, you land on an emerald green star landing pad. Step out of the elevator, knowing it will be there upon your return. You begin to walk along the iridescent pathway before you. You see the Emerald Temple glowing in the distance. Upon getting closer, you notice there are many steps up to the doorway to this temple. Begin to climb the steps, look down and notice your feet as you are climbing. With each step, you feel lighter and climb higher, up, up, up until you finally reach the doorway to the Temple. You walk through the doorway and one of your guides or angels may be there to greet you. Notice their appearance and you can ask their name if you like. Either way, you will be guided to the corridors of this temple. There are many special rooms in the Emerald Green Temple but you are guided to a special room called the Treasure Room. As you walk through the doorway, notice all of the beauty before you. Picture the incredible jewels, precious metals, gorgeous clothes; more than you could ever use. See yourself being given everything you could ever want, in much greater quantity than you could ever wish for. Enjoy it thoroughly. There are tables full of jewels and diamonds of every size and color. You pick them up and play with them, touch them, hold them, and delight in their shimmering colors and texture. You are handed a bag, so you can choose the most beautiful items and bring them with you. As you leave that area, you move to the other side of the room with beautiful fabrics and clothes. You try on whatever you like and choose which clothes you would like to take with you as well. You have fun frolicking in all of this abundance. As you leave this area, you see another table that has beautiful gift boxes. They are labeled with words like Joy, Divine Health, Agelessness, Nurturing, Great Success, Fulfillment in Career, Romance, and Intimacy. You think for a moment, what does my heart desire now? You pick up a box labeled Heart's Desire and settle into a luxurious comfortable chair. You close your eyes, and take a breath. As you lift open the lid to the Heart's Desire box, you open your eyes. A light shines from within the box and a three dimensional hologram is projected before you. What do you see? Enjoy the hologram of your Heart's Desire. When the projection is completed, close the lid to the box and add it to your bottomless bag to take home with you. Gather up each of these gift boxes that represent the areas of your life that you are ready to expand and enjoy. You are overjoyed and your heart feels like it is going to burst with excitement.

You are now ready to leave this room and you walk along the corridor and are guided to another special room in the Emerald Temple. As you enter the room, you see a large round pool in the center of the room with glistening, emerald-colored water. Around the room, there are all sizes of shining, awe-inspiring, emeralds. The room has an amazing energy of healing and abundance. You are guided to the pool area where you disrobe and step into a pool of warm, glistening emerald color water. As you immerse yourself, you feel any residual negative energy, fears, blocks, or anything holding you back from your total abundance, release into the pool. The emerald waters absorb these energies and fill you with the highest vibration of effortless manifestation. You stay for a few minutes, bathing and filling yourself with this healing energy, allowing yourself to have the emerald waters fill every cell, once and for all. cleansing your aura of *any negativity. As you feel this process complete you slowly stand up and get out of the pool where a beautiful robe, customized just for you is lying on a chaise lounge by the pool. You dry off and put on this robe that is made of otherworldly and incredibly beautiful material. Notice the colors and the fabric. This is your new abundance energy robe which you can put on at any time in the future. You leave the room wearing your abundance robe and as you move towards the doorway of the Emerald Temple, you see a beautiful shaft of white and gold light. You are drawn to this light, a light so bright like you have never seen before. Your guides tell you to step into this light and stand for a few minutes absorbing the energies of pure Source! You stand in the light, open to receive. While you stand in the light, ask your guides what you need to do to experience your heart's desire? Wait for the answer. Ask any other questions. After a few minutes, step out of the light, thank your guides, and walk through the doorway and begin your descent down the steps. Down, down, down the steps you descend. With each step down you are more grounded and feel more of your physical being, finally reaching the bottom step. Walk along the iridescent pathway until you see your elevator in the distance. You reach the elevator and step inside and see the numbers from 1 to 12 and you press number one. Your elevator begins its descent from the emerald landing pad, down through the stars as the numbers go from twelve, eleven, ten, nine, eight... into the clouds, seven, six, five, four... above the trees, three, two, and one... landing gently in your back yard. Step out of the elevator as it disappears. Imagine it is a warm spring day, kick off your shoes and dig your toes into the earth. Wiggle your feet and heels and imagine roots growing from the bottom of your feet that go all the way down deep into Mother Earth. Your roots connect you with Mother Earth, bring you into the present time, and bring you all the energy gifts you received from you journey. Take a breath, and open your eyes. Welcome back!*

Heart's Desire

Your Highest Self or soul comes in to this physical existence with a purpose, an agenda. There are certain contracts that you are here on this planet to fulfill. Your heart is like a compass that directs you to your soul's purpose.

When you know your heart's desire, and are doing, acting, and speaking from that place, you are aligned with the Divine. One of the best steps we can take on this Self-Love journey is to be acutely attuned to our heart's *true* desire. This will accelerate the process to alignment with the Divine, fulfillment of our purpose, and of course, blissful happiness. Your heart's desire is very important in the Creation Process; creation begins with the desire. When you are acting from the place of your true heart's desire, you are in sync and flow with the Divine; you are not taking many missteps. This is conscious creating! Many times we create from a place of what we think we *should do* or what we think we *should want* or from what we were *told* we should want. These desires are *from the neck up* – your mental concept. That is not your true heart's desire. Your heart's desire is made up of all your dreams. What is your true, authentic, aligned with purpose wish? It is important that you are honest with yourself about what you really, truly, in your heart of hearts, DESIRE. It requires that you go into your heart, connect with your true essence, and take a look at what you want your life to look like.

Discovering Your Heart's Desire

What if you do not know your heart's desire? That is o.k., we are on this path to discover our heart's desire. You might journal everyday and ask yourself the question, *What is it I really, really, really desire?* Ask your Highest Self, guides, Masters and teachers to show you what it is you should be and would enjoy doing. You can do this for all the different areas in your life generally, or specifically for one area, for instance, *What is my true heart's desire for relationship?* Wait to hear the answer. Have paper and pen handy and write what comes to you. The answers you receive may surprise you, allow for that. Hang out with your answers for a week or so and feel into it. *What would it be like if (blank) happened? What if (blank) was completely different than what I thought I wanted? What would that feel like or look like?* Did you get any feelings or impulses or images from the Emerald Temple? Conscious breathing and meditation are two more ways to your heart's desire. As we are truly quiet, we listen and learn our heart's desire. One of the purposes of all our clearing was to remove much of our unnecessary and/or detrimental chatter. We cleared to make room for the connection to the Divine and be able to actually hear what is being said, by the guides, Highest Self and soul. Make sure you are in as clear a state of mind as possible when you sit down to do this. You may want to even write out or speak what is going on in your life, and tell yourself that you will deal with all of it at a later time, but not now. Clear the decks! Sit quietly in that clear space and ask! The more you do this process, just like any other muscle, you will get better and better at it, and it will be easier to get to your true heart's desire. The Divine lives in the heart and when you connect in that place, and come from your true essence, you will answer the question for yourself from within.

How do we know if something is our true heart's desire? How do we know if it is in alignment with our soul's purpose? Knowing yourself, learning to love yourself and honoring your unique imprint on the planet enables you to tune into the higher frequencies of your authentic real mission. It is a good practice to close your eyes and think about your heart's desire and see yourself being, doing or living your heart's desire, and see how it feels in your body. There is a feeling associated with a full-body yes, and there is a feeling associated with maybe and no. Yes feels joyful, alive, energized and exciting. Yes feels good. Anything other than that is not a yes. If you are waffling and wavering it is a no. We do not always know whether we are living our heart's desire, or if we are in alignment with our soul's purpose, because we can only see from a limited perspective. Something may feel so right, in the moment, that you are absolutely 100% sure it is a part of your soul's path. If you feel it is a definite yes, then it is worth following that path wherever it leads you, even if it ultimately leads to a no manifestation or a creation in different timing than you had planned. Saying, "yes" and going for it, will keep you moving forward on your true heart's desire journey. This is the journey and ongoing process of Self-Love.

Your Consciousness Evolving

As you further evolve, continuing to do the techniques and processes, you will move up to higher levels of consciousness. Just like when you learn a new skill, like multiplication tables, for instance, you have that knowledge for the rest of your life. You may forget, for a moment, but the knowledge is always there. Consciousness works the same way. Once you know better, you do better, and you will feel better. You cannot go backwards in consciousness. You will recognize when you begin to come from old beliefs, your lower self, or ego. As you are working on the Clear, Connect and Create Formula, you will notice that as your consciousness evolves, so will your heart's desires. As you deepen who you are and become more clear, what you desire and what you manifest changes. As you move further from the desire to accumulate, control and manipulate, you move closer to living in the flow and being open to receive. You evolve from "not my will" to "thy will be done." You will not come from a place of what can I get, but how can I serve? From that place of service, comes that higher connection of Self-Love and Spirit – full circle. Sometimes, you may forget and have moments when you act from that lower place of consciousness or lower vibration. Eventually, you will remember and your consciousness will rise. As we enter the creation process, you may want to manifest the fancy car or more money than you need, and there is no judgment, here. The creation process works the same way. But, know, as you move to higher levels of consciousness your heart's desire will change and evolve with it.

CHAPTER 22

Opening to Create

We Are Ready to Create... But Wait

When we think we know what our heart's desire is, and we feel we are ready to create something new: such as a new home, business, job; writing a book; developing a website; a new relationship; the actual process of creation is a courageous act. When we are not in a place of connectedness, we can dream and vision and prepare to make our dream a reality, however, I suggest you wait until you feel connected. Being connected with your Self, feeling inspired by God, brings in aliveness and joy, vitality, vibrancy and the light of yourself forward. Doors will open, connections will be made. If you are not in alignment, it is more difficult to manifest and may take longer or not manifest at all. Getting into Connection with your Self and Source is the first step along the process of manifestation. It is necessary to prepare the way for your creation. Here are some suggestions to prepare the way...

Creating a Void

One of the first things we need to do as we begin to create is to make room. When you toss a pebble out into the lake, the ripples come back to you. If you toss out your pebble and it hits a branch or a rock, the ripples do not come back in the same way. This analogy describes how your intentions work. When you have an intention to create something and you are ready to "toss it out" to the Universe, make sure you have cleared out the rocks and branches, so your intention does not fall with a "thud" or get stopped. You want to create a void so that your intention can go out and come back to you like the ripples in the lake. If there is no void, the energy that you send out cannot come back. Creating a void is integral to the creation process because you cannot create on top of something else. In Clearing we worked on removing the weeds, rocks, and bramble of our psyches before planting our seeds. Creating a void is an extension of the clearing process. Clearing space helps to ensure that our intentions will come back to us like the ripples in a lake. When there is a void, the Universe rushes in to fill it. The Universe abhors a void. So when you have cleared space for your intentions to come back to you, the Universe will more easily respond with your manifestation.

Inventory Exercise

 We begin to create a void by taking an inventory of our life. I recommend that you take an inventory when you begin the creation process or any time you feel like things are not moving or flowing. Perhaps you are not getting that job; you are not receiving the money you are due; you are not creating the loving relationships you desire.

Step 1: Go through your address book.

Step 2: Read each name and think about that person and feel if there is any "charge" there.
* Is there any communication that I have withheld from this person?
* Am I in some way out of integrity with this person?
By going through your address book and making a list of the people you need to speak with, you are clearing your relationships.

Step 3: Consider what you want to do about these situations. You should forgive yourself and/or take some action to clear any blocks. These people or situations are blocks and may be acting as a boulder in your lake. By addressing each of the people you may be out of integrity with or by taking some action to clear, creates the void. When you have things that need to be cleared, it consciously or unconsciously occupies space in your mind, body, and soul – so we need to inventory the physical, mental, emotional, and the energetic. That pebble cannot go out and come back free and clear if there is something stuck in any of these areas. Take whatever action you need to clear any and all of your relationships.

Step 4: Look at your finances. Is there anyone you owe money? If you cannot pay the whole amount back now, call and set up a payment plan. Handle that which needs handling. Life does not just happen to you. There is something in your space that is clogging up the demonstration of your manifestation. When you clear up your space, and create a void, you will be amazed at how things start to move. You will see velocity occurring in your manifestation.

Clearing your Physical Space

Sometimes when you walk into a room, the air feels thick and the atmosphere does not feel good. Thought forms, negativity, fear, anger and stale energy can get trapped in a physical space. If you are creating something new, one of the first things to do is to clear your physical space. You may not yet be attuned to the lower vibrational or dark energy that you come in contact with, but just assume it is there. Taking the steps to clear it, demonstrates to the Universe your intention to create. This technique can be used anytime you enter into a new space. I do this regularly throughout my life; anytime I have a new living space, office or am staying in a hotel; anytime I feel a dark energy; anytime I have experienced any type of upset in my home. Water, salt and sage all have their value of cleaning and clearing. I mostly use sage. Sage is a sacred herb of indigenous people used to clear your space, aura and objects of any undesirable energy (not the sage you cook with). Buy yourself a sage stick, which you can purchase online, at a health food store or a metaphysical book store. Be focused that your intention is to clear the space. Out loud or in your mind. repeat the phrase, "I bless and dissipate," just as we did when we were clearing our chakras, you can also use the phrase, "I clear and release." First walk around the entire perimeter of the house with a lit sage stick. You want to have a continuous stream of smoke, making sure that every corner is touched and permeated by the smoke. Do that until you have come full circle. Inside the house, let the smoke into every room, closets, showers, passing through doorways, and (if the weather allows), through open windows. Repeat your mantra, "I bless and dissipate," and just let the smoke clear the energy.

We are going to go through your physical space two times. The first time was for cleansing the space, purifying and creating the void, and the second time is for sending out your intentions. Before you begin the second time through, take a moment and make a list of the qualities you desire to surround you. For example, you might want to have more harmony or peace in your relationships; you might want more abundance, more joy and aliveness. Any attributes your heart desires to manifest in your home, you can put into your space via your conscious intention. Your mantra as you walk around the perimeter and through your home the second time is your repeated intention. For example, "I am peace, I am health, I have more abundance, I have loving relationships." Get into the habit of doing this regularly to keep your space clear.

Other Ways to Create a Void

- Pay bills
- Outflow and circulate your energy by volunteering or helping another
- Clean your house
- Clean up your communications
- Get rid of things that you are not using
- Clean up your integrity
- Forgive yourself and others
- Make up any other ways you can think of to create a void and do a couple of them. See what happens!

Clearing the Body Temple

You can either do this clearing by itself for your own purposes or as part of a larger, more involved ritual. I clear the physical space of my body temple similar to the way I clear my home. If I have just gone through a troubling time or handled a major issue, or if I have been around someone negative, I clear my physical body to get more centered and grounded in my body. As mentioned, it helps to do this before any ritual to make sure that you are neutral before putting forth any intentions. You can do the chakra meditation from Connect, page 214, and add the smoke for a truly powerful clearing. You swirl the smoke around each of the chakra centers, clockwise, beginning at the head, pausing with the intention of blessing and dissipating at each of the chakra centers. Take the sage stick down the front of both legs and then up the back of the legs, knees, trunk and body, up the back of your neck, head, and complete at the top of the head at the crown. You can also just pass the smoke around your body, top to bottom, front and back, all the while holding your intention to clear your body temple.

Aligning Your Four Bodies Meditation

Throughout the book we have cleared and connected using these four areas, Relationship, Career/Finance, Health/Wellness, and Spirituality. The reason we have used those four areas is because these are the areas that most people want to create in. When we are learning the creative process, we will use the framework of the physical, emotional, mental, and spiritual parts of our being. We are made up of these four bodies and they each have their own role, forming a unique pattern that we draw from in the creative process. Similar to clearing your body, this is a technique to align the four bodies of your Self so you have the maximum potential to be the most connected and clear. Anytime you experience upset, trauma or grief and you want to shift those feelings, you can do this technique to get your body in alignment. This is also the place from which you want to create.

Sit down and close your eyes and take a few deep breaths to become more present in your physical body. The way you do this is to be aware of your breath as your chest rises and falls. Take a couple of breaths with the intention to connect to the physical. Feel the different parts, notice your heartbeat, feel your fingers and toes and bring your awareness fully into your body. The next thing you are going to do is to call forth your emotional body into alignment with your physical body. Imagine your emotional body as a full body jumpsuit that you put on and zip up. Imagine a cord reaching from your root chakra leading to your solar plexus and fasten it in, by tying it, or anchoring it, whatever image you want to use. Now your emotional body is in alignment with your physical body. Call in your mental body to be aligned with your physical and emotional body. Again put on the jumpsuit of your mental body which goes from your head to your toes, and zip it up. Now imagine a cord from your solar plexus to heart and fasten it in. Now your mental body is in alignment with your emotional and physical body. Now we are calling in the spiritual body. Zip it up like a jumpsuit and create a cord from the heart chakra to the crown chakra and intend that your physical, emotional, mental, and spiritual bodies are aligned. Take a breath. How do you feel? You have all your bodies aligned and connected. Take another breath and open your eyes.

Creating From the Highest Place

In all literature from the bible to modern day writing, there is a theme of mountains or very high places being the metaphor for a high vibrational, spiritual experience. For example, Moses received the Ten Commandments on top of Mt. Sinai. As we move forward to create, we want to make sure we, too, are coming from an elevated place to put forth our intentions. Creating is a spiritual, sacred act and we want to be sure your state of mind reflects that highest, clearest vibration. If you are coming from a place of survival, or have just undergone a trauma, your creations may take much longer, or be much more difficult to manifest. If you are not in a higher frame of mind and frequency, then wait and work on your consciousness before you put forth your intentions. These are big steps we are taking. When I desire to expand my consciousness, I recommend the following:

- Go through the Connecting exercises again.
- Meditate
- Go to your favorite masters' and teachers' websites or books and get inspired.
- Read something that lifts your spirit.
- Go to a place in nature where you can see the magnificence of God's creation.

These are some examples, but you can create your own way of finding what is uplifting for you. Now you are ready to put forth your intentions for your own creation!

CHAPTER 23

The Create Process

Introducing the Creation Process

We have cleared that which no longer serves us, we have connected with our highest Self, and from that place of connectedness, we are ready to put forth our authentic heart's desire. When you are aligned with who you really are, there is a knowing of what is for your highest good. Self-Love and the creation process are one and the same. People are creating all of the time, but when it comes from the place of a sacred relationship with Self, it becomes a powerful path!

The Creation Process

First comes the impulse, the desire, the idea of wanting something new to come into your life. It begins to formulate in your mind and thoughts and you get a picture of the way your life could be. Ideas begin to come to you on how you could create your wish. In your mind, you begin to see it. Your mental body takes hold and begins to form the idea of what steps you need to take to create that desire. Your mental body is great at this, it takes the initial idea and runs with it. You begin to see it, and you begin to have ideas about how to make it happen; people to talk to, things to do to bring it about. Instead of just jumping in and running with it I suggest we pause here, and utilize the Law of Attraction and your subconscious to give you a better chance of manifestation. So, here we go!

Pick One

Throughout this book, we have looked at all areas of your life. You may have many changes you want to make and many ideas of what would make all the areas of your life be different or better. Eventually, as you become a master of manifestation you will create in all the different areas simultaneously. For now, as we begin to play with the Creation process, I would like you to limit your creation to one desire so you can really practice this process and focus all your energies on making this one desire appear. You might want to start small. For instance, manifest a great parking space the next time you go shopping; or as in the book by Richard Bach, *Illusions*, his character manifested a blue feather; something you can see in your mind that appears as if out of nowhere. We are just playing here, so have fun with it!

Placing Your Order with the Universe

The next step is to let the Universe know what it is you want to create. You will be putting forth your request. I call this process Placing Your Order with the Universe. The best way I can describe this is through the following scenario.

Imagine that you are going to an old fashioned diner to have dinner. You skipped lunch so you are very hungry by the time you sit down to have your meal. The waitress comes up to your table and is ready to take your order. Because you are famished and can barely even think of what you want to eat, you let her know, "I am starving, bring me whatever is your special of the day." Time passes and you are getting hungrier and hungrier and finally the waitress arrives with the special, liver and onions, mashed potatoes, and green beans. The smell alone, repulses you, and given that you do not even eat meat anymore, you realize this will not do. You realize that in order to get what you want you need to be very specific. At this point, you pick up the menu and decide on what you really want and let your waitress know, "grilled salmon, baked potato, and peas, and carrots." When the food arrives, you are very happy because you placed your order in much detail and got exactly what you wanted.

This metaphor came to me one day when I realized that my clients were saying to me, "I need money," "I want a relationship," "I want to be happy." In observing this phenomenon, I realized that their requests for the Universe were too general. They might get that man, but he was not at all what they were looking for. Money came, but in much smaller amounts than they desired. It became apparent to me, that in order to create what you want and desire, the more specific you have to be in placing your order with the Universe. The more specific you are, the better the outcome! Now, when I teach people how to manifest, I emphasize, to order exactly what you want instead of saying, "I am hungry bring me whatever." For example, you want more money? How much and by when? You want a new, loving relationship? What is on your list for that ideal mate? His age, his looks; his character; list the qualities that are important to you. Sometimes the Universe has bigger and better plans for us that we cannot see. When I am placing my order, I always add, "This or something better, and so it is," or "that which is in the highest good for me will occur." Adding these phrases "leaves the door open" allowing Spirit to orchestrate a more wonderful, extraordinary experience than we could even imagine ourselves. Begin formulating the details to your vision of what you want to create. Jot them down in your journal so you have them available when you are ready to write your visions.

Visioning - See It & Feel It!

We are very specific about what we want to create, and now I want you to see it. You already have gotten some pictures in your mind, and I want you to really tell a story with those pictures. This process is called Visioning. Here, the mental and emotional bodies work together to form the pictures. Our subconscious is the vehicle by which our manifestations come to us. Our subconscious does not understand what is happening in reality, present time vs. what is happening in our thoughts or emotions. This is the reason why we worked so diligently on Clearing our past. Just to refresh, if you are reactivated by a childhood trauma, it feels as if it is happening again for you in the present, until it is dealt with and cleared. So, too, we can create wonderful experiences in our mind as if it is happening in the present. As you imagine your creation, the subconscious body will bring you that. The more we can activate our subconscious to get behind our creation, the quicker our creation will manifest. The words *I am* invoke God, the Universe, your highest self and the universal flow of energy, energizing whatever words follow to manifest. It also invokes your own power of who you are. *I am* aligns you with Source, it is the presence of Source in action and invokes the full activity of God. When you say and feel "I am" you open wide the door to natural flow. When you say "I am not," you shut the door. I always begin my visions with *I am*. At the end of all my visions, say the phrase, *This or something better, and so it is.* This statement opens up the possibilities of even greater manifestations that the Universe has for you that you may not have even conceived of.

Focus on the End Result

In order for visioning to work, you have to be clear on the end result. Your subconscious needs to know what is at the finish line. Know your goal. If you do not have a goal, you will be running around in circles and your manifestation will not be what you desire. As you begin to create your goals, recall and re-embrace all of our deserving exercises, where we stretched our worth. Extend beyond what you think is possible.

Visualizing Your Creation

Picture yourself being, doing and having your creation. How does it feel? How does it smell and taste? Really get into the feeling aspect, the satisfaction, the accomplishment, and the good feelings that come from getting what you desire. Look

outward at the world - the media, movies, a book, people you know – to create a model of what you want to create for yourself. Close your eyes and imagine that this energy is filling your body from head to toe. As you imagine having this creation of yours, imagine having a nob where you can turn up the feeling! Look at your creation from all aspects and create a handful of scenarios where you are being, doing and having your creation. So, if it is a job you want to create, picture yourself getting the call from your new supervisor letting you know your start date. You call your friend and tell them the news and you go out to celebrate. Imagine yourself on your first day, what are you wearing, how are you feeling? Picture yourself putting your first check in the bank (and for what amount?). See your bank account filling up and how much peace, joy and security that brings you. Begin acting and feeling in your daily life as if all of this has already occurred, feeling the abundance now before it has manifested, feeling grateful for the divine fulfillment of your manifestation, NOW, even though it has not yet occurred. Now, I want you to write your visualization, but before that...

A Word... about the Words

There is tremendous power in your words. The Bible says, "First, there was the word." The word was used in the creation process. There is something to that. Words have power to shift our circumstances. Through our words, we can let the Universe know what we want and not just be at the effect of our circumstances. I spoke earlier about the importance of being careful about your speech and to watch your thoughts, and you know how to write an affirmation. We will be creating a vision for our lives, and writing more affirmations, using these words to create our new reality. As a thought begins in your mind, as does your creation, you give that thought power by speaking and writing about it.

We have mentioned the use of the term "I AM" in creating our affirmations. This phrase is so powerful because it brings forth the power of the creator. In the Bible, when Moses gets a demonstration of Gods presence and power at the burning bush, Moses asks God for his name. God responds,

Yahweh, or translated, *I AM that I AM,* or, *I shall be that I shall be.* It is the name for God. It invokes the power and energy and creative ability of Divinity. Every time you use the words, "I AM," you bring forth all of that power in front of whatever follows. For example, I am healthy verses I am sick is a much more empowered use of this energy. You are literally calling forth divine health. *I AM* in the spoken word is a statement that merges yourself, YOU, with your God-Self, your highest Self. We use the phrase so often we have actually diminished and misdirected this energy. We put this phrase in front of all the things we do not want. "I am sick, I am poor, I am tired." I would like you to contemplate your use of the words *I AM.* Think of the power of saying, "I am so sick of (fill in the blank)." You are calling in illness. Here I will ask you to begin to have a consciousness of the power of your words. If someone asks you how you are feeling and you really do not feel great. Instead of saying, I am sick, try saying, "I am feeling better and better." That will start the flow in the direction you want to go, instead of the opposite. Wayne Dyer suggests that you use I AM statements in the last 5 minutes of your day saying affirmations before you go to sleep to literally reprogram your subconscious mind evoking this power of your God-Self. Speak I AM statements, such as "I am loved, I am healthy, I am prosperous." This is one of the most effective ways to bring forth your creations and your desires. Know that who you *really* are is the energy of the I AM Presence. The more you step into this awareness, the easier it is to create.

As you have negative occurrences going on in your life, be careful to not speak of it by whining or complaining about it. These are things that should be thought of as *that which should not be spoken,* because by speaking it, you give it power. As I am speaking to someone about something troubling me, I can literally *feel* my energy dip. One might think I am contradicting myself here, in that, throughout this book I have asked you to clear, clear, clear. And one of our main processes of clearing is through our Be-With Communication. But, again, in communicating for clearing there is an intention. The intention of clearing is the key. And even in your clearing communication, I ask you to be careful in making statements that use the *I AM.* Even if you feel the need to complain or express negativity, do it with the intention to clear. Instead of tossing around the *I AM* everywhere, try to only use it when decreeing and affirming what you do desire, giving the statement and yourself, even more power.

Integrity of Visioning

I have had clients ask me whether it is proper to include another person in their visions. This is a good question because everyone has free will and while you have your intentions, they may inevitably include others. Be sure when including someone else in your vision that your energy is coming from the highest place. Check for yourself whether your intention is to control someone else or control the outcome, this becomes a manipulation or interfering with someone's free will. But as we have said, like energy attracts like energy, if you are coming from a sincere place of good intention, your vision is in integrity. Also be sure, if you are including someone in your vision, that you are not fixated on just this one avenue of manifestation. Are there other ways your creation can come to fruition without the involvement of this person? If you are including a spouse in your vision, see if you can also get your spouse to hold that vision (e.g. to stop smoking or lose weight). If you both are aligned in this vision, this gives it power and is not controlling or manipulating. There is nothing wrong with putting out an intention, and asking for what you desire. You can hold the vision, and you cannot guarantee an outcome. We do not know what the highest good is for another, in many cases, we do not always even know what is in the highest good for ourselves. I am sure you have had instances in your life where you have been disappointed, maybe you did not get a job, or a relationship did not work out, and at the time it was devastating and you just could not see why this circumstance did not work out the way you wanted. Many times we will get the bigger picture later, realizing that this scenario really was not for your highest good. In all visions, I suggest you put in what I call, the highest good clause at the end of each affirmation or visioning statement, *"For everyone's highest good involved."*

The following are the different types of visualizations you can practice. See which one sounds the most fun for you to do!

Movie Screen Visualization

Your visualization is the end result of the story you wish to create. Creating your visualization is like playing a movie on the screen of your mind. It is flush with details. Be sure to feel the feelings as you watch your movie in your mind allowing yourself the joy and fulfillment of your dreams coming true.

Here is an example of a relationship visualization. *I see my mate (with all the attributes you assigned him) coming to the door with flowers. He smells good, the flowers are beautiful, he is so attentive and he intuitively knows my favorite flower! He takes my arm and opens the car door for me. We go to a fabulous restaurant. I smell the delicious food as I walk in the door. I see the waiters, the tables, the other guests. I catch a glimpse of myself in a mirror and I look beautiful and radiant. My new man is looking at me adoringly from across the table. I am laughing, as he is talking because he is so charming. He is listening intently as I speak. I feel so joyful that I have found the man of my dreams. This or something better, and so it is!*

Affirming Visualization

Another way to visualize is to make a detailed list of what you want to create. This type of visualizing is like an affirmation which we talked about in Clearing when you are trying to change a thought or belief. Affirmations are similar to visualizations in that they are positive statements you make to yourself and the Universe in the area you are working on. Affirmations are what we use to proclaim something you may not believe for yourself right now, but something you want to bring in and make true for yourself. So, for example, if you really do not like public speaking and do not feel you are very good at it, you can make an affirmation that you say to yourself out loud several times a day, "I am a confident, accomplished speaker in front of hundreds of people!" If you are looking for a job, you might affirm for yourself, "I meet people everyday who bring to me my perfect job, now!" A good affirmation uses all the same parameters as the visualizations but is more succinct. You may have several affirmations you say together several times a day. Here is an example of one of my affirming visualizations in the area of career and finance:

- *I am debt-free.*
- *I have a minimum of $500,000 in the bank or more, now!*
- *I receive an annual income of $1,000,000 or more.*
- *I get regular, huge royalties from the best-selling book I have written.*
- *I have 20 premier coaching clients on year long contracts.*
- *I have sold-out auditoriums of people coming to hear me speak.*
- *I do regular speaking engagements for huge corporations teaching the Clear, Connect, Create Formula.*
- *I generously contribute to the charities of my choice.*
- *I am able to travel to two of the places on my "travel-wish" list every year; for example, Paris, Italy and Greece.*
- *I have a fabulous leather jacket.*
- *I have five or more pairs of Jimmy Chu gorgeous high heels.*
- *I have a wardrobe, and hair and makeup consultant.*
- *My beautiful home in a warm climate is fully paid off and I have another home in Chicago.*
- *I am able to be fully generous in all areas of my life.*
- *I am completely at peace about my finances with full financial freedom, now and forever!*
- *I am connected and aligned with my highest Self!*
- *This or something better, and so it is!*

Catherine Ponder was one of my first teachers of prosperity and I used her work *The Dynamic Laws of Prosperity* as my manifestation bible throughout the years. The following are some of the affirmations from that book that have really supported me throughout my life. I put them here for you to use as suggested general affirmations to speak aloud. Add your own that fit and support you to create what you desire.

* *Vast improvement comes quickly in every phase of my life now. Every day in every way, things are getting better and better for me right now.*
* *I am rich, well and happy and every phase of my life is in divine order right now.*
* *I praise my world now. My world is full of wonderful people who now lovingly help me in every way.*
* *Divine love, working through substance, prospers my financial affairs making me free, rich and financially independent right now. I am financially independent now. I am, I am, I am.*
* *I am receiving. I am receiving now. I am receiving all the wealth that the Universe has for me now.*

Story Time Visualization

Another way of visualizing is to create a story, or many stories of HOW your specific desire comes into fruition. The trick here is to look at what and who is in your life everyday and make them a part of your visualization. You want to make this story just like you are talking to your best friend relating what actually happened WHEN your dream came true! So you will be writing and reading it to yourself in the past tense. You will want to write several of these, maybe one a day several days in a row. There are many of you who may be single and interested in finding your partner and I, too, have been in that position. This is the exact way this type of visualization worked for me (a week to the day after I started writing these stories each day). I first looked at what I do every day in my life. I go biking or walking; I go to the pool and the movies, and I go out to dinner with friends while I am at my Florida home. These are normal, regular actions for me on a day to day, week to week basis. You want to make it as real an experience as possible so your mind and subconscious completely get on board. So one of your stories might be...

I woke in the morning with a feeling of excitement and I did not know why.

While getting ready for my daily swim at the pool, I decided I better shave my legs. I felt good and fit and just had a feeling of anticipation. I found my usual spot by the pool and sat down and in walks a man I had never seen before. He is a tall man, handsome, and I found myself extremely attracted to him and hardly able to concentrate on my swimming. I swam a few laps and got out of the pool and felt his eyes on me. We started talking and it was an easy conversation. The more I learned about him, the more attracted I was. By the end of the conversation, he had asked me to go on our first date to go biking. This or something better. And so it is!

Write a different version everyday of how your wish comes to you until it manifests. Another one, might be similar, but I go walking. Another one might be about meeting someone's eyes across the restaurant. The visualization above, was exactly how I met the man currently in my life. It worked for me, and it can work for you!

Using Visualizations with Others

When I was diagnosed with breast cancer, it was shocking to me and my family because I had been so healthy and vital and no one had ever had cancer in my family. My family members and friends were especially rocked and reeling from the diagnosis. I could hear the fear in their voices when they called me. I wrote a vision for myself. My vision was as follows:

I am going to have the surgery and the doctors are going to get all the cancer out of my body. The doctors and nurses will be at their best and they will treat me with the utmost care and compassion. It will be their best surgery ever and my healing will be rapid. The result of the surgery will be the best case scenario. When they do the biopsy the cancer will be contained and will not have spread and will be the most non-aggressive of cancers. Aftercare will be minimal. There will be no re-occurrence. And from this experience I am healthier with more vitality and in optimal well-being. I am better than ever. This or something better, and so it is!

I sent this vision out to the people I loved and read it to myself several times a day. I told my friends and family if they could hold this vision with me they could be around me. I needed only positive people and emotions around me. If they could not hold this vision for me, I would be in touch with them at a later time. The result and the experience was exactly as I had intended and visualized. First, and foremost, especially when dealing with your health, do not worry about ruffling feathers. I had enough to deal with my own fears that crept up regularly (I am not a superhuman, after all, I was scared). I could not deal with assuaging the fears of everyone else too. It was right for me in this circumstance to put up boundaries. Asking those around me to hold my highest vision empowered me to create my desired outcome.

Writing Your Visualization

Now, it's your turn! Writing your visualization of what you want to create is a great technique to connect with yourself, raise your vibration and to bring into physical form your intention. What do you really want to create? What is it that you long for? What is your true heart's desire? If it is for your highest good, know that it will manifest. Make a list about what it is you want. Be very detailed and very specific. Go through the list and add the vibrant details of how your manifestation will look, feel and taste.

Visualization Parameters:
* Write your vision as if it is occurring now, in the present tense. Use the word *now* in your vision to pull it into the present, as opposed to something you desire in the future. If you picture your creation occurring in the future, that is where it will stay, it will always be in the future. "I am living in my beautiful home with my divine mate, now!"
* Use the words *I am.*

- Never write what you do not want. If you write, *I do not want this type of man xxx, or I do not want a job that is not close to my home, or I never want to be as unhealthy as my mother*. If you put out to the Universe what you do not want, it does not know the difference and the Universe will rush to fulfill the request, giving you more of what you do not want. Phrase your visualization to what you do desire, for example, *I am in a relationship with a peaceful, stable, handsome man, now! I have landed the perfect job which is close to my home. I am healthy, fit and vibrantly alive, now!*
- Write it in as much detail as you can imagine utilizing all your senses.
- As we have said before, the feelings you bring to your visualization are one of the most important aspects. Get in touch with the joy and the excitement of the creation you are visualizing. Feel what it is like to have your creation. Turn up the dial of that high joy vibration filling every cell in your body. You want to put that feeling into your visualization as well, using the words, *I feel so joyful...* The emotion is the attractor, it is the emotion's vibration that calls in what you desire to create.
- At the end of your vision, use the phrases, *"For the highest good of all,"* and *"This or something better. And so it is!"*

Ceremony

Take your list of what you want to create and do a ceremony. Connect with yourself and get into a high, joy vibration. Create sacred space. Read your vision out loud. When you are done, place your vision on the alter where it will stay for 30 days. Take time out for each day to read it. Meditate first, getting yourself into a calm space of receiving, read your vision and take a few minutes every day really visioning it happening. At the end of each day at your alter do a ceremony where you offer up to the Divine and your guides your vision. Surrender, "thy will be done." Let go and let God. To strengthen the experience of your vision every day, have your vision board or treasure map (explained in the next chapter) close by so you can sit and gaze at the pictorial representation of your vision.

....

CHAPTER 24

Taking Action

Everyday Visualize

What do you do with your visualizations?

* Everyday intend that your visualization is occurring for you.
* Believe it.
* Read it to yourself several times a day, especially upon waking, sometime in the middle of the day and before you go to bed.
* Keep it in front of you in the forefront of your mind. Some people put it on their computer's screen saver.
* You can speak it into a recorder and listen to it several times a day. This is especially helpful because the mind is not engaged. You are feeding your message directly to the subconscious.

First thing in the morning, create a visualization of how you want your day to be. This could be one of your visualizations coming to fruition. It could be what you desire for this day, and how your interactions shall go. This is not a to-do list for yourself. This is not an exercise in organization or making your day more efficient. This is an exercise in the power of your intention. We will use the same parameters for the visualization of our creation as we did to visualize our day. I used these visualization techniques in my event planning business. I used to produce huge events for large corporations. I was responsible for all the details – food, music, activities, décor. I would write a visualization for the best case scenario for how I wanted the event to go. I would share this visualization with my assistant and my team so they, too, could be aligned with the vision. I would start with how I felt the day of the event upon waking up that morning, the weather, the ride to the event. Then I would move through the entire party. I would see the staff, clean and polished, the event personnel, the band, the caterers, the food, the equipment, the entertainment. My visualization would be very detailed, several pages, all very positive. I included how I and my assistant would feel, how the guests would feel, and the staff's excitement. The conclusion would always be that my client would say to me, "This was the greatest party ever!" I would read my visualization the day of the event, on the way to the event and try to read it one more time at the party to anchor it into my subconscious. From the time I started this practice, these parties would be very smooth and successful. When I did forget to include a detail in the visualization, like the DJ arriving on time, there was always some kind of glitch with that aspect. But for the most part, these events unrolled, eerily and miraculously, exactly as I had envisioned, sometimes even better.

Taking Action

Visioning and affirming is not just about saying the magic incantation and ta-dah, your wish appears! We have been talking a lot about the inner processes of creating – making sure you are clear, connected with the Divine part of yourself and watching your thoughts and words; as well as seeing your manifestation as if it has already happened. Given that we are spiritual beings having a physical experience, it is necessary to take physical actions to support your manifestation arriving. When you are in alignment with the Divine, you will be guided to take outer actions that will move you closer to your heart's desire. This is why it is so important to be connected and aligned during this process. The more that you follow through with these actions, the more guidance you will be given.

Listen. When we listen, and quiet our minds it allows the Universe a few seconds to "download" information to us. In that moment we may not get the answer we are seeking, but trust that it will come through. Later, throughout the day, a person you have not thought of in a while may pop in your head and you will feel directed to call them. This could be just the person that knows about your future job. If you are trying to find a mate, and you see a commercial for a dating site that touches you, go online and post your profile. If there is a party or dance you were not going to attend, and at the last minute feel prompted to go... GO! *Every time you feel inspired to follow through with one of the impulses you receive, not only does your intuition get stronger, but you are consistently demonstrating to the Universe that you are serious about bringing forth your creation.*

Follow your inspiration. Being connected means that you are taking the steps to listen to the inspiration coming to you from the Universe. We do this with the Meditation and Mindfulness Exercise.

Meditation & Mindfulness Exercise. Get quiet everyday for at least a few minutes and consciously be with your breath. Be mindful throughout the day. Whatever the task is at hand, you are focused on that task. Clear your mind of the clutter. If you are doing dishes, your mind is completely focused on doing the dishes; the feel of the water, the smell of soap, the glint of light on the dishes. If your mind wanders, just bring it back to your breath and/or the task at hand.

Do something every day that supports your manifestation. If you want to be a famous published author, and you do not sit down every day and write your book, you are not giving the Universe the chance to respond and support you. You can affirm and vision until the cows come home, but if there is no book to publish, it would be difficult to manifest that dream. If you want a new job and you do not network or keep an eye out for new opportunities, it may be difficult to get that new job. You have to put forth the physical actions that support your dream.

290 · CLEAR · CONNECT · CREATE

Not every action you take in the physical world will result in the culmination of your dream as you perceive it. There is no harm in putting yourself and your manifestation out there. You are saying, "I am open to all the opportunities!" "I expect my creation to appear today, now!" This is where a co-creation of Spirit and matter comes together.

Here is one of the many examples of manifestation when I have followed my intuition: *Some time ago, I had to give up my home in Florida for the winter because we had rented it out and I really wasn't looking forward to spending another winter in Chicago. I visioned that I had a beautiful home in Florida. One morning, as I was puzzling about what to do about my living situation, I had an intuition to walk across the street to my neighbor that I did not know and introduce myself. This woman not only became a close friend, she became my advocate, searching for places for me to live, finally leading me to a beautiful home that perfectly fit my vision, where I spent a fabulous, warm, winter in Florida.* Following those intuitive prompts can support you, accelerating the timing of your manifestation, as well as, demonstrating to you that you are not alone in the manifestation process. This is how it works!

Keep that notebook handy. As you meditate, daydream on the train, and upon waking, write down any suggestions that you receive and feel. And then do it if it resonates as a yes for you! Call that friend, go to that restaurant, do what you are prompted to do. Take action on these things, because this is your guidance coming through to support you.

Call on your guides. When you are in the process of manifesting what you desire, read your vision every night before you go to bed. Before you fall asleep, ask your guides to give you support and to work on your creation while sleeping, and give you any information you need upon arising. This is something that I have put into practice and it works amazingly. I have had answers to questions and ideas come through upon waking that I, literally, would have never dreamed of! Then, when you wake, ask your self, "What do I need to do today to support my vision to bring it into physical form?" Write down the response in your notebook.

Keep a dream journal and write any dreams you may be having. Look for the messages and symbols that can support you.

Create a Vision Board. A vision board, also known as a treasure map, is a visual display of the end result of your creation. You are already meditating daily on your visualizations, and we want to tap into your subconscious. The subconscious dramatically responds to pictures. You will need a poster board, some magazines, scissors and a glue stick. We will be creating a collage of the life you love. Begin to flip through magazines, cutting out any images or words that speak to you and represent the goals you want to achieve. You could even put a picture of yourself in the middle as if all the visual images of desires are coming to you. Let yourself be creative and have fun with your collage. Be flexible, if you change your mind on something, or find a more powerful image, remove the old picture and replace it with something new. When finished, place it where you see it every day. It will feed your subconscious. For some, it might be easier to have a notebook with clear inserts so you can carry it with you and flip through the pictures you collected throughout the day. The mind's imaging has magical power! Each day focus on your vision board. Breathe slowly and go within. Use it as a focus of your meditation, calling upon your guides and highest self to guide you in the manifestation of it. Feel the joy of your creation. You will be programming your subconscious to bring that creation to you.

Have Laser-like Focus. There are two approaches to manifesting, Laser-like Focus and Soft Focus. In some respects you have to do them both at the same time, and it has to do with how you "hold" yourself and your vision while in the creative process. After many, many years of studying and teaching manifesting, I have realized something very important for the process. I am, and I believe most women, are multi-taskers to say the least. Where men can get a hold of that bone and chew it down to a nub, women will take a little nibble, put it down, do the laundry, the dishes, balance the check book, rake the leaves, sew a button, make dinner, workout and then come back to the bone. In the past, I would put a plan that I wanted to manifest out to the

Universe and do many other projects simultaneously. I would be working on the book, putting together a class, calling people for my event business, and trying to enroll 20 clients for my new coaching practice. Then, at the end of the month, I would look around, exasperated and wonder why the Universe was not responding? I laugh at it now, but at the time I did not understand that my focus was completely fractured by all I had intended. I have already suggested, here, that in the beginning you focus on only one creation at a time. Being clear and in a state of connectedness while you are playing the game of manifesting, is a wonderful, empowering experience. Do all that I suggest and play with it, watch all that shows up for you, it will feel as if you are creating your Universe... and you are!

Soft Focus. When you are in the space of manifestation, you are aligned, grounded, connected, and trusting the universe. When in a space of trusting you are not pushing or forcing it to make it happen. This is Soft Focus. How does nature create? Grass does not try to grow. How does the universe create? Planets effortlessly stay in their orbit. There is no pushing, struggling, controlling or worry, it just happens naturally, it flows. When I am controlling or manipulating, my manifestation process is challenging. When I am in a high joy vibration, and I want to create more clients, for example, I hold my intention in a light way. I move forward in my day, all the while *connecting* with Self and keeping my intention in soft-focus. I still visualize my 20 premier coaching clients and I still take the action steps to speak to people about my work. By using soft focus, the Universe responds. There is a difference between manipulating and grasping at your prize versus just *knowing* that it is coming. It is the softer touch rather than the aggressive energy associated with MAKING it happen. Keep it in your consciousness. My intention is still 20 clients, and everyday as I say my visions, I have my focus on the finish line. I know where I am going, and I am not calling 200 people every day to make it happen. I am in the space of it happening. I am knowing it is happening.

Watch Your Thoughts While In Action. While you are in the creating process, you will need to watch your thoughts and words while you are taking action to manifest your dream. For example, if you want to lose weight and you are taking all the right steps; you are saying your visions and affirmations daily, you are meditating and visualizing your new body, your vitality, etc., but then you break your food regimen and have a piece of birthday cake. I have heard people say, "Oh, it is so bad for me," or "it always goes straight to my hips." By having this internal dialogue, and especially by saying it out loud, you are affirming and creating that result. After that piece of cake are you berating yourself in your mind? Are you now feeling like you have ruined everything from your little slip up? Be kind to yourself. It is not necessarily bad to eat birthday cake. Maybe what works is to enjoy the dessert and then return to your food plan. Being loving to yourself during the creation process will get your farther.

It is also important that you remain vigilant to monitor your mind, your thoughts, during the creative process. When you are manifesting something new, the mind attempts to sabotage you, bringing in old thought forms, even those you thought you had cleared. Adopt some "go too" affirmations when the mind takes over, something more positive like, "Everything I eat turns to health and beauty, even when I'm eating that birthday cake!" Watching your thoughts and your words ultimately might lead you back to the Clearing chapters. If your belief really is that every time you eat anything sweet, it goes to your hips, then that thought will need to be cleared. You might find throughout this process that you are moving back and forth between the previous sections. Check in with yourself regularly to make sure you are Clear and Connected during the Create Process. Notice what your thoughts and words are when you are involved in the action of creating your manifestation and write down anything that you think is negative. See if next to the negative you can create a more positive thought just as we did in Clearing. *Thoughts: OMG this is fattening, I should not be eating this! New Thought: Everything I eat creates health and beauty.*

Be present while taking action. If you are looking for a new job and sending out resumes via the internet, take a few breaths before hitting send. See the vision in your mind of the end result you are trying to create. If you are beginning a new exercise regime, be fully in your body, feeling what it feels like to be fit with tremendous energy.

Get a Creation Buddy. Share your goals, your visualizations and affirmations with your creation buddy. Share your treasure map, and explain the symbols and what you have pictured. Set up a weekly support call for at least six weeks, at a designated time, sharing what actions you have taken. Keep each other accountable!

* Discuss what you have done to manifest your dream
* Share the intuitions that have shown up for you
* Discuss any "dips" in connection or anything that might need to be cleared (dips are covered in the next chapter)
* Express the miracles!

Create new commitments for each week and support each other until both of your visions are achieved.

Aligning With Your Vision Exercise

 This is a great exercise to do with your creation buddy or someone close enough to you that they are a source of support for you. You want to choose someone who can "hold" your vision with you. This exercise can be done either in person or on the phone. Even if your friend has not read this book, you can share with them how to do this exercise. The ground rules are similar to the Re-Creation Process (page 23). Ask your partner to:

* Be silent while you read your vision to him/her.
* In their silence, imagine what it is you are sharing.
* See in his/her mind's eye your creation.
* Support your desire to create this manifestation with no doubt and no judgment.
* See it happening, feel it happening, and act as your silent cheerleader.

Your job in reading your vision, is to:

◆ Speak it with enthusiasm and tremendous positive feeling behind your words.

◆ Visualize it yourself as you express, bringing joy and aliveness to every syllable.

Once you are finished, close your eyes and ask your partner to do the same. Take a moment and feel what it is like to speak your vision into existence. What does that feel like in your body? Let yourself enjoy the feeling of your vision. Open your eyes. If you would like, you can now ask your partner for feedback. It is not necessary, but it can be extremely helpful. For instance, one time when I was reading my vision to one of my creation buddies, she noticed that in a certain area of speaking my vision, I started speeding up and my voice sounded tight. Sure enough, I was blazing through that area of my vision because I had some energy that I needed to clear. Be open to hearing how your vision came across, so that you can tweak anything that needs strengthening. By sharing it with another, you can also analyze for yourself whether you believe, and if you do not believe it yourself, change your vision to be an accurate reflection of what you desire to occur. Next, you can switch and be the listener for your partner. It is just as much fun to hear what it is they are working on. Notice how uplifted you both feel. Speaking your visions to each other will bring you both into that high joy vibration where manifestation occurs. Speaking it and feeling it turns you both into magnets for your good. You might want to schedule a time to do this regularly.

Aligning Your Will with God's Will Meditation

This meditation connects your vision with God's will. This is another powerful exercise, which again, might bring up some lingering emotions about God which need to be cleared. Begin by asking yourself these questions:

* Do you think God would want you to be happy, healthy and abundant?
* Do you embrace the concept of a benevolent, supportive God?
* What would it look like to align your will with God?

If nothing glaringly comes up for you, proceed, and have your visualization close by. If something does feel "very charged" go back to the Clearing Religion and Spirituality chapter and do a clearing exercise around those thoughts and beliefs.

Sit quietly in a comfortable chair. Take three deep breaths and clear your mind. When you are ready, imagine a clear tube the width of your hips reaching down to the center of the earth. Anchor your tube there. If you had any fears or resistance come up for you from the questions, send them down the tube. Bring to mind your visualization, and see if you have any fears, resistance, or doubt with regard to that; if you do, send them down the tube as well. Now, enthusiastically speak your vision for yourself out loud.

Once complete, ask yourself: Why would God's will be aligned with my vision? Speak out loud for yourself why this is true.

Now imagine that the Divine is all around you, surrounding you. Picture a tube of light from the heavens entering your being through your crown chakra and illuminating each of your chakras. Go slowly and let the light linger at each energy center until it feels ready to go to the next. Fill your whole being with this heavenly light, all the way down to the soles of your feet. You are now completely connected to the Divine! Say out loud, "I have aligned my will with God's will. And I am praying for the knowledge of God's will to carry it out." Now that you are aligned with, trusting, and connected with the Divine, re-speak your vision, seeing it, hearing it and feeling it.

Take a deep breath. How are you feeling after the second time you expressed your vision? Did it feel different from the first time? My experience when doing this meditation is a feeling of filling places within my body with that Divine Light, which were empty and are now full. It helps me feel more resilient, more solid in my commitment and my desire. It is not a feeling of density, but more able to refract, have things bounce off and not permeate me as much. I feel more centered and grounded. When I speak my vision the first time, I experience it *as coming from myself, from a mental place or from a lower body state. When I speak my vision after the alignment, it feels like my vision is being spoken from my heart, from an inner place of strength, a place that trusts that God will help me to manifest my vision.*

Touchstones. We have worked with touchstones in other areas, and they are just as powerful in the creation process. Find a touchstone for yourself, a small stone, or crystal, something that feels good in your hand and that easily fits into your pocket. Hold your stone and intend to infuse that stone with your visualization. Recall your visualization to your mind, replay it with the most emotion you can muster, and imagine all of that emotion and energy filtering into the stone. Be fully present in the energy of your success and feel that stone absorbing all of those good feelings and great energy. End your visualization knowing that your stone is a physical reminder of your visualization, anchoring you in the knowing that your wishes are fulfilled.

CHAPTER 25

Dipping & Fear

Dipping

Y ou have been practicing all the tools. You have been speaking your vision. You have been doing your daily practice. You have been a diligent, joyous student in the creation process. And you wake up one morning and you just feel down. You begin to feel some old emotions; like a victim, anger, frustration. You begin looking at the gap from where you were to where you are now. You begin to judge yourself. You are dipping!

What is dipping? Dipping is a phrase I coined to describe what happens when we periodically "dip" out of that high vibrational state we have worked so hard to get into. When we are in the creation process, we want to be in that high, positive vibration because that attracts more good into our lives. But dipping out of that state happens from time to time. We can do something as minor as cutting our self while shaving and that can cause us to dip, and lead to a cascade of unwanted feelings to surface. We can dip by something actually tragic or bad happening. The following are some reasons when and how we dip:

* A major happening can lead to a dip: an injury, a family drama, a financial setback
* A minor happening can occur (like cutting your self shaving)
* You wake up and suddenly you just feel worse

- The "Yes... Buts" surface
- You find yourself in fear, lack, or worry
- You find yourself experiencing a loss
- Your patterns are triggered, old emotions or an old wound resurfaces
- You realize you are having extreme emotional responses to minor events
- You are triggered by negative people
- You are in physical pain

Dipping is like slipping back into an old way of consciousness. *It is not bad to dip.* The feelings you are experiencing may bring up something you need to learn or feel, or point to something that needs to be corrected in your life. It is time to re-engage that 'Psyche Detective' to discover what this is all about. The key here is to realize you are dipping and feeling bad, and not to then just plaster a smile on it. It is Self-Loving to investigate it. Remember that a negative, fear-based energy is a much lower vibration and more difficult from which to create. From the perspective of what you focus on expands, continual negative thoughts or fearful emotions on any subject will bring you more of the same. We want to shift back to a place of love, acceptance, and trust. Discovering what is really going on, will also allow you to more quickly get back into the high joy vibration and move you towards your creation.

First and Foremost – Allow Your Feelings

The first thing to do when you realize you are dipping is to be Self-Loving and to allow your feelings to "be" without jumping in and changing them. In this culture, most people are busy making themselves feel better, pushing through, making it go away. If you are feeling that something is off, it might be giving you information that you need. You might be in this space for a reason. We are emotional creatures, in most cases, in need of nurturing. I invite you to increase your Self-Love practices. Let your Self be. Take a nap. Give yourself permission to comfort your Self. Play. Put down your to-do list, your creation, your job and whatever else has been occupying your mind and take some Me-Time.

Do Not Judge

Several things could be occurring when we dip. When you feel yourself start to dip the key is to not judge. It is not bad or negative. One of the things you can do is to observe your thoughts and watch to see if you are scaring yourself or giving yourself negative statements that are perpetuating the state of dipping. This is where you can "cancel" that conversation and re-write the script.

Acknowledge It

Another thing to do is to acknowledge how you are feeling, do not shove it under the carpet or pretend you are feeling fine. Look within and try to put words around what you are feeling. You need to look and see what is going on with you because that will give you an indication of what is the best thing to do to get back to that higher state of connectedness. Ask yourself these questions:

- Can I trace these feelings back to when they began?
- What is this dip in consciousness telling me?
- Is there any action that needs to be taken?
- Am I out of integrity somewhere in my life?
- Did something recently happen that I glossed over?
- Do I have any unspoken communications with anyone?
- Did I recently say, "yes" to something, where I really wanted to say, "no"?
- Where am I over-doing or under-doing (avoiding) in my life?
- Have I not given myself enough space to create?
- Am I eating and sleeping well?
- Do I need to ask others in my life to take more responsibility?
- Has what I wanted to create changed in some way, or have I changed my mind?
- Is there an old story that keeps running through my mind?
- Is there a phrase that keeps re-occurring? For instance, "I can't," or "I never will," or "who do I think I am?"

Physical Pain

Feeling physical pain is one of the easiest ways for us to take a dip. The mind can immediately bring up feelings of victimization, a "poor me" attitude. Address your body's physical needs. What can facilitate physical healing? When our attention is not on the pain, most people generally are not aware of the physical pain. Nurture yourself more than you normally would through this period. Ask in meditation what your body is trying to tell you. Refer to Louise Hay's book, *Heal Your Body*, this gives metaphysical explanations of what different ailments mean with a corresponding affirmation. In my experience Hay's descriptions are spot-on and provide information about yourself you may not have realized.

The Mind/Ego Dip

When we are in the creation process, we are moving to higher, vibrational states. Beware! The mind and the ego will get louder as we get stronger. It is as if the mind/ego gets threatened. As we are moving to higher states of consciousness, it can be compared to climbing a mountain. You are going along and you feel good, you are happy that you have achieved your first 500 feet and you feel "in the zone." You keep going. As you climb higher, you find you are out of breath, your legs hurt, you start thinking, what is wrong with me, what happened to that zone? It is similar on our path of Self-Love. As you reach new levels of consciousness, you begin to feel empowered, strong, and you get comfortable there. As your consciousness continues to grow, the mind/ego gets threatened and begins to fight you for control. The mind/ego wants to be in control and is going crazy like a pack of wild horses. When you are connected and empowered, YOU are in control. You are reigning in that pack of wild horses. Like most humans, we used to be ruled by the mind/ego. Those conversations that were going on in your head seemed real. In the past, you may have reacted to circumstances, rather than controlling your reactions and your feelings around them. Now, you have observed the mind, cleared a lot of space, and you operate more and more from higher levels of consciousness. The mind/ego can get louder because it is threatened as you reach for the next level on your consciousness journey. It appears as a dip, as if you are in a funk, easily triggered. Pat yourself on the back, this is actually a sign that you are more in your power. Recognize it for what it really is, the mind/ego's struggle for survival.

As you begin to pay attention to your thoughts, you may hear: "no you can't do that," "who do you think you are?" or whatever the rest of the old tapes playing in your mind are repeating. By listening to that conversation, you can see it for what it is, just the threatened mind/ego. Nothing has occurred to make you less empowered or less likely to achieve your goals. Thank your mind for sharing, and return to your I AM statements. Meditate and continue to visualize to let the mind know, YOU are in charge! Mastering the mind in the face of fear is a discipline. Continue to use your tools for connecting even while in your dip. Many times you can push through the dip just by continuing your positive ascent. Continue to do something every day to reach your goals. Even when you feel discouraged and downhearted, especially then! Sometimes the only way to achieve those big results in life is to have that level of discipline.

The "Yes... But" Dip

When you are ready to create something new in an area, the limiting mind may step in and start to tell you what you cannot have and why it will not work. If you have already broken through that initial resistance and decided to attempt that manifestation anyway, good for you! Many times, as we get into the creation process, those "yes... buts" get louder. So, if you want a new job, and you have written your visualization and are working on that creation, your mind might now step in and say, "yes, but the economy is so bad I better stay where I am at." Or, you want a new relationship and the mind says, "yes, but all the good ones are already taken." The mind/ego will be very clever and bring up all the limiting thoughts, such as, why you cannot have this, that, or the other, and why your creation will never come to fruition. How do we get around a mind that tells us all the reasons why we can't?

The Magic Wand Technique

A technique I have used is the Magic Wand. It is very simple. You can use it with a literal wand from a new age, or metaphysical book store (all Master Manifestors have their own magic wand), you can make one, or you can just imagine it. For those of you who remember the 1970's TV show Bewitched, Samantha would concentrate on what she desired and wiggle her nose, and tah-dah, it would appear! A magic wand is the same concept, when an all powerful-wizard, YOU, waves his/her magic wand, whatever she/he desires appears; no mind interference, no yes... buts, just a wave and tah-dah! So, you have your magic wand or you imagine it in your hand. Close your eyes, and take a few deep, conscious breaths. You know your manifestation will come to you, it has to because you have your potent magical tool, your wand. Magic, manifestation, and the Universe's power know nothing of the economy. The concept of "not enough" is not in the Universe's language. The Universe knows and is all abundant. You are a child of the Universe. You can be anything, have anything and do anything your heart desires. Feel the power in your hand! Speak your visualization out loud from the powerful place of having a magic wand in your hand. Wave your wand, and know that your heart's desire is here, NOW!

You Find Yourself in Fear, Lack or Worry

The type of fear we are talking about here, is not the boogey man or the monster under the bed. I am talking about fear of unknown, fear of the future, and the "what ifs" worry cycle. In the next chapter, we will discuss surrender and trust, and fear more in depth. Finding yourself in fear can easily lead to dipping. For instance, you receive word that you might be laid off. That kind of experience in lack and worry can cause a dip in your consciousness. Receiving that notice can be scary and trigger your feelings of survival, the fight or flight instinct. What goes on? Some people get nervous, have full body sensations, their stomach churns, their heart pounds, they feel anxious. Their thoughts are desperate; what is going to happen to me and my family? If the thoughts are followed through, tracing them where they lead, they may take them to: we are not going to survive, we are going to lose our house, ultimately seeing themselves as destitute. This is a dip that goes pretty far down. In those fear-based moments, one is not thinking about consciousness or creation. The fear and the mind has taken over, throwing worst case scenarios at you.

Don't give into the fear. Not giving into the fear, not going where the mind wants to go, holding in your mind's eye a perfect vision of the best possible scenario, remaining focused on the desired end result... these are the ways you can stay conscious. By controlling the fear you change your energy.

Reign in those wild horses! Ask yourself, "Is that really true?" to quiet the mind. Get practical. Before you do anything, take some deep breaths and relax so you can think clearly. What is real and what is not? When we have a problem, or fear and worry around a situation, we are conditioned to handle it on our own. Handle the immediate circumstances. You have heard this rumor, and it is not necessarily true. Is there a way to get more facts? Try to calm your mind and let it know that this may or may not happen. Once you have handled the immediate situation, see what you can do to take yourself up the vibrational ladder, so to speak, and get yourself back into a higher place. It is very important that even though you dipped very far, the quicker you can acknowledge it and release it, the better, as you can now get into a higher vibration to attract your good.

In order for us all to learn the important lessons in life, we must each day surmount a fear. – Ralph Waldo Emerson

Loss

When one has lost a pet or loved one, there can be a deep feeling of loss and grief. This can cause an emotional dip that is real and understandable. Acknowledge for yourself that you are going through a serious emotional time and you will need to create or carve out space for yourself and your feelings. Do not rush to get through it. Allow the grief to be there until it is complete. It requires expressing what is there with a friend or in writing. Whatever you can do to put words to your feelings is helpful. Pamper yourself during this time. Rest more. We have a tendency in this culture to push away our unwanted feelings, especially grief. Fully feeling the feelings can help it move through. We feel grief in our heart and solar plexus. Breathe into these areas and let the energy circulate around your body and out. Crying is a good way to release. If you are not a person that cries often, or cannot bring yourself to cry for your own circumstance, watch a movie that is related to your topic. For instance, if you lost a pet, watch a movie like *Marley and Me* to get your emotions up and out. Feel sad as long as you need to, allow your feelings to flow. Once you start to feel better, do all the things that can help you climb the vibrational ladder.

Your Patterns are Triggered

You realize your old wound has been triggered and you are dipping. You engage the Psyche Detective, retracing your steps and your feelings through the day. When did this begin? Sometimes you cannot always pinpoint the exact event, yet you can see a pattern. Sometimes it is a very subtle change of feelings. For instance, if you are not in a relationship and want to be, you realize you saw happy couples everywhere you went. Or, if you have father issues, you remember walking by a park earlier, seeing a father engaged with his children. Begin the clearing process to rise from the dip. Write in your journal about when and why you believe the dip began. Express how it triggered your old wound, what was similar and what feelings have resurfaced. Many times that is all that needs to be done. By recognizing the connection between your past and present feelings or events, you can pass through the dip. After you have cleared, take whatever steps you can to get yourself back into your high, joy vibration.

> *If you are distressed by anything external, the pain is not due to the thing itself, but to your estimate of it; and this you have the power to revoke at any moment. - Marcus Aurelius*

Extreme Emotional Response

Co-writer Margaret's dipping story: My son had an opportunity to try out some instruments at his school and join the music program which he was very excited about. The line was long for the instrument he wanted to try and his class was moving on. Instead of raising his hand and asking for more time, he just went on with his class. I heard this story and was ENRAGED! I was really angry at my son for not raising his hand and asking for more time. I could not seem to let it go. I had yelled at him and there was nothing more to say, but I was still so mad! I left the house to take a drive and try to cool down. I took some deep breaths and asked myself, what is really going on here? I realized I was in the middle of a dip. There were several things happening. First, I realized I was feeling overwhelmed. By him not signing up for the music program at his school, this put another engagement on my calendar, because I would need to sign him up at a later date. Underlying these thoughts and feelings was my little girl feeling like a victim, "it's all on me," she was crying. Where was my husband in all this? I also desired my son to be empowered and take more responsibility and not rely so much on me. I could have just taken him to the music event myself, all the while with a big chip on my shoulder from "walking with my cross," but this was an opportunity to make a correction. I asked my husband to take him to the music event, and he readily agreed. Problem solved with an easy communication. I wondered, however, what would have happened if I had taken him to the event? How angry would I have been? How might I have further hurt my son's feelings because of the state I was in? That dip was an opportunity, and while difficult, I welcome the growth that came from it.

In looking at Margaret's story, there is another point that is important to note. A dip will generally be caused by several things happening at one time. For instance, Margaret was a) feeling overwhelmed, b) feeling a victim, c) wanting her son and husband to take more responsibility, d) feeling resentment for doing too much. Even in the highest of states, when faced with all these feelings, the most conscious of us would go plummeting down. But the thing Margaret did to begin her ascent back up the mountain, was to take some time for herself to really investigate her feelings and get clear about all that was going on, as well as to look and see what actions she needed to take to shift them. Asking her husband to help, took care of three things, feeling overwhelmed, feeling like she had to do it all and getting her husband more involved. She also used it as a teaching opportunity for her son, explaining that he needed to speak up for himself to get what he wanted. When I acknowledged her for handling this situation with so much Self-Love, I asked her how she felt afterward. She expressed that the dip was done, the negative feelings had passed through, and she felt back to herself.

Triggered By Negative People

As outlined in the last paragraph, being triggered by negative people is usually a cascade effect, meaning there is usually more than one incident which sends you on a dip. We have all had the following day: you wake to a rainy, gray day; everywhere you go people seem like they woke up on the wrong side of the bed; you watch or read something depressing; you speak to your mother and she starts complaining; people are rude to you in a store; somebody calls you in a rant. It just feels as if you are surrounded by negativity that day. My prescription for this type of dip is to remove yourself from the negativity because it can affect your overall consciousness. Put on some beautiful music, read or watch something inspiring, listen to one of your favorite teacher's online, workout, take a walk. Keep doing your affirmations and your daily regimen moving towards your creation goals.

This Too Shall Pass

When you realize you are in a downward spiral and are really having difficulty shifting, I love the saying, "This too shall pass." Knowing that whatever is going on is not permanent, can help. Repeat this to yourself. You have not always been in this situation, without finances, or without a lover, or sick. There was a time when you were not experiencing these circumstances. Realize that this is just what you are experiencing right now. Sometimes when you are experiencing something that still feels negative to you, it feels like it has been with you forever, and always will be. Truthfully, that is not the case if you really look at the facts. List out five thoughts you can have that would make you feel better about this subject. For instance: *This too shall pass, it has not always been this way; this too shall pass, I could get a new job tomorrow and start on Monday; this too shall pass, I could meet my new relationship at the movies later on tonight.* Change could be just around the corner, be open to it, expect a miracle! When I say these possibilities to myself, it opens me up. I begin to have better feeling thoughts which lead to good things coming. Thoughts equal things. Positive thoughts equal good things.

When You Are Dipping

Overall, when faced with a dip, for whatever reason, take some of the following actions. Many of these can be found in the Connect section as well.

- Acknowledge it and adopt an intention to release it.
- Do not judge it or see it as a set back. Hold it as an opportunity to get yourself back into alignment.
- Never skip over your feelings, however negative, and pretend they are not there. The key is to honor yourself and your feelings.
- Nurture. Sometimes we feel this negative way because we are tired or not feeling good. We need to pay attention to that.
- Write about it or speak it to the re-creating/be-with partner. In doing so, you are validating your feelings but not adding to the downward spiral. Honoring your feelings is important, but wallowing in them is not the best choice. After feeling sufficiently cleared, I suggest you return to practicing one or more of the techniques that you have found helpful in getting yourself back into alignment.
- Close your eyes, and feel gratitude. Gratitude is a great practice to move you out of your dip. Refer to your gratitude journal or just begin listing in your mind all of the things in your life for which you are grateful. When you are vibrating in a place of gratitude and having enough, it is difficult

to have your attention on lack. Being grateful brings in a higher vibration that magnetizes all the good in your life.

- Watch a CD or read something about the laws of attraction or something inspirational.
- Speak your vision again.
- Have some fun. Go to a movie. Do something that takes you out of thinking and feeling negative.
- Offer yourself some Self-Loving tools. Review the list of Acts of Self-Love (page 34) and do a few things on the list.
- Do something physical, stomp around if angry or frustrated.
- Get into nature.
- Take a bike ride or a walk. Deep breaths and exercise calm down the nervous system and bring you back to your center.
- Pray, not to receive something, but for peace. Light candles. Do a ritual.
- List five or more things for yourself that make you feel peaceful. Some suggestions might be music, gardening, journaling, being in nature, or exercise.
- Do one of the guided visualizations in this book.
- Meditate.

Clearing, connecting and creating are about fine-tuning the instrument, YOU. We are strengthening you, aligning you with God and trust. With my clients, I sometimes see them come to me in a crisis. We work through it and they may come back four months later with the same issue. While in the create process, it may feel like you are taking two steps forward, and four steps back, but if you really commit to the practices, you can make tremendous progress. People who really want to make a change in their lives, must commit to do the work regularly. Everyone has their own pace. Some will go slow and others will go fast. It depends on your level of commitment. It depends on what you want to create and manifest in your life. It requires you to be vulnerable and go deep and be invested in your Self. It requires Self-Love.

CHAPTER 26

Trust & Surrender

The act of trusting and surrendering is an integral part of the creation process. In the Connection chapter, we actively worked on our relationship with our Self, our Highest Self, and God. I gave you exercises to explore that relationship and make it stronger. Trust and surrender work together, hand-in-hand, and are an outcome of our work to connect with the Divine part of our Self.

Trust

Trust is to have confidence, belief and faith that our creation is on its way. You must absolutely believe, in your visualizations, prayers, and affirmations that it is true, that it has already happened. Your creation is for your highest good and you have firm reliance that this creation is here now. Trust in a Higher Source and power is important here for all the same reasons. Trusting that God, the Universe or Source has got your back, is supporting you, and wants the highest good for you is the same vibration that will bring you your heart's desire. When we feel that, and believe in that support, then there is something bigger than our human self that is with us guiding the way. Then, no matter what happens, there is the confidence that our highest good is being brought forth. Bad things can still happen along the way, but trust allows us to know that, no matter what, things will be ok. In the relationship between trust and surrender, trust comes first, without trust we cannot surrender. Think about the fear involved in jumping off a high diving board and being afraid of heights. In order to make that jump, you have to trust that you will be ok, that you will not die, that nothing bad will happen. Only then, can you surrender to the fear and take the proverbial "leap." When you have that trust, you can fully surrender.

Do You Trust?

Journal the answers to these questions to see if you have trust issues.

- Where have you trusted in your life and got burned?
- Who have you trusted and then betrayed you?
- Did this experience make you feel like you did something wrong, by picking the wrong friends or mate?
- Are you still blaming the person, yourself or God for this experience?

If you can pinpoint a time in your life when you trusted and had been deceived, see if the following is true for you:

I cannot really trust them, therefore I cannot really trust myself.
The next level: I cannot really trust God.

There is your lack of trust. Now the flip side, what have you dreamed into existence? What good have you created? We tend to focus on what we did not manifest. When we focus on the good, and see where we created something wonderful, with very little effort, that awareness lifts us up. We can again trust that we are supported by the Universe and allow that which is there for us to come.

Exercise To Build Trust

In the Connection chapter, we began to build the energetic container to make and strengthen our relationship with the Universe and our Highest Self. Now, we want to start building this container of trust, so we have a trust reservoir to draw upon. So, for example, in looking at my own life, one of the most powerful experiences I went through was when I had breast cancer. While it was hugely fearful, dramatic and traumatic, it shaped the person I am today. It was an opportunity for me to absolutely put into place all of the techniques of Self-Love that I knew to be true. I am stronger, I am vibrant and vital and in the best shape of my life, physically, mentally and emotionally. I owe my current state of optimal health and well-being, as well as this book and my coaching career to this gift of my experience with cancer. No matter what area of your life you choose to draw from, relationship, health, financial, or career, write a story or make a list of the expected or unexpected good that has come to you. Share this story with your creation buddy. Looking at the gifts that you have created for yourself and writing about them or speaking about them regularly will strengthen and develop that trust muscle.

Surrender

The word surrender has a lot of "charge." Think of the word "cancer." It brings forth images and fear for many people. Surrender is a word with the same amount of charge or feeling behind it. We imagine criminals with their hands up, surrendering their freedom, or waving the white flag in battle. The actual definition of surrender is, "to relinquish possession or control of something." We will be looking at our attachment to these images and letting go of the negative charge and beliefs surrounding surrender. When we think of times in our life when we have done things that are beyond what we think we are capable of, or words come to us that we later pause and say to ourselves, "who said that?", we begin to see there is something acting in our lives beyond our understanding. An example of that force coming through is when we are faced with a synchronicity that can only be directed by Divine intelligence; when we ask for support from the Universe and it comes; or when we listen to our inner wisdom or gut instinct and it proves reliable. When we give that Divine force and power permission to come through, we are saying YES to it. You are trusting it and you are surrendering to it, which allows your creation to come through ten-fold with ease.

- **Take a moment here and examine for yourself what the word surrender means to you, and journal about it. What images and feelings come up for you just saying the word? What about when you say the phrase, *I surrender*, out loud? Let go of the negative charge and beliefs of what surrender is and open yourself up to something greater.**

Surrender means:
- You are coming from a higher perspective releasing any and all control and manipulation.
- You are choosing to come from SELF versus your self, your larger, whole Self with Spirit, rather than your smaller self.
- You are letting go of the idea that you have to do it yourself; that you have to MAKE it happen.
- Merging with your God Self to allow the creation to happen.
- Giving your Self and your creation up to the universe and allowing the Universe to fulfill your request.
- Allowing the Creator to come forth and illuminate what action steps in the inner and outer parts of yourself for YOU to take.
- Releasing the attachment of the particular way you are holding your creation. For example, if you are looking for a job and you go on an interview, you may feel like this is the only way you can get a job. We get attached to the form, and not the desired outcome. If you are looking to make a specific amount of income, being attached to one possibility could block the Universe's bigger plan for you. There may be something bigger and better for you.

When does one need to surrender?

◆ When you find yourself in fear
◆ When you are in times of crisis
◆ When you are dipping
◆ When you are in the process of creating and your manifestation is not arriving
◆ When you are attached to one particular outcome
◆ When you feel frustrated

Fear

In the last chapter, we talked about fear and said that it is more difficult to manifest your creation when you are in a place of fear. There was a time in my life when I wondered why I was, periodically, without a close, loving relationship or had family issues. For me, these issues would bring up fear and feelings of being stuck. My chest would feel tight, I felt like crying everyday. I could feel the fear underneath all my words, and I sometimes felt paralyzed. All I wanted to do was escape into the TV, to shut my mind completely off. What happens when you are in fear? If the fear is financial or work related, you might feel as if your clients are falling away, ideas and opportunities are drying up, the phone stops ringing. Things you were counting on do not manifest, the money dries up. It may feel like all the doors are being slammed. One can feel like they want to give up; these can all be manifestations of a serious dip. So what do you do now?

Surrender

When faced with the premise of surrendering to these challenges, I originally balked. I realized I personally had a huge charge on the word surrender. I would think, "So I just give up? Give up my dreams? Stop making plans? Lay down?" I felt as if I was letting go of my will. When I talked about surrender with some of my clients who were experiencing a financial dip, for example, they would respond, "I can't surrender, who's going to pay the rent? What about my kids? Don't tell me to surrender, I need to take action, tell me what to do." Surrendering can be a very scary proposition. If you are a take charge, take action kind of person, like I am, the mind is always focused on the next thing to do. In order for me to survive, I felt I had to control. I had to *make* things happen. We were conditioned by our families and culture to make it on our own. But after some serious contemplation and meditation on the concept of surrender, I came to this conclusion: *If you believe you have to do it all, then you do not feel you have the support from others and from God.* With that belief, that is how your Universe shows up. You *do* have to do it all.

Ultimately it is a decision of faith over fear (e.g., fear of the unknown, the what-ifs). Faith, trust, and surrender is *knowing* that you are taken care of. Your life may be changing and you think it is for the worse. You may lose your job, you may lose your way of life as it exists right now. And as much as you want to hang onto that identity, that way of being that is right now, ultimately, it does not matter. There is a greater plan for you. The growth is in the journey. When you are at your lowest, the real you is not far behind.

> The Universe has a plan that will take you to all the places
> within yourself you could not get to on your own.

You Are Not Alone

The Universe and your Celestial team are always with you. Your intuition, support, and inspiration are always available to you. You need only call upon it. If you believe you have to do it yourself, then you *do* have to do it yourself. You have already discounted the support you could receive. You have closed the door on the support that is there for you. Going back to our mountain climbing motif... it's like trying to climb that mountain without the proper gear. You might be going along fine by yourself for awhile, periodically falling down, and getting back up. Sheer will power can take us so far. Halfway up the mountain you realize you do not have the training, gear, or a guide to be able to do this by yourself. You were not designed to do it yourself. Without the support, without opening to those channels and trusting there is a force that will provide you something better from the larger vision of your life, you fall down a lot. You get frustrated. You need the support, faith, trust and inspiration to make it to the top. But, worry not! You are not alone and there is a larger vision and meaning to your struggle.

Turn it over to the Universe, being open to receiving
the answers to all of your questions.

I can already hear some of you, "Well, that is all well and good, Cindy, but what do I *do????*"

Express Fear. The first thing we have to do when in fear and desperation is to acknowledge it and to express the despair. Choose this person wisely and make sure they have the time and space to really hear you. Many people find it difficult to hear fear and despair without being activated. There are not a lot of places to express without the person you are speaking to, consciously or unconsciously, adding mass to your speaking. This goes back to the parameters outlined for the Re-Creation Exercise. Let me further explain. When you are sharing an especially difficult situation and the person you are speaking to emotes with you, saying things like, "I'm so worried for you," or "I'm so angry that you are going through this." While they are being supportive with their speaking and saying what they think you need to hear, their worry, regret, fear and anger just adds those feelings on top of your already full plate of emotions. Stop and notice when speaking about a certain situation will add mass and create more fear for yourself. When you are so deep in a place of fear that you intuitively know that you cannot speak about it using the Re-Creation parameters for yourself, DON'T! Doing so will only "feed" the fear, make your mind louder, and exacerbate the problem. Wait until you are in a clearer space to do the Re-Creation with a partner.

What to do instead is to write about it. Express your feelings of fear and despair and outline all the what-ifs. Turn off the phone. Light a candle and do prayers for gratitude, surrendering or a ritual. Your energy will be different. You will feel stronger, clearer and you can make different choices.

By not adding mass, you are not putting negative feeling and thoughts together and sending that out to the Universe. Fear comes up, it is the human condition. You may have to go back to do some Clearing exercises. Once you are again clear in your vision, do not feel badly if this is in an area that has been difficult for you to create in. This may become an area in which you achieve the greatest amount of growth. Surrender is working on and with your consciousness. Clearing and surrendering brings you into vibrational attunement.

Divine Timing

Our thoughts do not manifest instantly which is a good thing. If a random thought like "I could hit a bump and fall off my bicycle" enters your mind, it is good that all thoughts do not manifest immediately, especially the negative ones. There is a time gap which allows us to refine our thoughts, to have a higher thought, and get more clarity of what we really want. Other times, we get frustrated because our thoughts do not manifest instantly. We begin to doubt that it is ever coming at all. We begin to think that our prayers and requests have not been heard. Again, here, we do not have the bigger picture. So, sometimes, if what you ask for is not in Divine timing for you now, that may mean that Spirit sees your manifestation would be better a year from now. Maybe that job that is perfect for you is not even available yet. Perhaps your perfect mate is in an unhealthy relationship with someone else at the moment. Should you meet him/her now, the timing would be off.

> *One of the main aspects in the co-creating relationship with*
> *Spirit is to keep asking, maintaining your energetic container,*
> *and letting go, to allow the wisdom of your Spirit to fulfill*
> *your dreams in its own way and in its own Divine time.*

The path to Self-Love and spiritual health is the path to connection and love. Is it Self-Loving to berate yourself because your creation has not arrived? In co-creation, we set out our intention, we vision, and we request.

Now we need to let go and let God. You are allowing that highest Source energy to handle the details knowing that that spiritual essence has the broader picture of all that is occurring.

Letting go of the attachment to the thing you desire is necessary for your manifestation to come to you. As the Buddha says, attachment to a certain thing or outcome is a primary source of suffering. In this game of manifestation that we are playing, it may be hard to get there, but that is the trick, you need to be fulfilled without it.

- Go back to the basics in Connecting. Getting very strong with Spirit will allow you to surrender more and know in your heart of hearts that you are fine now, with or without the manifestation.
- Refocus on the good you have and be grateful for what you do have. I am alive, I am breathing, and I am healthy. When you are fine with yourself, you are not coming from a place of desperation.
- If your creation is not arriving in your timing, look at your life and see what good is happening now. Open to receive the good.

Natural Law

Be open, trust, allow, give it to God and let it go. I speak intimately about the difficulty of surrender, because this for me has been a personal challenge for me. When I would set an intention for myself, my mind at times would take over and I would feel the need to fuss with everything, especially when the results I desired did not come. Nature, and fertile rebirth is the natural order of things and is the perfect example to teach us about surrender. Do the flowers try to bloom? Do the trees worry about coming back to life next spring? When you plant your seed in the sun and water it, do you then the next day dig it up to see if it has grown yet? Of course not, that would kill any chances for your seed to take root. Do you hover over it, blocking out the sun? No, you leave it, you trust that nature (God) will take its course and it will root, sprout and flower. This is a natural law of the Universe.

The Mind

Our mind tackles each situation like a puzzle, analyzing, picking it apart, trying to find a loophole, trying to discover an action we can take to resolve it. When there is no resolution, when the only solution is to wait and see, or accept our situation as it is, our mind can literally "drive us crazy" seeking out something, anything to do, do, do. It creates scenarios, what ifs, scenes of cause and effect, "if this happens, then, this… and I will be fine." At this moment, we are writing the script to resolve our problem, and we are not trusting that this situation is for our highest good. We are not trusting that God has a solution for our situation. We do not believe that God's solution is better than our own. Give permission to allow that power to be here. Say YES! to that bigger part of yourself and Divine intervention. You are activating that energy as your own Highest Self.

Allowing

Allowing is an energy, a state of mind that creates an opening, so your manifestation *can* come in. Allowing can be scary. Investigate further why is it uncomfortable for you? Is it because you feel the need to control it, fix it, or do something to make it happen? Nine out of ten times, the bottom line will be that you do not *trust* it will happen without you controlling it. Trusting the Universe to provide exactly what you need in the perfect time is the action of being in alignment with the Universe and *allowing* the natural Flow. You are not stepping in your own way, not forcing, or pushing. Imagine in your mind's eye a closed fist. Now imagine an open hand. Each image brings up a different feeling. To open your hands to receive rather than having a closed fist (e.g., to control and hang on) demonstrates the energy to allow, trust, and surrender.

Affirmations to Surrender

Here are some affirmations to say when that niggling problem re-enters your mind and threatens to take over. Saying something to master your mind can bring you back to the peaceful place of trust and surrender.

The Serenity Prayer
God, grant me the serenity to accept the things I cannot change.
The courage to change the things I can.
And the wisdom to know the difference.

I surrender I let go.
It is complete, now rest in peace.
I am done, the angels come.
I let go and let God.
I trust my Celestial Team is at work.
I trust the Universe to provide exactly what I need in the perfect time.
I leave it, I receive it.
I give it away, my worry is at bay. I can play!
I let go, I am in the flow.

Surrendering Your Creation

According to the angel experts, angels cannot enter our lives without our expressed permission. By holding onto your problem you prevent Divine Intervention (see *Healing with the Angels* by Doreen Virtue). Pause for a moment to call in the highest part of your Self. By giving yourself permission to step into that part of yourself, you begin the process of surrendering your creation or problem. Giving up your problem or creation to your Celestial Team is like mailing a letter. You have to release the letter from your hand before the post office can deliver it for you. You are giving away your problem or creation. We take it back, every time we have worry and fear. Once you have completed this visualization, your job is to mindfully control your worry.

When you begin to worry about this problem again, you have, in effect told the Universe and your Celestial Team, "you are not handling this fast enough, and I think I can do a better job anyway, so I am taking my letter back." When we surrender and trust, we give up our script on how to resolve the issue. Your Celestial Team and God have a much better plan for fixing the problem! God's will is that you be happy. If you totally trust and surrender all concerns, a solution will come, and most likely it is even greater than you could have imagined.

Visualization to Surrender Your Problem or Creation

 Close your eyes and take three deep breaths to center yourself. Imagine yourself sitting down at a desk, the desk can be as simple or ornate as you desire. You pause for a moment, pen in hand, to fully reflect on your problem, fully experiencing all the emotions, sorrow, fear and worry this problem is causing in your life. You look down at your paper (parchment, scroll, papyrus, again, whatever you desire), and as you look down at your paper, it is as if your Soul is writing the letter in a beautiful gold script. Your prayer to your Celestial Team fervently composes itself before your eyes. When you feel complete, you thank the Team for their assistance. And you end the letter with the phrase, "This or something better is now manifesting for me in totally satisfying ways." You fold the letter and place it in an envelope and seal it. You walk out of your home and there is a mail box. It can be a traditional mailbox, or since this is a heavenly request your imagination can create any kind of mailbox you desire. You drop your letter into the mailbox. As soon as the letter has left your hand, you rest assured that your Team has received your letter and has heard your prayer. You no longer need to worry over this problem. You have released it to the Universe. You are at peace. Feel the inner peace that the situation has been perfectly handled. When you feel ready, open your eyes.

CHAPTER 27

Receiving

Receiving may be difficult if you are not open to allowing it to flow. It is very helpful to be in a positive energetic vibration in order to receive. When you are in a place of worry or lack, it can be difficult to manifest. If you are trying too hard to make something happen in your life, this too, blocks the receiving. People can feel your desperate energy and they do not feel attracted to it. There may have been times when you have tried all the manifesting techniques we have discussed: thought positively, visualized and written about your heart's desire, with no result. Fear, worry, desperation or trying too hard is a much lower vibration and trains your nervous system to expect lack. It can be difficult to manifest anything in this state.

This is why we, yet again, go back to Clearing and why clearing is so important and why the Clear-Connect-Create Formula is unique to manifestation techniques. Thoughts create things; this is true. But it is not the mind, it is not your thoughts, it is not your do-do-doing that brings it to fruition. It is the *feeling* and the *feeling* is all from your heart center. This is why the Clear-Connect-Create Formula and the Path to Self-Love work together. When you begin nurturing your Self, focusing your thoughts, managing the mental body, you begin to feel better. You begin to tap into your joyful aliveness, and you *feel* like all your needs are met. You *feel* like your manifestation is already present. You *feel* grateful for it already being here.

Practice feeling like this on a regular basis, and flood your nervous system with these feelings.

The following visualization helps you to anchor Self-Love feelings, and manifest feelings which you desire in your being. Use any, or all, of this visualization daily for at least five minutes. Even if you just spend time bathing your heart center in love, this practice will train your nervous system and your body to exist in a state of relaxation, love and receiving, creating a receptive environment for your manifestation. Feeling those feelings allow the wonderful things to come in. As Michael Beckwith's mantra says, "All your needs are abundantly met." If you truly believe and feel that in your heart, that all your needs are abundantly met, you now can come to a place of full receptivity.

Creating from the Heart Center Visualization

 Get into a comfortable place where you will not be disturbed. Close your eyes and take three deep breaths, and get present and connected. Imagine a cord, the width of your hips going down, down, down into the center of the Earth, and anchor it there. Now, bring your attention to your heart center, the spiritual heart which is located behind the breastbone. It is a soft pink color, illuminated by all the love in your life and the light of the Divine. Breathe into it and expand it. Spend some time being in that space of your heart center and open it up. Continue to breathe into that area, expanding it, bigger than your body, bigger than the room, bigger than your whole house. You are surrounded by the loving energy of your heart center.

Now imagine, just above your head a light pink rosebud. As you are watching it, it begins to open, unfurling its petals, one by one, opening, opening, until it is bursting with aliveness. Once it is as wide open as it can possibly get, it begins to glow, radiating a soft pink light, getting brighter and brighter. It is almost too bright to keep looking at it, but you do, and soon its shimmering pink light turns into a shower that begins to gently rain down on your head. This beautiful, shimmering pink light comes into your crown chakra and begins to fill up your

head, raining down into your third eye, awakening and opening the third eye to the perfect balance of openness. Now, the light moves into your throat chakra, the place of power, where you speak your world into manifestation. It fills that area, bathing your throat chakra in the pink light. From your throat chakra, the pink light spills over into your heart. Your heart knows this light, the light of Divine Love. You see your heart expanding once again with this light and love. If you see any darkness, or blocks, anything that keeps you from experiencing yourself as Self-Love, send that image down the grounding cord, into the Earth. Now, send the pink light down into the stomach and your organs around the stomach bringing that part of you into healing alignment and know that you deserve! Bring the light down into the second chakra, located below the belly button, this is the seat of your creativity. As you infuse it with all the love available from the pink light, your intuition and creativity are nurtured, and begin to pulsate with a powerful vibration. The shimmering shower of pink light is now moving all the way down to the root chakra (the lowest point of the trunk of your body), the area that is the flight or fight survival part of your being sending it the message that all your needs are abundantly met. Watch as this pink soft light infuses your whole being, with the love of Self, the love of Source. Bring your awareness back to your heart chakra and see this light at the center of your being filling you and anchoring you in Divine love, fully aligning you with your commitment to Oneness with Source through Self-Love. As you are bathed in the soft pink light of the spiritual heart center, notice how this feels, and enjoy.

We will now be travelling to the Pink Palace. Imagine yourself standing outside, alone and undisturbed in a green, lush, grassy field. Your eyes are closed and you are basking in the warm sunlight. You feel the grass tickling your feet, a soft breeze on your skin. You see a soft pink mist begin to roll in before you. It begins to surround your feet, becoming thicker, and before you know it, you can no longer see your bare feet. It is as if you are standing on a pink cloud. The pink mist is cool and damp on your feet and legs and you feel a sense of oneness with the cloud. There is no fear, only a sense of belonging and coming home. Soon the cloud begins to lift you off the ground and you feel excitement for your journey. It is as if your pink cloud has become a magic carpet. You look down at the trees.

You can see your house. You sit down in the mist and enjoy the journey, looking down at the sites below as you climb higher and higher into the sky. Soon you are amongst the stars. In the distance, illuminated by a soft pink glow, you see a palace in the clouds, and you know this is your true destination. Your pink cloud connects to a pathway to the palace, and you walk along the beautiful pink road before you. There are amazing trees, flowers, birds, and insects all around, the vividness of the colors are the likes you have never seen. You take in the smells and sights, opening up all your senses as you walk along the pathway. It looks so beautiful, you are anxious to get to the Pink Palace. You see many steps to the doorway to the temple. As you begin to walk up, up, up the steps, you feel lighter than air. When you reach the doorway you are greeted by a beautiful pink angel, with huge, soft, pink wings. Her face is gentle and she has kind bright blue glowing eyes. She is so happy to see you. She takes your hand and walks you through the corridors of the temple. There are many doors that you may enter but you are guided to one special room. The ceiling and walls are made of pink marble with gold inlay. Flowers surround you perfuming the air. Take a moment to look around and let your imagination fill in the details of all you see, feel and experience in this Divine temple room. In the center of the room is an elevated platform with beautiful pink quartz and jeweled steps. You step up each step, and as you get to the top of the steps and look down, you see it is a pool, that must be made for a king or a queen, it is, YOU! You walk up the steps to the pool and take off your clothing. You step into the pink, warm, bubbling waters and relax in the sensation of this nurturing pool of Divine waters. To the side of the pool is a goblet with a pink bubbling elixir. You take a sip and it sends an amazing warm feeling down your throat, to your stomach. As you relax in the pool, think of the journey you have been on while working with this book. Remember all of the work you have done, thoughts and realizations you have had. You have travelled through clearing and connecting with Your Self, and creating your heart's desire. It is now time to fully connect with who you really are and your own Self-Love. Contemplate your beautiful journey. Acknowledge your commitment to your Self and your Spirit. Leave in the pool any false ideas, beliefs, fears, or anything left in your being that may be in the way of you fully embracing your own Self-Love. Stay in the pool as long as you like, this water will never get cold. When you are ready, step out of the pool and don your priest/ priestess robe on the side of the pool. Notice the colors and the soft, comforting material as you put it on; it is a perfect fit. Your angel reappears and guides you through the corridors. She leads you to another room. As the door opens, you feel a rush. There is an amazing powerful pink light in the center of the room coming from a skylight in the ceiling. This light is shining on a gold throne, made out of a material you have never seen before. You see flecks of gold swirling in the light, and as you take a seat in the throne, bathed in this gold and pink light, your vibration rises to its most powerful ascension. You have never felt such Love! You are fully connected with your Source and with Love. Feel it in every cell, vibrating and expanding. By the throne, there is a table with a wand. You pick up the wand. This is your wand for manifestation that you can use at any time. You waive your wand in front of you, and a huge screen framed in a soft, pink, giant heart appears. Bring to your heart the feeling of what it feels like for you to be, feel and express Self-Love in every area of your life. In the area of relationship, see the Divine relationship you are creating with Self. How does it look, your life expressed as a Love of Self? Picture the people in your life. How do the relationships in your life look when completely Self-Loving? Remember how your heart bursts open when seeing a newborn baby or a puppy. Give that Love to your Self as you honor yourself, respect your Self and deserve perfect Divine health, fulfillment of finances and career, creative expression, and completely loving relationships. You are, in this moment, completely aligned with Source. You know who you are fully and completely. Imagine your life with great detail and watch the movie of your life framed by this pink heart. Infuse it with the feeling of love and gratitude. Think and feel about every area of your life. When you are complete, close the screen. Sit for a moment feeling the great feeling of knowing who you are as Self-Love, letting that feeling expand in your heart. Step down from the throne taking your wand with you. Walk out of this room towards the entrance, the doorway of the temple. At the door, your Self-Love Angel is waiting for you. She puts out her arms to hug you and her nine foot wings spread out behind her. You step in for the embrace and her soft wings close around. You feel so much love and gratitude in your heart for your life. Does your angel have any words for you now? Listen with your heart as you gaze *into her deep blue eyes. What do you see there? She hands you a pink rose. Walk through the doorway and walk down the steps, with each step down becoming more grounded and in your body. You step off the steps on the pink pathway which leads back to your pink cloud. You sit down on your cloud and begin the descent down through the stars, down into the white clouds, above the trees... down until your pink cloud lands softly in the green grass of the yard where you began. You wiggle your toes in the grass and the pink mist of the cloud begins to dissipate. You feel the solidness of the earth beneath your feet. You feel the sun's warmth on your face again, and a slight breeze in your hair. From your feet, you feel roots growing out of the soles of your feet. The roots are growing down in to the earth, grounding you in your physical body. Welcome back into your physical home, back to your chair, wiggle your fingers and toes bringing you back to your body. Take a breath to presence yourself here. When you are ready, open your eyes, and come back into your life anchored in Self-Love.*

> *Appreciation and Self-Love are the most important tools that you could ever nurture. Appreciation of others, and the appreciation of yourself is the closest vibrational match to your Source Energy of anything that we have ever witnessed anywhere in the Universe. – Abraham*

Morning Prayer to Receive

I was given this prayer by a spiritual counselor of mine, America Martinez. She received this prayer for me from Spirit to support me during a big transition and financial challenge that was occurring for me at the time. It really worked! She introduced this to me by saying that it would help me reclaim my good. Abundance surrounds us all, all of the time, we just need to open up to receive it. This prayer is also used to reframe your energetic responses and patterns to receiving. Say this prayer every morning upon rising for a minimum of 30 days. Open your arms and face the horizon, taking three deep breaths. While saying this prayer, focus on really opening up your heart and soul to the words herein.

I welcome in the Goddess of Abundance and the Divine Mother. In the presence of these Divine beings I am making a statement today. That statement is to impact the ongoing evolution of my soul and the ongoing experiences that I am to have in this lifetime and beyond this lifetime. I am responding positively! Let it be known to myself and to the Divine and to the helpers of the Divine, that I am now embracing that which comes to me, that overflows to me: whether it be financial windfalls, talents, opportunities, inheritances, abundances of all forms and shapes, I am now responding to those gifts with no hesitation involved. On the contrary, I have a willingness to joyfully receive, knowing that I have generously given. And so I now sit in a moment in time, in the evolution of my soul, that welcomes me to joyfully receive, calmly receive, knowing that that is the correct action to take spiritually.

So I stand in my life, making a commitment to myself and my God, that I will do the action of receiving joyfully and collaborating with abundances sent my way. And that I will know myself to be someone who is to receive God's graces, for God wishes that for me! Blessed be!

CHAPTER 28

Reaching Your Destination

The Formula

We have come to the end of the path, at least in the form of this book. I hope this is the beginning of your journey. The Path to Self-Love is a winding road. The Clear, Connect, Create Formula helps you to navigate this path, so you can be your most empowered Self! Here is a quick recap of the formula, so you can review and apply the necessary tools and techniques when needed.

Clear
- Acknowledge your feelings
- Journal and do the "Re-Creation" process
- Utilize the Psyche Detective for yourself when you are triggered
- Apply clearing tools and techniques when you feel stuck, when you see a pattern, when something from your past comes up for you
- Continue to analyze your thoughts and beliefs and implement changes when needed
- Continue to do releasing techniques, such as: letter writing, journaling, burning rituals, breath, meditation, dance, stomp, and more
- Express your true authentic Self

- Recognize and manage energy drains
- Communicate your needs in relationships and set boundaries
- Forgive yourself and others daily

Connect
- Nurture Love of Self
- Continue the relationship with the child within
- Get into and stay in integrity
- Have integrity with your word
- Take responsibility
- Listen to your intuition
- Take a daily dose of happy
- Continue to do connecting techniques, such as: meditate, listen to inspiring speakers, read uplifting material, walk in nature, maintain your alter
- Manage your physical, mental, emotional, and spiritual bodies
- Be in gratitude
- Call on your Celestial Team for guidance and support
- Do rituals
- Do the "Approaching the Day" Techniques

Create
- Notice when you do not feel you deserve something, and affirm you do!
- Continue to expand your Abundance Barometer
- Create voids before manifesting techniques
- Place your order with the Universe
- Create visual cues to align with your vision
- Vision
- Affirm
- Do something every day to manifest your goal
- Manage dipping
- Surrender and trust
- Open to receive

Cindy and Margaret's Path

Clear · Connect · Create: A Powerful Path to Self-Love may look like a book, but it was a life ~ both of our lives. The Self-Love Path has been our blue print. We have personally and professionally traveled this experiential, multi-dimensional path together. Over the past eight years as we wrote this book, we have lived this journey. Every tool, technique, and realization has come from our own experience. We have supported each other, recreated each other, created boundaries with each other and others. We have cleared/made space in our lives for each of our heart's desire – to be successful published authors and to make a difference in the world with the Clear · Connect · Create Formula. Our lives, now, do not resemble our lives at the start of the book. Cindy closed her event planning business and launched her coaching career; left her beautiful apartment in Chicago and moved to Florida; completed family history and healed past wounds; became physically active and is now in the best shape of her life; transformed the "m & m's" – men and money; and is now feeling Self-Love and abundance in every area beyond her wildest dreams. Margaret returned to the workforce after being a stay at home mom for several years; cleared and healed her relationship with her mother; learned to balance her family relationships and set boundaries; left her marriage and moved out of the home she had built with her husband; created a new way of eating and exercising; has gotten into financial integrity and has fulfilled a dream to be a published writer. We have laughed at how our lives have paralleled the section we were working on at the time; almost as if the Universe were nudging forward our own healing in that area, and it was! We laughed even more when this phenomenon also occurred for our editor. One of the reasons this book has taken so long to finish is because we applied our own formula – we wrote this book with Self-Love, meaning we did not push ourselves. If one of us did not feel well emotionally or physically, we did not work that day and suggested rest and restoration. We practiced loving our Selves and each other. We contracted to do it. This work has been the guidepost to transform our lives, and we hope, yours as well.

Your Journey

For you, our dear Reader, we hope this book has given you a place to stop, and step away from your life as you know it. We hope you have taken a look at your Self at the deepest of levels to see who you are, what you believe, and what you desire in this life. Most people never take the time in a lifetime to do this, and this is the path you have been on. You have demonstrated the courage, willingness and commitment to clear out your history, your beliefs, and fears and to step away from that defining reality. You have connected with the deepest and most powerful part of yourself which people read and hear about, and may never do the experiential work to have that manifest as a reality for them. You have searched for your true heart's desire and come away with your authentic passion. You have a vision, you have a glimpse into your sacred contract. If you feel you have not come that far yet, this book is on no timeline. Learn and work with the tools in this book to manifest your dream. This is huge for you, reader, to step away from your normal waking consciousness and allow yourself to stand in the knowing that you are a spiritual being having a human experience. You are here to enjoy, celebrate, and manifest the glory of God and who you really are! This is where you are on this journey, and where you take it from here is your choice. You now have the tools, space, and roadmap to fulfill your destiny!

The greatest way one can be an inspiration and impact the world is to be an example of the Light. The Divine Light knows that it is sacred, knows that it deserves, and knows that it is here to fulfill and express the power within. You are this Light, and you uplift all in your circle and beyond. Your light creates a ripple effect that touches countless numbers of people. As you realize your true identity, your true essence, and act from Source and demonstrate Self-Love, the Universe transforms!

There is nothing to do except be Self-Love and clear that which no longer serves. Connect to your Highest, most Divine Being and Self. Create that which you are here to be, do and have.

Our first and last love is - self-love. ~ Christian Bovee

Final Thoughts

We began this book with a discussion of my first experience with Self-Love and my realization that we are spiritual beings having a physical experience. I will now leave you with my heart's desire for you, dear Reader:

* Remember who you are, a powerful being having a human experience.
* Continue to love your Self. Do something every day to nurture your Self-Love; as this is the key to your empowerment
* Support your Self on this path of life. Reach out to others who are on a similar path or have read this book.
* Continue the journey with me by visiting my website at www.cindypaine.com and become a member of my community. You can receive my inspirational quotes via email, sign up to receive my blogs, download some of the visualizations, and enroll in my workshops or online classes for more support to manifest your heart's desires. You are a work in progress. Be kind to yourself.

My heart's desire for each and every one of you is to Love your Self beyond what you think is possible and know that you are on this path to CELEBRATE YOUR MAGNIFICENCE!

Blessings,
Cindy Paine

Index